Chinese Odyssey

Volume 5

Cheng & Tsui Publications of Related Interest

The Enduring Legacy of Ancient China
Primary Source Lessons for Teachers and Students
Comp. by Primary Source, Inc.
Pbk. w/CD-ROM   ISBN-13: 978-0-88727-508-1
                       ISBN-10: 0-88727-508-7

Cheng & Tsui Chinese Character Dictionary
Wang Huidi, Editor-in-Chief
Paperback   ISBN-13: 978-0-88727-314-8
                   ISBN-10: 0-88727-314-9

Pop Chinese, 2nd Edition
A Cheng & Tsui Bilingual Handbook of Contemporary Colloquial Expressions
Yu Feng, Yaohua Shi, Zhijie Jia, Judith M. Amory, and Jie Cai
Paperback   ISBN-13: 978-0-88727-563-0
                   ISBN-10: 0-88727-563-X

Masterworks Chinese Companion
Expressive Literacy through Reading and Composition
Comp. by Qin-hong Anderson
Paperback   ISBN-13: 978-0-88727-435-0
                   ISBN-10: 0-88727-435-8

Open for Business, 2nd Edition
Lessons in Chinese Commerce for the New Millennium
Jane C. M. Kuo
Vol. 1 Textbook & Workbook   ISBN-13: 978-0-88727-456-5
                                    ISBN-10: 0-88727-456-0
Vol. 1 Audio CD   ISBN-13: 978-0-88727-411-4
                                    ISBN-10: 0-88727-411-0
Vol. 2 Textbook & Workbook   ISBN-13: 978-0-88727-626-2
                                    ISBN-10: 0-88727-626-1
Vol. 2 Audio CD   ISBN-13: 978-0-88727-410-7
                                    ISBN-10: 0-88727-410-2

Please visit www.cheng-tsui.com for more information on these and many other language-learning resources.

通向中国

Chinese
Odyssey

Innovative Chinese Courseware

Xueying Wang, Li-chuang Chi, and Liping Feng

王学英　　　祁立庄　　　冯力平

CHENG & TSUI COMPANY　Boston

Chinese Odyssey Volume 5 Textbook

The contents of *Chinese Odyssey* were developed in part under a grant from the Fund for the Improvement of Postsecondary Education (FIPSE), U.S. Department of Education. However, these contents do not necessarily represent the policy of the Department of Education, and you should not assume endorsement by the Federal Government.

20 19 18 17 16   2 3 4 5 6 7
2nd Printing, 2016

Published by
Cheng & Tsui Company
25 West Street
Boston, MA 02111-1213 USA
Fax (617) 426-3669
www.cheng-tsui.com
"Bringing Asia to the World"™

Wang, Xueying.
Chinese odyssey : innovative Chinese courseware / Xueying Wang,
    Li-chuang Chi, and Liping Feng.
        p. cm.
    Includes an index.
    Chinese and English.
    ISBN 0-88727-514-1
    1. Chinese language—Textbooks for foreign speakers—English.
I. Chi, Li-chuang. II. Feng, Liping. III. Title.
PL1129.E5W385 2004
495.1'82421—dc22

                                        2004063504

Simplified and Traditional Character Edition
ISBN-13: 978-0-88727-514-2
ISBN-10: 0-88727-514-1

Printed in the United States of America

Chinese Odyssey includes multimedia products, textbooks, workbooks, and audio products. Visit www.cheng-tsui.com for more information on the other components of *Chinese Odyssey*.

Publisher's Note

Despite the increasing use of technology in foreign language education, there have been few multimedia courses in Chinese that focus on all four skills and span all levels of language instruction. At long last, we are pleased to present *Chinese Odyssey*, unique because it is the first stand-alone multimedia series designed for multi-year classroom instruction. *Chinese Odyssey*'s pace and oral/aural emphasis are geared to the American high school and college instructional environments, and its combination of multimedia, audio, and book products allows educators the flexibility to use it independently as a multimedia course, or to combine multimedia and paper formats.

In this edition of *Chinese Odyssey*, we combine both simplified and traditional characters in the same book. In Volumes 1 & 2, which cover the first year of study, we present the traditional and simplified character editions in separate sections. This layout is meant to provide ready access to both traditional and simplified characters without overwhelming beginning students. In Volumes 3–6, which cover the second and third years of study, we present the two character sets together on facing pages. We switch to facing pages in the higher levels in order to encourage fluency for intermediate and advanced-level students who wish to study and compare both character sets.

The Cheng & Tsui Chinese Language Series is designed to publish and widely distribute quality language learning materials created by leading instructors from around the world. We welcome readers' comments and suggestions concerning the publications in this series. Please send feedback to our Editorial Department (e-mail: editor@cheng-tsui.com), or contact the following members of our Editorial Board.

Contents

Acknowledgments

I would like to thank Li-chuang Chi and Liping Feng, the other two authors of the *Chinese Odyssey* series, for their hard work in writing the manuscripts. Together, we have completed three years of Chinese language instructional materials for a total of six volumes. This project stimulated constant debate among the three of us, who miraculously still very much enjoy working with each other.

Special thanks also go to the following institutions and individuals whose contributions helped to push the project along and to make this multimedia courseware the best it could possibly be:

Thanks to the Fund for the Improvement of Post-Secondary Education (FIPSE) of the U.S. Department of Education for its generous funding. Thanks to the Dean's Office of the School of Arts and Science, whose support made this project possible; thanks also to the Johns Hopkins University students who beta-tested the book and provided valuable feedback.

Thanks to our publisher Cheng & Tsui Company for their kind editing and tireless reviewing of the manuscript. Thanks also to Blueshoe Technologies, Inc., our partner for developing the courseware, for adding additional features to the software in order to meet our needs and for providing technical support for the software.

Special thanks to Xi'an International Studies University and its School of Chinese Studies for their collaboration in filming the video clips for all six volumes. Their filming project started in the scorching summer heat of China, resulting in several project members falling ill because of heat stroke. Yet, under the superior leadership of Li Changxing, Director of the Center of Educational Technology, our university collaborators still completed a high quality project while maintaining a willing attitude. Thanks also to Jiang Xiaomin, Deputy Director of the School of Chinese Studies at Xi'an International Studies University, who always worked with the best interests of this project in mind.

Thanks especially to the following individuals who made significant contributions to the project:

- Chris Vee, Senior Technology Specialist at Johns Hopkins University, for his amazing talents in audio/video editing, shooting, and recording, and for his skills in troubleshooting all kinds of mysterious technical problems that we encountered during the course of the project. It seems like there is no problem he can't solve;

- Jesse Warford, Computer Support Specialist at the Johns Hopkins University Language Lab, for his technical support, advice, positive attitude, and encouragement;

- Graham Bouton, Manager of Desktop Computing Services at Johns Hopkins University, for providing us with technical support, manpower, and moral support;

- Luping Chen, for her involvement in writing during the early stages of the grant;

- Lillian Tian, for her involvement in writing some of the lessons in volumes three, four, five, and six during the early stages of the grant, for her constant constructive criticism of the content, and for her melodious voice, recorded in our audio and multimedia CDs;

- Project team members Risa Lin, Zheng Wang, Huang Lu, Yow-Ning Wan, Huiping Liu, Ronghua Yang, past employees such as Dennis Chi, Jolene Porter, Ruyin Xue and many others, for their tireless efforts, attention to detail, ability to meet deadlines even if it meant working overtime, and constant suggestions on how to further improve the quality of the project;

- Sheng Xu, Ph.D. computer science student at Johns Hopkins University, for taking the time during his dissertation writing period to create an installer for our multimedia courseware;

- Cindy Simpson, the Language Laboratory Coordinator at Johns Hopkins University, and the lab student employees for their suggestions on the improvement of the project.

- Carol Young, the Language Teaching Center Administrator at Johns Hopkins University, for all her administrative assistance to the grant, including management of the grant budget, grant staff, and student payroll.

- Marina Koestler, a former Johns Hopkins University student, for her wonderful editing of the English portions of our manuscript.

Special thanks to my husband, Fanjiu Wang, for putting up with me over the last few years while I ignored him on weekends and evenings to work on this project. Special thanks also to my daughter, Jingya Wang, who took the time out of her busy college life to read and comment on the manuscript. Similarly, the other two authors would like to thank their family members for their moral support.

Due to limited space, we could not list everyone who made contributions. However, we extend thanks to everyone for anything s/he may have done for the project.

Xueying Wang, Ph.D.
Principal Investigator of the Grant Project

Introduction

Welcome to *Chinese Odyssey*, an innovative multimedia language courseware for learning Chinese. *Chinese Odyssey* is designed to provide a comprehensive curriculum, laying the groundwork for building your Chinese language skills from beginning to advanced levels over a period of three years. Designed for high school, college, and adult learners, *Chinese Odyssey* teaches the full scope of language learning skills—listening, speaking, reading, and writing—in addition to grammar. And because it is completely multimedia-based, *Chinese Odyssey* provides unique access to video, audio, and interactive exercises, adding a new dimension of flexibility and richness to the language learning experience.

Year-by-Year Learning Objectives

First Year (Volumes 1 and 2)

The first year is designed to teach the basic survival skills you will need to communicate in Chinese. The exercises concentrate heavily on spoken language and pronunciation, with a special focus on pinyin and tones in Volume 1. In Volume 2, pronunciation exercises are gradually replaced by more communicative and grammar-based exercises.

Second Year (Volumes 3 and 4)

In your second year of studying Chinese, you will complete the basic groundwork in Chinese, and you'll learn more about Chinese grammar. At this point, you should become more comfortable with Chinese customs and will be able to communicate about daily tasks with Chinese people. By the end of this year, you will have gained the necessary language skills for living in China.

Third Year (Volumes 5 and 6)

At this level, you will be continuously honing your language skills and cultural understanding. You will develop the skills necessary to carry on a high-level discussion in Chinese, expressing your opinions as you talk about issues related to current events, Chinese society, politics, economics, the education system, and aspects of Chinese culture such as food, holidays, and Chinese medicine. You will also begin to learn the written form of Chinese (书面语/書面語), which is different from the modern spoken form of the language.

Chinese Odyssey's Pedagogical Approach

Why Multimedia

In the past, most education took place in a classroom environment and was based primarily on interaction between the teacher and student. Today, people of all ages and backgrounds are seeking to enhance their language experience with multimedia tools. As a completely stand-alone multimedia courseware, *Chinese Odyssey* lets you effectively manage your own learning. Using the multimedia CD-ROMs, you can instantly see whether you've completed an exercise correctly, get explanations of answers, and record your exercise scores. You can participate in a variety of interactive situations that allow you to practice what you have learned. Thus, you can set your own pace and focus on your perceived areas of weakness.

The multimedia format easily accommodates students of varying backgrounds, skill levels, and aptitudes. For example, beginning students can spend more time learning to write Chinese characters by following animated stroke order, or focus on pronunciation drills. In the second and third years, students can take advantage of online resources—such as links to Internet pages related to lesson topics—which will enrich their learning experience. In short, for students, using the multimedia courseware is like having a private tutor.

Within the realm of traditional classroom-based instruction, the *Chinese Odyssey* courseware enables instructors to more effectively use their limited instructional hours for interaction with their students rather than for mechanical drills. For example, using the multimedia CD-ROM, students can do drills and exercises as well as review the lesson on their own time. This frees up class time for more meaningful interaction between teachers and students. Because the courseware contains a score-keeping function, language instructors don't have to spend lots of time grading students' homework. Instructors can simply ask students to print out their exercise score reports, which will automatically indicate the students' performance as well as the time taken to complete the exercise. Moreover, students absent from class can take their portable CDs with them in order to keep up with lessons, without having to use too much of the instructor's time to make up the class.

A Note about the Exercises

Chinese Odyssey contains sophisticated multimedia exercises in grammar and the four basic language skills—listening, speaking, reading, and writing. In order to prepare you to take the *Hanyu Shuiping Kaoshi* (HSK), the Chinese Proficiency Test given by the Chinese government, some of the exercises are in HSK format (see "How *Chinese Odyssey* Provides Preparation for the HSK" on page xiii). Other multimedia exercises include matching games and pre-recorded dialogues that you can engage in with the computer; we hope that such activities are able to bring some fun and interaction to Chinese learning.

Why We Introduce Conversational Chinese and Idiomatic Colloquial Speech

The dialogues in *Chinese Odyssey* are written in conversational Chinese, the language that people in mainland China use in their daily interactions. This differs from the standard textbook language found in most Chinese language learning materials. Some of the expressions may also differ from the language used in Taiwan.

We take this approach because we believe that the standard textbook language is heavily limited by vocabulary and grammar, and that it does not reflect natural spoken Mandarin Chinese. In the written passages, we use more formal language and less conversational language.

In addition to conversational Chinese, we also introduce authentic idiomatic colloquial speech to make learning more real and the everyday spoken language more accessible. These idiomatic expressions are explained in the notes that follow the dialogues. Heritage students and those who are highly motivated to learn can simply memorize the colloquial speech without a need to analyze the grammar. Those who have limited time do not have to memorize the idiomatic colloquial expressions.

Topics in *Chinese Odyssey*

The course material contains practical topics such as greeting people, entertaining guests, opening a bank account, or going to the post office, as well as contemporary topics such as dating and opening a cell phone account. The grammar points and vocabulary are introduced based on the content of the topics. Before writing *Chinese Odyssey*, we held a series of discussions with our students in order to select topics that would be, from a learner's perspective, both interesting and practical. For example, dating is a topic that students love because it helps to bring Chinese learning from academia into their everyday world.

Settings in *Chinese Odyssey*

The settings in *Chinese Odyssey* are designed to mirror the real experiences of students learning Chinese. In the first year, most students begin their language-learning journey in their home country. During the second and third years, however, students tend to travel abroad to enhance their language-learning experience in the target country of their chosen language. Thus, in parallel, our courseware begins in the home country of the novice Chinese learner, and then shifts to China, with increasingly sophisticated scenes as the students themselves advance in their language skills.

Curriculum Planning

Each year of *Chinese Odyssey* covers two volumes of material, with 20 lessons for each of the first two years (approximately 5–6 instructional hours per lesson), and 10 lessons for the third year (approximately 9–10 instructional hours per lesson). To facilitate learning and teaching, we have tightly controlled the number of vocabulary words and the length of the text in each lesson. Grammar is graded in terms of level of difficulty, and difficult grammar points such as 的, 了, and verb complements usually appear more than once: first to introduce basic concepts, and later with increasingly detailed explanations and practice.

How *Chinese Odyssey* Provides Preparation for the HSK

In addition to providing a rigorous Chinese language course, *Chinese Odyssey* is designed to prepare you for taking the *Hanyu Shuiping Kaoshi* (HSK), a proficiency-based, standardized aptitude test issued by the Chinese government. If you want to study abroad or work in China, you will eventually have to take this test. *Chinese Odyssey*'s testing software is modeled after the HSK, to give you a sense of what the actual exam is like and help you prepare for the exam.

A Tour through *Chinese Odyssey*

Textbook

Text

Each lesson is introduced with a dialogue, which we refer to as the lesson's "text." Based on the experiences of a group of friends studying Chinese, the dialogues reflect the daily life of a typical university student.

The situations in each of the lessons are real-life situations that you might encounter upon visiting or pre-paring to visit China, such as asking for directions, ordering food at a restaurant, or applying for a visa to study abroad. We have also incorporated a range of cultural material, including common idioms and slang, to enhance your working knowledge of Chinese culture and tradition.

Vocabulary

Because Chinese is a non-alphabetic language, it is often fascinating but time-consuming for beginning stu-dents to learn the written form. To make it easier, we have divided the vocabulary in Volume 1 of the first year into the following two types:

- Basic: Basic vocabulary consists of common words that are used in everyday conversation. You will practice listening, speaking, and reading these words, but will not be responsible for writing them by hand.

- Core: From the pool of basic vocabulary words, there is a smaller set of core vocabulary, which you should learn to write. In the vocabulary lists, these core vocabulary words are starred.

Throughout *Chinese Odyssey*, you'll also find the following lists of words in the Vocabulary section.

- Notes: Explain special expressions or idioms that appear in the texts. These special expressions are not required learning, but because they are fun and convey something interesting about Chinese culture, most students enjoy learning them.

- Spoken Expressions (口头用语/口頭用語): Part of the required basic vocabulary, these are collo-quial expressions that you will encounter frequently in everyday conversation.

- Featured Vocabulary (词汇注解/詞匯注解): Contains further explanations and examples for the more difficult-to-use or commonly confused words and phrases.

- Supplementary Vocabulary (补充词汇/補充詞匯): Additional words related to the lesson topic. Not required learning.

Starting in Volume 3 of the second year, as a preface to the opening dialogue we have included a back-ground paragraph that provides additional information related to the topic. In the third year, the opening passages become more sophisticated as more written language is introduced, and the dialogues are short-ened accordingly.

Phonetics

This section (Lessons 1–8 in Volume 1) teaches you how to pronounce Chinese using pinyin, the standard romanization system. This section includes phonetic presentations along with exercises such as distinguishing tones, distinguishing sounds, pronunciation practice, and sight reading to help you master pinyin.

Character Writing

This section (Lessons 2–8 in Volume 1) presents Chinese character composition, stroke types, stroke order, and radicals along with a Chinese character box for handwriting practice.

Grammar

This section presents three to five grammar points related to the text in each lesson. The structures are introduced progressively from simple to complex and are displayed in chart form with plenty of supporting examples, making them accessible and easy to use for reference or self-study. You will start by learning parts of speech and the basic word order of a Chinese sentence. Gradually, you will begin to form more complex sentences using new grammatical structures, learn more function words (words with no substantial meaning, but specific grammatical roles), and more complex conjunctions unique to the Chinese language. Throughout the grammar sections, there are short "Practice" exercises that allow you to apply the grammar points you've just learned.

Textbook Exercises

In each lesson of the textbook for volumes 1–4, we have added some classroom-based exercises to give you an opportunity to practice what you have learned with your teacher and your classmates. The textbook exercises focus on grammar and general understanding of the lessons. This allows the teacher to check whether you understand the materials presented in class and give you feedback as you develop your skills. In Volume 5 & 6, the textbook exercises are expanded so that contextualized practice sections immediately follow each major section. After the vocabulary lists, there are related vocabulary exercises. And after grammar patterns are introduced, likewise there is a section of related grammar exercises. This structure accommodates more focused and contextualized language practice for students at the higher skill levels.

Workbook

Volumes 1–4 of *Chinese Odyssey* each include a workbook that contains four sections: listening, speaking, reading, and writing. Each section has two to four tasks, starting at an easy level and gradually becoming more difficult as your skills progress. For example, in the listening section you first might be asked to listen to a set of Chinese phrases and select the corresponding English. Later on, you might hear a short conversation or monologue and be asked to respond to questions based on the text. Speaking exercises emphasize pronunciation, intonation, and conversational skills along with correct grammatical structure. Reading and writing exercises measure your ability to respond to authentic sections of Chinese text in real-life situations you might encounter (writing an e-mail, filling out a form, writing a summary based on Web research, etc.).

In Volumes 5 & 6 of *Chinese Odyssey*, the organization of exercises changes to allow for more integrated practice of all four skills. Instead of a separate workbook with exercises divided by skill type, the exercises in Volumes 5 & 6 combine at least two, and usually three, of the different language skills together. You will have the opportunity to listen and speak, or to read, speak, and write, for example, in a series of integrated tasks.

Multimedia CD-ROM Set

The multimedia CD-ROM is a stand-alone courseware, and includes the same wide range of activities covering listening, speaking, reading, writing, and grammar that you'll find in the textbook and workbook. In addition, the multimedia CD-ROM includes interactive activities and detailed explanations for the practice material, and offers the following technological advantages to help you further improve your language skills:

- A variety of images, video, audio, and readings that incorporate all the basic language skills in a dynamic multimedia environment.

- An interactive platform that allows you to engage in pre-recorded dialogues with the computer.

- Voice-recording capability that allows you to compare your pronunciation with that of a native speaker.

- The flexibility to optimize activities to your own personal skill level, for example by choosing to hear audio clips at different speeds, and choosing to show or hide pinyin.

- Vocabulary lists that feature step-by-step demonstration of character creation and stroke order.

- Immediate feedback on exercise results, with relevant explanations.

- Video clips and authentic materials that help broaden your understanding of life in contemporary China.

- Easy-to-follow navigation and attractive layout.

For more information on the multimedia CD-ROM, please see "The *Chinese Odyssey* Multimedia CD-ROM" on page xvii.

Audio CD

The audio CDs includes all lesson texts and vocabulary in the textbook, as well as all listening exercises and some speaking exercises in the workbook. The audio CDs can be used in addition to the Multimedia CD-ROM Set for students who would like extra speaking and listening practice, or they can be used as the primary source for audio content for students who prefer not to use the multimedia CD-ROMs.

Using the Materials in *Chinese Odyssey*

There are three major ways to utilize the materials in *Chinese Odyssey*.

Multimedia CD-ROM Set

This is the primary element, and includes all lessons, grammar, vocabulary, and exercises in the program. It can be used as a stand-alone set, or in conjunction with other elements.

Textbook/Workbook + Multimedia CD-ROM Set

The workbook allows you to do listening, reading, writing, and some speaking exercises without a computer. It includes all the workbook exercises on the CD-ROM, with the exception of some speaking exercises that require voice recording and playback.

Textbook/Workbook + Audio CD Set

This combination works well for people who aren't utilizing the multimedia CD-ROMs. The audio CD set contains audio content for all lessons, plus listening exercises and some speaking exercises.

Chinese Odyssey is an excellent courseware package, but like any teaching tool, it's only half of the equation. We've provided you with the materials, and now it's up to you to make the best use of them. Remember, the more you practice your Chinese, the better you will become. We wish you the best of luck and hope that you enjoy *Chinese Odyssey*.

The Chinese Odyssey Multimedia CD-ROM

The Multimedia CD-ROM is the primary element in the *Chinese Odyssey* courseware, and may either be used as a stand-alone set or, for those who prefer to work with pen and paper, supplemented with the textbook and workbook. Directly correlated with the textbook and workbook, the multimedia CD-ROM allows you to practice listening, speaking, reading, and writing Chinese in an interactive format at your own pace.

Texts

- Read and listen to each lesson's text.

- Show or hide pinyin.

- See a video in which speakers enact the dialogues.

Phonetics

This section appears in Lessons 1–8 of Volume 1.

BlueGLAS

| MAIN MENU | VOCABULARY INDEX | GRAMMAR LIST | HELP | QUIT |

Phonetics

Presentation | Tones | Pinyin Review | All Pinyin

I. Review of Initials and Finals

The initials and finals selected for review here are based on vocabulary learned in this lesson. We have included initials and finals from previous lessons in parentheses, to be used with those that we covered in this lesson.

Initials: ch   p   (b   zh   sh)
Finals: -i   iao   ua   uang   (ao   an   ang)

II. Phonetic Spelling Rules

A. When There are No Initials

iao --> yao   When -iao does not have any initials, i changes to y.

ua --> wa   When -ua does not have any initials, u changes

5s | TEXT | PHONETICS | VOCABULARY | GRAMMAR | EXERCISES

- Learn new sounds and tones.
- See a table containing all sounds in the Chinese language.
- Click on any word to hear its pronunciation.

Vocabulary

- View each lesson's vocabulary list.

- Click on any character to see how it's written.

- Click on any pinyin word to hear how it's pronounced.

- Record your voice and compare your pronunciation to that of a native speaker.

Grammar

| MAIN MENU | VOCABULARY INDEX | GRAMMAR LIST | HELP | QUIT |

Grammar

Review | **I** | **II** | **III** | **IV**

I. Using Time-Phrases

In Chinese, expressions of time are usually nouns (今天 jīntiān, 现在 xiànzài, etc.). A time phrase indicating the time of an action can go in one of the following two places:

A. Before the Subject at the Very Beginning of a Sentence

Time word	Subject	Verb/Adjective Predicate	
现在	我	做作业。	Now I will do my homework.
现在	我	很忙。	I am very busy now.

B. Between the Subject and the Verb or Adjective Predicate

Subject	Time word	Verb/Adjective Predicate	
我	今天	不工作。	Now I am not working.
我	现在	很顺利。	Now everything goes smoothly with me.

6s | TEXT | PHONETICS | VOCABULARY | GRAMMAR | EXERCISES

- Review each lesson's grammar points.

Exercises

BlueGLAS   _ | □ | ×

| MAIN MENU | VOCABULARY INDEX | GRAMMAR LIST | HELP | QUIT |

Textbook: Paraphrase Task

Previous Task   Next Task

Paraphrasing - Task 1: Paraphrasing
Exercise 1/2. Translate the following dialogue into Chinese, using your own words. When you are comfortable with your translation, record yourself speaking. To check your pronunciation, listen to the dialogue between the two speakers.

Exercise 1/2 (Step 1 Oral) ◁ ▷

Record

Stop

Playback

Submit

| Script | Key | Text | Voc | Gram |

Script 1/2 Returning the notes

A: Where are you going?
B: I am going to return the Chinese notes.
A: You are not using them now. Is it okay if I use it for a second?
B: Sure.

| 6s | TEXT | PHONETICS | VOCABULARY | GRAMMAR | EXERCISES |

- Do exercises in the textbook and workbook.

- See a key with explanations of correct answers.

- Record your voice and compare your pronunciation to that of a native speaker.

- Easily reference the lesson's text, vocabulary list, and grammar notes.

- View your scores.

List of Abbreviations

General Abbreviations

Abbreviation	Full Word
gram.	grammar
lit.	literally
met.	metaphorically
sb.	somebody
sth.	something
voc.	vocabulary
vs.	versus

Part of Speech Abbreviations

Abbreviation	Full Word
adj.	adjective
adj. phr.	adjective phrase
adv.	adverb
adv. conj.	adverbial conjunction
attr.	attributive
aux.	auxiliary verb
b.f.	bound form
conj.	conjunction
demon. pron.	demonstrative pronoun
interj.	interjection
interrog.	interrogative
m.w.	measure word
n.	noun
n. part.	noun particle

Abbreviation	Full Word
num.	number
part.	particle
phr.	phrase
pref.	prefix
prep.	preposition
pron.	pronoun
prop. n.	proper noun
p.w.	place word
s.e.	spoken expression
sent.	sentence
suff.	suffix
t.w.	time word
v.	verb
v. comp.	verb complement
v. obj.	verb object
v. phr.	verb phrase

41

中国饮食

Chinese Food

In this lesson you will:

■ Use proper etiquette and culturally appropriate Chinese meal behavior.

■ Describe and differentiate Chinese foods from different regions in China.

■ Compare Chinese food with food from your own country.

中国文化里很重要的一部份就是饮食，所以又叫做饮食文化。中国饭有主食和副食两种。主食一般是用粮食做成的。例如，米饭、馒头、饼、面条和饺子等等。副食就是我们常说的中国菜。中国地方大，不同地方的人由于受到气候、风俗习惯、特产等的影响，饮食的口味也不同。例如，南方人爱吃米饭是由于南方水多，生产大米的关系；北方生产麦子，所以北方人爱吃面食。另外，中国各地的风味也不一样。比方说，南方菜常带甜味，北方菜比较咸，四川的菜很辣，山西的菜比较酸。随着历史的发展，慢慢地形成了四川、湖南和广东等菜系。这些菜系有不同之处，也有相同之处。不管是哪个菜系，好的中国菜都讲究色(颜色)、香(香味)、味(味道)、形(形状)这四大特

Xueying Wang

The entrance to a Chongqing-style restaurant in Xi'an, China.

41

中國飲食
Chinese Food

> **In this lesson you will:**
> - Use proper etiquette and culturally appropriate Chinese meal behavior.
> - Describe and differentiate Chinese foods from different regions in China.
> - Compare Chinese food with food from your own country.

　　中國文化裏很重要的一部份就是飲食，所以又叫做飲食文化。中國飯有主食和副食兩種。主食一般是用糧食做成的。例如，米飯、饅頭、餅、麵條和餃子等等。副食就是我們常說的中國菜。中國地方大，不同地方的人由於受到氣候、風俗習慣、特產等的影響，飲食的口味也不同。例如，南方人愛吃米飯是由於南方水多，生產大米的關係；北方生產麥子，所以北方人愛吃麵食。另外，中國各地的風味也不一樣。比方說，南方菜常帶甜味，北方菜比較鹹，四川的菜很辣，山西的菜比較酸。隨著歷史的發展，慢慢地形成了四川、湖南和廣東等菜系。這些菜系有不同之處，也有相同之處。不管是哪個菜系，好的中國菜都講究色(顏色)、香(香味)、味(味道)、形(形狀)這四大特

The entrance to a Chongqing-style restaurant in Xi'an, China.

点。另外，饭后饮茶是中国人的习惯之一。中国人喝茶也很讲究色、香、味。很多人都认为茶叶对身体好。中国南方产的茶很有名，例如龙井茶、茉莉花茶等。

　　近几年来，人们的饮食习惯也有了很大的改变。以前一般人都自己买菜做饭，或者去单位的食堂买饭。现在由于很多人都忙得没时间做饭，所以各种半成品，速食店就越来越多，不但方便，而且便宜。自从中国开放以来，中国人由于受到西方文化的影响，现在也开始吃西餐和喝咖啡。中国各大城已经有了麦当劳和肯得鸡。当然，无论如何，中国人最喜欢的还是中国菜。下面请看李丽莉和吴文德在中国饭馆点菜的小故事：

吴文德：看菜单跟看天书一样，我根本不知道应该点什么？

李丽莉：那你就看看照片，望梅解渴[1]吧。我在离开美国以前，背了一些菜单，比如宫保鸡丁、干扁四季豆、陈皮牛、雪豆虾、鱼香肉丝。在这儿的菜单上，怎么看不见那些菜呢？

陈小云：你说的那些是已经美国化了的中国菜。这儿是真正的四川饭馆。看，这是有名的重庆火锅，麻婆豆腐，红油抄手，水煮牛肉。

李丽莉：现在大家都讲究健康饮食，豆腐有营养，我来个麻婆豆腐吧。

吴文德：红油抄手在美国是头台，在这儿是主菜。我来一碗，看看有什么不同之处。对了，这儿有什么汤，我习惯先喝一碗汤再吃饭。

李丽莉：中国人习惯先吃饭，后喝汤。我们应该入乡随俗[2]，按照中国人的方式吃饭。

Enjoying hot pot in Hangzhou, China.

點。另外，飯後飲茶是中國人的習慣之一。中國人喝茶也很講究色、香、味。很多人都認為茶葉對身體好。中國南方產的茶很有名，例如龍井茶、茉莉花茶等。

　　近幾年來，人們的飲食習慣也有了很大的改變。以前一般人都自己買菜做飯，或者去單位的食堂買飯。現在由於很多人都忙得沒時間做飯，所以各種半成品，速食店就越來越多，不但方便，而且便宜。自從中國開放以來，中國人由於受到西方文化的影響，現在也開始吃西餐和喝咖啡。中國各大城已經有了麥當勞和肯得雞。當然，無論如何，中國人最喜歡的還是中國菜。下面請看李麗莉和吳文德在中國飯館點菜的小故事：

吳文德：看菜單跟看天書一樣，我根本不知道應該點什麼？

李麗莉：那你就看看照片，望梅解渴[1]吧。我在離開美國以前，背了一些菜單，比如宮保雞丁、乾扁四季豆、陳皮牛、雪豆蝦、魚香肉絲。在這兒的菜單上，怎麼看不見那些菜呢？

陳小雲：你說的那些是已經美國化了的中國菜。這兒是真正的四川飯館。看，這是有名的重慶火鍋，麻婆豆腐，紅油抄手，水煮牛肉。

李麗莉：現在大家都講究健康飲食，豆腐有營養，我來個麻婆豆腐吧。

吳文德：紅油抄手在美國是頭檯，在這兒是主菜。我來一碗，看看有什麼不同之處。對了，這兒有什麼湯，我習慣先喝一碗湯再吃飯。

李麗莉：中國人習慣先吃飯，後喝湯。我們應該入鄉隨俗[2]，按照中國人的方式吃飯。

Enjoying hot pot in Hangzhou, China.

陈小云：其实南方有些地方，也先喝汤，后吃饭。有些中国人喝汤和吃饭的时候嘴里都出声，这表示吃得很香。

吴文德：说起"餐桌礼节，"我听说吃饭的时候，筷子不能直插在饭上，也不能用筷子敲碗。对吗？

陈小云：对。但是，我们别光说"餐桌礼节"了。再不点菜，我们就得画饼充饥[3]了。

Notes

1. 望梅解（止）渴 (wàng méi jiě[zhǐ] kě)

   The visual image of what one desires can be a source of relief. (Lit.) Seeing the plums from afar can relieve thirst. For more information, please see Task 4 in 听说读写练习.

2. 入乡随俗 (rù xiāng suí sú)

   When in Rome, do as the Romans do. (Lit.) Enter a region, follow the customs.

3. 画饼充饥 (huà bǐng chōng jī)

   To feed on illusions; (Lit.) Draw a pancake to fill one's stomach. For more information, please see Task 4 in 听说读写练习.

课文问答 *Questions and Answers*

1. 中国各地的菜有什么不同之处？
2. 中国人现在的饮食习惯和以前一样不一样？为什么？
3. 中国人和你们那里的人饮食习惯有什么不同？
4. 你喜欢吃南方菜还是北方菜？为什么？你最喜欢吃的中国菜是什么？为什么？

A home-cooked feast prepared by a Hangzhou family for their guests.

陳小雲：其實南方有些地方，也先喝湯，後吃飯。有些中國人喝湯和吃飯的時候嘴裏都出聲，這表示吃得很香。

吳文德：說起"餐桌禮節，"我聽說吃飯的時候，筷子不能直插在飯上，也不能用筷子敲碗。對嗎？

陳小雲：對。但是，我們別光說"餐桌禮節"了。再不點菜，我們就得畫餅充饑³了。

Notes

1. 望梅解（止）渴 (wàng méi jiě[zhǐ] kě)

The visual image of what one desires can be a source of relief. (Lit.) Seeing the plums from afar can relieve thirst. For more information, please see Task 4 in 聽說讀寫練習.

2. 入鄉隨俗 (rù xiāng suí sú)

When in Rome, do as the Romans do. (Lit.) Enter a region, follow the customs.

3. 畫餅充饑 (huà bǐng chōng jī)

To feed on illusions; (Lit.) Draw a pancake to fill one's stomach. For more information, please see Task 4 in 聽說讀寫練習.

課文問答 *Questions and Answers*

1. 中國各地的菜有什麼不同之處？
2. 中國人現在的飲食習慣和以前一樣不一樣？為什麼？
3. 中國人和你們那裏的人飲食習慣有什麼不同？
4. 你喜歡吃南方菜還是北方菜？為什麼？你最喜歡吃的中國菜是什麼？為什麼？

A home-cooked feast prepared by a Hangzhou family for their guests.

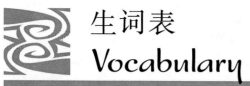

生词表
Vocabulary

Character	Pinyin	Part of Speech	English Definition
1. 饮食	yǐnshí	*n.*	food and drink

中国人的饮食习惯和西方人的很不一样。

饮		*n.*	drinks
		v.	to drink
食		*n*	food

2. 主食	zhǔshí	*n.*	staple food (rice, noodles, bread, etc.)

我们常常去食堂买主食。

3. 副食	fùshí	*n.*	nonstaple food (soup, vegetables, meat, pastry, etc.)

你们去哪儿买副食？

副		*pref.*	side (effect), minor, marginal, vice-

4. 粮食	liángshi	*n.*	grain, provisions

我们不应该浪费粮食。

粮		*n.*	grain, cereals

5. 例如	lìrú	*conj.*	for instance, for example

这家店有很多种甜点，例如日本甜点，法国甜点等等。

6. 同	tóng	*adj.*	the same as

这本书跟那本书不同。

7. 由于	yóuyú	*conj.*	because, thanks to, as a result of

由于那儿饭馆很多，所以大家都不做饭。

8. 受	shòu	*v.*	to be the recipient of (an action), to receive

我不想再受苦了。

9. 气候	qìhòu	*n.*	climate

你们那儿气候怎么样？

10. 特产	tèchǎn	*n.*	product of a specific area

这儿有什么特产？

特		*b.f.*	special, particular
产		*b.f.*	product

生词表
Vocabulary

Character	Pinyin	Part of Speech	English Definition
1. 飲食	yǐnshí	n.	food and drink
中國人的飲食習慣和西方人的很不一樣。			
飲		n.	drinks
		v.	to drink
食		n	food
2. 主食	zhǔshí	n.	staple food (rice, noodles, bread, etc.)
我們常常去食堂買主食。			
3. 副食	fùshí	n.	nonstaple food (soup, vegetables, meat, pastry, etc.)
你們去哪兒買副食？			
副		pref.	side (effect), minor, marginal, vice-
4. 糧食	liángshi	n.	grain, provisions
我們不應該浪費糧食。			
糧		n.	grain, cereals
5. 例如	lìrú	conj.	for instance, for example
這家店有很多種甜點，例如日本甜點，法國甜點等等。			
6. 同	tóng	adj.	the same as
這本書跟那本書不同。			
7. 由於	yóuyú	conj.	because, thanks to, as a result of
由於那兒飯館很多，所以大家都不做飯。			
8. 受	shòu	v.	to be the recipient of (an action), to receive
我不想再受苦了。			
9. 氣候	qìhòu	n.	climate
你們那兒氣候怎麼樣？			
10. 特產	tèchǎn	n.	product of a specific area
這兒有什麼特產？			
特		b.f.	special, particular
產		b.f.	product

11. 影响   yǐngxiǎng   *n.*   influence, effect, impact

我受了他的影响，所以现在也爱吃中国饭了。

                                v.   to influence

不好好吃饭会影响你的身体。

12. 南方   nánfāng   *n.*   south, southern direction

我们家是南方人。

13. 生产   shēngchǎn   *v.*   to produce, to manufacture

这个地方生产些什么？

14. 大米   dàmǐ   *n.*   rice

这儿主要生产大米。

米   *n.*   rice (uncooked) (= 米; 大米 is used to distinguish it from other grains)

15. 北方   běifāng   *n.*   north, northern direction

我朋友家是北方人。

16. 麦子   màizi   *n.*   wheat (the crop)

这儿不生产麦子。

17. 面食   miànshí   *n.*   food made out of wheat (noodles, bread, buns, dumplings, etc.)

你爱吃面食吗？

面   *n.*   wheat flour, flour, noodles

18. 另外   lìngwài   *conj.*   in addition, moreover, on the other hand

我们家人都爱吃米饭，另外我们也爱吃面食。

                                adj.   other

我有两把椅子。一把在书房，另外一把在卧室。

19. 比方说   bǐfang shuō   *phr.*   for example, for instance

南方人都喜欢吃甜的，比方说，我们家就每次炒菜都要加糖。

比方   *n.*   example, illustration

20. 随着   suízhe   *conj.*   following, along with...

随着这里中国饭馆的增加，越来越多的人都开始吃中国饭。

                                v.   to follow

学生都随着老师走出了教室。

11. 影響   yǐngxiǎng   *n.*   influence, effect, impact

我受了他的影響，所以現在也愛吃中國飯了。

                                             v.   to influence

不好好吃飯會影響你的身體。

12. 南方   nánfāng   *n.*   south, southern direction

我們家是南方人。

13. 生產   shēngchǎn   *v.*   to produce, to manufacture

這個地方生產些什麼？

14. 大米   dàmǐ   *n.*   rice

這兒主要生產大米。

米   *n.*   rice (uncooked) (= 米; 大米 is used to distinguish it from other grains)

15. 北方   běifāng   *n.*   north, northern direction

我朋友家是北方人。

16. 麥子   màizi   *n.*   wheat (the crop)

這兒不生產麥子。

17. 麵食   miànshí   *n.*   food made out of wheat (noodles, bread, buns, dumplings, etc.)

你愛吃麵食嗎？

麵   *n.*   wheat flour, flour, noodles

18. 另外   lìngwài   *conj.*   in addition, moreover, on the other hand

我們家人都愛吃米飯，另外我們也愛吃麵食。

                                             adj.   other

我有兩把椅子。一把在書房，另外一把在臥室。

19. 比方說   bǐfang shuō   *phr.*   for example, for instance

南方人都喜歡吃甜的，比方說，我們家就每次炒菜都要加糖。

比方   *n.*   example, illustration

20. 隨著   suízhe   *conj.*   following, along with...

隨著這裏中國飯館的增加，越來越多的人都開始吃中國飯。

                                             v.   to follow

學生都隨著老師走出了教室。

21. 历史   lìshǐ   *n.*   history

我今天有历史课。

历   *b.f.*   experience

史   *b.f.*   history

22. 发展   fāzhǎn   *v.*   to develop, to expand

现在中国发展得很快。

n.   development, growth

这个城市的发展很快。

展   *b.f.*   to unfold, to put on display

23. 形成   xíngchéng   *v. comp.*   to take the form of, to develop into

人们的饮食习惯就是这样形成的。

24. 菜系   càixì   *n.*   culinary system, culinary tradition

中国有几大菜系，你知道吗？

25. 不管   bùguǎn   *conj.*   regardless of

不管你是哪儿人，你都会喜欢这个菜。

26. 相同之处   xiāngtóng zhī chù   *phr.*   similar traits, resemblance

这些菜有不少相同之处，因为都是我做的。

相同   *adj.*   same, identical

27. 讲究   jiǎngjiu   *v.*   (of taste) to be particular about, to be fastidious about

他这个人不讲究吃的。

adj.   fastidious, artistic, sophisticated

这个人生活特别讲究。

28. 形状   xíngzhuàng   *n.*   form and shape

这个甜点的形状很像一个葡萄。

29. 特点   tèdiǎn   *n.*   characteristic, trait

这家饭馆的特点是价格便宜。

30. 改变   gǎibiàn   *v.*   to alter, to change

你为什么总是想让我改变自己的习惯？

n.   change

近几年来我们学校有很大的改变。

21. 歷史　　　　　lìshǐ　　　　　　*n.*　　　　history

我今天有歷史課。

歷　　　　　　　　　　　　　*b.f.*　　　experience

史　　　　　　　　　　　　　*b.f.*　　　history

22. 發展　　　　　fāzhǎn　　　　　*v.*　　　　to develop, to expand

現在中國發展得很快。

　　　　　　　　　　　　　　n.　　　　development, growth

這個城市的發展很快。

展　　　　　　　　　　　　　*b.f.*　　　to unfold, to put on display

23. 形成　　　　　xíngchéng　　　*v. comp.*　to take the form of, to develop into

人們的飲食習慣就是這樣形成的。

24. 菜系　　　　　càixì　　　　　　*n.*　　　　culinary system, culinary tradition

中國有幾大菜系，你知道嗎？

25. 不管　　　　　bùguǎn　　　　　*conj.*　　regardless of

不管你是哪兒人，你都會喜歡這個菜。

26. 相同之處　　　xiāngtóng zhī chù　*phr.*　similar traits, resemblance

這些菜有不少相同之處，因為都是我做的。

相同　　　　　　　　　　　　*adj.*　　same, identical

27. 講究　　　　　jiǎngjiu　　　　　*v.*　　　　(of taste) to be particular about, to be fastidious about

他這個人不講究吃的。

　　　　　　　　　　　　　　adj.　　fastidious, artistic, sophisticated

這個人生活特別講究。

28. 形狀　　　　　xíngzhuàng　　　*n.*　　　　form and shape

這個甜點的形狀很像一個人。

29. 特點　　　　　tèdiǎn　　　　　　*n.*　　　　characteristic, trait

這家飯館的特點是價格便宜。

30. 改變　　　　　gǎibiàn　　　　　*v.*　　　　to alter, to change

你為什麼總是想讓我改變自己的習慣？

　　　　　　　　　　　　　　n.　　　　change

近幾年來我們學校有很大的改變。

31. 半成品   bànchéngpǐn   *n.*   (lit.) half-finished product

这是半成品，你回家以后热一热就可以吃了。

   成品   *n.*   ready-made product, finished product
   品   *n.*   article, product, commodity

32. 速食   sùshí   *n.*   fast food

我们去速食饭馆买点东西吃吧。

   速   *b.f.*   rapid, speedy

33. 开放   kāifàng   *v.*   to open to the public

这家公园今天是第一天开放。

34. 西方   xīfāng   *n.*   the West, Western countries

很多西方人都喜欢吃四川菜。

35. 西餐   xīcān   *n.*   Western food

他不爱吃西餐。

36. 无论如何   wúlùn rúhé   *conj.*   in any case, no matter what

无论如何我今天得吃一点面食。

   无论   *conj.*   regardless of
   如何   *interrog.* (written) how

37. 化   huà   *b.f.*   -ise, -ize

我现在的饮食习惯都已经中国化了。

38. 营养   yíngyǎng   *n.*   nutrition, nourishment

你应该注意营养。

39. 按照   ànzhào   *prep.*   following the pattern of, according to

我的这个菜是按照我爸爸教我的方法做的。

40. 方式   fāngshì   *n.*   method, pattern, mode; (lit.) direction and pattern

你这种喝汤的方式很像中国人。

41. 嘴   zuǐ   *n.*   mouth

我的嘴很疼。

42. 表示   biǎoshì   *v.*   to express, to show, to demonstrate, to indicate

这种声音表示他已经吃饱了。

                                   n.   indication

这种表示方法很清楚。

31. 半成品　　　bànchéngpǐn　　*n.*　　　　(lit.) half-finished product
　　這是半成品，你回家以後熱一熱就可以吃了。
　　成品　　　　　　　　　　*n.*　　　　ready-made product, finished product
　　品　　　　　　　　　　　*n.*　　　　article, product, commodity

32. 速食　　　sùshí　　　　*n.*　　　　fast food
　　我們去速食飯館買點東西吃吧。
　　速　　　　　　　　　　　*b.f.*　　　rapid, speedy

33. 開放　　　kāifàng　　　*v.*　　　　to open to the public
　　這家公園今天是第一天開放。

34. 西方　　　xīfāng　　　　*n.*　　　　the West, Western countries
　　很多西方人都喜歡吃四川菜。

35. 西餐　　　xīcān　　　　*n.*　　　　Western food
　　他不愛吃西餐。

36. 無論如何　wúlùn rúhé　*conj.*　　in any case, no matter what
　　無論如何我今天得吃一點麵食。
　　無論　　　　　　　　　　*conj.*　　regardless of
　　如何　　　　　　　　　　*interrog.*　(written) how

37. 化　　　　huà　　　　　*b.f.*　　　-ise, -ize
　　我現在的飲食習慣都已經中國化了。

38. 營養　　　yíngyǎng　　*n.*　　　　nutrition, nourishment
　　你應該注意營養。

39. 按照　　　ànzhào　　　*prep.*　　following the pattern of, according to
　　我的這個菜是按照我爸爸教我的方法做的。

40. 方式　　　fāngshì　　　*n.*　　　　method, pattern, mode; (lit.) direction and pattern
　　你這種喝湯的方式很像中國人。

41. 嘴　　　　zuǐ　　　　　*n.*　　　　mouth
　　我的嘴很疼。

42. 表示　　　biǎoshì　　　*v.*　　　　to express, to show, to demonstrate, to indicate
　　這種聲音表示他已經吃飽了。
　　　　　　　　　　　　　　n.　　　　indication
　　這種表示方法很清楚。

43. 礼节   lǐjié   *n.*   manners, courtesy, social formalities

这是中国人的礼节，你不知道吗？

44. 插   chā   *v.*   to stick (something) in, to insert

请你把这些花儿插得好看一点。

饭名和菜名 Names of Some Foods and Dishes

A. 饭名（主食）

1. 米饭	mǐfàn		rice
2. 馒头	mántou		steamed bun (without filling)
3. 包子	bāozi		steamed bun (with filling)
4. 饼（子）	bǐng (zi)		pancake
5. 面条	miàntiáo		noodles

B. 菜名

1. 家常豆腐	jiācháng dòufu	home-style tofu
2. 宫保鸡丁	gōngbǎo jīdīng	gongbao chicken
3. 干扁四季豆	gānbiǎn sìjìdòu	crispy beans
4. 陈皮牛	chénpí niú	orange beef
5. 雪豆虾	xuědòu xiā	shrimp with snow peas
6. 鱼香肉丝	yúxiāng ròusī	fish-flavored pork
7. 麻婆豆腐	mápó dòufu	mapo tofu
8. 红油抄手	hóngyóu chāoshǒu	dumplings in hot and spicy oil
9. 水煮牛	shuǐzhǔ niú	Sichuan-style beef

专有名词 Proper Nouns

1. 山西	Shānxī	Shanxi Province
2. 四川	Sìchuān	Sichuan Province

43. 禮節　　　　　　　lǐjié　　　　　　*n.*　　　　manners, courtesy, social formalities

這是中國人的禮節，你不知道嗎？

44. 插　　　　　　　　chā　　　　　　　*v.*　　　　to stick (something) in, to insert

請你把這些花兒插得好看一點。

飯名和菜名 Names of Some Foods and Dishes

A. 飯名（主食）

1. 米飯　　　　　　mǐfàn　　　　　　　　　　rice
2. 饅頭　　　　　　mántou　　　　　　　　　steamed bun (without filling)
3. 包子　　　　　　bāozi　　　　　　　　　　steamed bun (with filling)
4. 餅（子）　　　　bǐng (zi)　　　　　　　　pancake
5. 麵條　　　　　　miàntiáo　　　　　　　　noodles

B. 菜名

1. 家常豆腐　　　jiācháng dòufu　　　　　home-style tofu
2. 宮保雞丁　　　gōngbǎo jīdīng　　　　　gongbao chicken
3. 乾扁四季豆　　gānbiǎn sìjìdòu　　　　　crispy beans
4. 陳皮牛　　　　chénpí niú　　　　　　　orange beef
5. 雪豆蝦　　　　xuědòu xiā　　　　　　　shrimp with snow peas
6. 魚香肉絲　　　yúxiāng ròusī　　　　　　fish-flavored pork
7. 麻婆豆腐　　　mápó dòufu　　　　　　　mapo tofu
8. 紅油抄手　　　hóngyóu chāoshǒu　　　　dumplings in hot and spicy oil
9. 水煮牛　　　　shuǐzhǔ niú　　　　　　　Sichuan-style beef

專有名詞 Proper Nouns

1. 山西　　　　　Shānxī　　　　　　　　　Shanxi Province
2. 四川　　　　　Sìchuān　　　　　　　　　Sichuan Province

3. 湖南	Húnán	Hunan Province
4. 广东	Guǎngdōng	Guangdong Province
5. 龙井茶	Lóngjǐngchá	Dragon Well Tea, a famous green tea
6. 茉莉花茶	Mòlihuāchá	Jasmine tea
7. 重庆	Chóngqìng	Chongqing, formerly a city in Sichuan Province, now a district under national jurisdiction
8. 麦当劳	Màidāngláo	McDonald's
9. 肯得鸡	Kěndéjī	Kentucky Fried Chicken

口头用语 Spoken Expressions

1. 天书	tiānshū	writing that is too difficult to read and comprehend; (lit.) heavenly scripture
2. 头台	tóutái	appetizer, starter
3. 主菜	zhǔcài	entrée

书面语 vs. 口语 Written Form vs. Spoken Form

In Chinese, the "written form" preserves a lot of words and expressions from Classical Chinese and is therefore more concise and formal. As its name implies, the "written form" is used primarily in writing, but it occurs frequently in speech as well.

书面语	口语
1. 各地	各个地方
2. 不同之处	不一样的地方
3. 相同之处	一样的地方
4. 饭后	吃完饭以后
5. 近	最近
6. 无论如何	不管怎么样

3. 湖南	Húnán	Hunan Province
4. 廣東	Guǎngdōng	Guangdong Province
5. 龍井茶	Lóngjǐngchá	Dragon Well Tea, a famous green tea
6. 茉莉花茶	Mòlihuāchá	Jasmine tea
7. 重慶	Chóngqìng	Chongqing, formerly a city in Sichuan Province, now a district under national jurisdiction
8. 麥當勞	Màidāngláo	McDonald's
9. 肯得雞	Kěndéjī	Kentucky Fried Chicken

口頭用語 Spoken Expressions

1. 天書	tiānshū	writing that is too difficult to read and comprehend; (lit.) heavenly scripture
2. 頭檯	tóutái	appetizer, starter
3. 主菜	zhǔcài	entrée

書面語 vs. 口語 Written Form vs. Spoken Form

In Chinese, the "written form" preserves a lot of words and expressions from Classical Chinese and is therefore more concise and formal. As its name implies, the "written form" is used primarily in writing, but it occurs frequently in speech as well.

書面語	口語
1. 各地	各個地方
2. 不同之處	不一樣的地方
3. 相同之處	一樣的地方
4. 飯後	吃完飯以後
5. 近	最近
6. 無論如何	不管怎麼樣

词汇注解 Featured Vocabulary

1. 例如／比如 (lìrú/bǐrú) vs. 比方说 (bǐfang shuō)

比如	*conj.*	for example, such as (formal)
例如	*conj.*	for example, such as (formal)
比方说	*phr.*	for example (casual)

2. 等／等等 (děng/děngděng) vs. 等一下儿 (děng yīxiàr)

等	***n. part.***	etc.

This is usually used at the end of a list of nouns and may be followed by a summing-up term.

北京上海等地现在都有这种饭馆。

This kind of restaurant can be found in Beijing, Shanghai, etc.

等等	***n. part.***	etc.

Same as 等 above, but it stands alone at the end of the sentence.

今年他去的地方有西安、上海，等等。

This year the places he went to included Xi'an, Shanghai, etc.

等（一下儿）	*v.*	to wait

请等一下儿。

Please wait a minute.

3. 影响 (yǐngxiǎng)

影响	*n.*	influence

As a noun, 影响 is frequently used with the verb 受（到）to form the pattern 受（到）…影响, which describes a subject being influenced by something or someone. It is often paired with a sentence describing the result of this influence. The result can be placed in the first or second clause.

Placed in the first clause:

由于受到了西方的影响，现在喝咖啡的人越来越多了。

Because of Western influence, more and more people now drink coffee.

Placed in the second clause:

他喜欢吃辣的，是因为受了他爸爸妈妈的影响。

He likes to eat hot and spicy food, because he is influenced by his parents.

影响	*v.*	to influence, to affect

This is usually used to describe a negative situation.

工作太多影响到了他的身体健康。

Too much work has affected his health.

辭彙注解 Featured Vocabulary

1. 例如/比如 (lìrú/bǐrú) vs. 比方說 (bǐfang shuō)

比如	*conj.*	for example, such as (formal)
例如	*conj.*	for example, such as (formal)
比方說	*phr.*	for example (casual)

2. 等/等等 (děng/děngděng) vs. 等一下兒 (děng yīxiàr)

等	**n. part.**	etc.

This is usually used at the end of a list of nouns and may be followed by a summing-up term.

北京上海等地現在都有這種飯館。

This kind of restaurant can be found in Beijing, Shanghai, etc.

等等	**n. part.**	etc.

Same as 等 above, but it stands alone at the end of the sentence.

今年他去的地方有西安、上海，等等。

This year the places he went to included Xi'an, Shanghai, etc.

等（一下兒）	*v.*	to wait

請等一下兒。

Please wait a minute.

3. 影響 (yǐngxiǎng)

影響	**n.**	influence

As a noun, 影響 is frequently used with the verb 受（到）to form the pattern 受（到）…影響, which describes a subject being influenced by something or someone. It is often paired with a sentence describing the result of this influence. The result can be placed in the first or second clause.

Placed in the first clause:

由於受到了西方的影響，現在喝咖啡的人越來越多了。

Because of Western influence, more and more people now drink coffee.

Placed in the second clause:

他喜歡吃辣的，是因為受了他爸爸媽媽的影響。

He likes to eat hot and spicy food, because he is influenced by his parents.

影響	*v.*	to influence, to affect

This is usually used to describe a negative situation.

工作太多影響到了他的身體健康。

Too much work has affected his health.

4. 另外 (lìngwài)

另外	*adv.*	additionally

This word introduces a supplement to what has already been mentioned, often occurring with 又，还，再, etc.

他炒了一个菜，另外又做了一个汤。
After he finished cooking the main course, he made a soup.

另外	*demon. pron.*	another

This is often placed before a numeral + measure word and possibly a noun as an addendum to the initial statement.

我的一个姐姐在美国，另外一个(姐姐)在日本。
I have one older sister in America and another in Japan.

5. 南方/北方 (nánfāng/běifāng) vs. 东方/西方 (dōngfāng/xīfāng)

南方/北方	*n.*	South/North

These are usually used to designate two regions in a country.

东方/西方	*n.*	East/West

These are usually used to designate two different regions in the world.

In contrast, 南部，北部，东部, and 西部 are all used to designate regions in a country.

6. 化 (huà)

化	*v.*	-ize or -ify

化 can follow a noun or an adjective to transform it into a verb or an adjective.

中国人现在的饮食习惯已经非常现代化了。
The eating habits of Chinese people are already very modernized.

为了绿化城市，中国到处都在种树。
In order to make cities greener, people in China are growing trees everywhere.

7. 方式 (fāngshì) vs. 方法 (fāngfǎ)

方式	*n.*	a way or a pattern of doing something

饮食方式
the pattern of eating

方法	*n.*	the method used to solve problems or to do things

烧菜的方法
the method of cooking

4. 另外 (lìngwài)

另外	*adv.*	additionally

This word introduces a supplement to what has already been mentioned, often occurring with 又，還，再，etc.

他炒了一個菜，另外又做了一個湯。
After he finished cooking the main course, he made a soup.

另外	*demon. pron.*	another

This is often placed before a numeral + measure word and possibly a noun as an addendum to the initial statement.

我的一個姐姐在美國，另外一個（姐姐）在日本。
I have one older sister in America and another in Japan.

5. 南方/北方 (nánfāng/běifāng) vs. 東方/西方 (dōngfāng/xīfāng)

南方/北方	*n.*	South/North

These are usually used to designate two regions in a country.

東方/西方	*n.*	East/West

These are usually used to designate two different regions in the world.

In contrast, 南部，北部，東部，and 西部 are all used to designate regions in a country.

6. 化 (huà)

化	*v.*	-ize or -ify

化 can follow a noun or an adjective to transform it into a verb or an adjective.

中國人現在的飲食習慣已經非常現代化了。
The eating habits of Chinese people are already very modernized.

為了綠化城市，中國到處都在種樹。
In order to make cities greener, people in China are growing trees everywhere.

7. 方式 (fāngshì) vs. 方法 (fāngfǎ)

方式	*n.*	a way or a pattern of doing something

飲食方式
the pattern of eating

方法	*n.*	the method used to solve problems or to do things

燒菜的方法
the method of cooking

8. 表示 (biǎoshì) vs. 表达 (biǎodá)

表示	*v.*	to express one's feelings

我们对你的帮助表示感谢。
We thank you for your help.

表达	*v.*	to express, to convey

如果你不能用中文表达你的意思，就用英文说吧。
If you cannot express yourself in Chinese, just use English.

表达	*n.*	the act of expressing

他的中文表达能力很好。
His ability to express himself in Chinese is very good.

词汇练习
Vocabulary Exercises

🎧 🀄 TASK 1. 组词 WORD AND PHRASE COMPOSITION

Use the given bound form on the left as a guide to help you think of other, similar compound words. Feel free to use a dictionary when needed. Then write down the English definition of each of the compound words you've created.

1. 化 (-ize): 美国化   Americanized

    _____化

    _____化

    _____化

2. 品 (product): 成品   ready-made product

    _____品

    _____品

    _____品

3. 食 (food): 主食   staple food

    _____食

    _____食

    _____食

8. 表示 (biǎoshì) vs. 表達 (biǎodá)

表示	*v.*	to express one's feelings

我們對你的幫助表示感謝。
We thank you for your help.

表達	*v.*	to express, to convey

如果你不能用中文表達你的意思，就用英文說吧。
If you cannot express yourself in Chinese, just use English.

表達	*n.*	the act of expressing

他的中文表達能力很好。
His ability to express himself in Chinese is very good.

辭彙練習
Vocabulary Exercises

🎧 🖊 TASK 1. 組詞 WORD AND PHRASE COMPOSITION

Use the given bound form on the left as a guide to help you think of other, similar compound words. Feel free to use a dictionary when needed. Then write down the English definition of each of the compound words you've created.

1. 化 (-ize): 美國化   Americanized
   _____化
   _____化
   _____化

2. 品 (product): 成品   ready-made product
   _____品
   _____品
   _____品

3. 食 (food): 主食   staple food
   _____食
   _____食
   _____食

4. 特 (special): 特产   local specialty

   特 _____

   特 _____

   特 _____

5. 单 (single): 单位   unit

   单 _____

   单 _____

   单 _____

6. 表 (to express): 表示   to express

   表 _____

   表 _____

   表 _____

🎧💠 TASK 2. 搭配 MATCHING

A. 近义词

Match synonyms from among the following words and phrases.

1) 速食	a) 比如
2) 不管	b) 发展成
3) 形成	c) 快餐
4) 无论如何	d) 吃的主食
5) 粮食	e) 不管怎么样
6) 例如	f) 无论

B. 动宾词组

Match verbs in the left column with nouns in the right column to form phrases.

1. Verbs	Nouns
1) 形成	a) 营养
2) 随着	b) 那种方式
3) 按照	c) 四大菜系
4) 讲究	d) 历史的发展

4. 特 (special): 特產   local specialty

   特 _____

   特 _____

   特 _____

5. 單 (single): 單位   unit

   單 _____

   單 _____

   單 _____

6. 表 (to express): 表示   to express

   表 _____

   表 _____

   表 _____

🎧 TASK 2. 搭配 MATCHING

A. 近義詞

Match synonyms from among the following words and phrases.

1) 速食	a) 比如
2) 不管	b) 發展成
3) 形成	c) 快餐
4) 無論如何	d) 吃的主食
5) 糧食	e) 不管怎麼樣
6) 例如	f) 無論

B. 動賓詞組

Match verbs in the left column with nouns in the right column to form phrases.

Verbs	**Nouns**
1) 形成	a) 營養
2) 隨著	b) 那種方式
3) 按照	c) 四大菜系
4) 講究	d) 歷史的發展

2. Verbs   **Nouns**

1) 表示   a) 一些改变

2) 有   b) 什么形状

3) 受   c) 感谢

4)（不管）是   d) 气候的影响

🎧 TASK 3. 填空 FILL IN THE BLANKS

A. 句子

Read the following sentences and fill in each blank with the appropriate word or phrase from the given options.

生产   另外   讲究   发展   表示   形成

1. 随着几千年来的 _____，喝茶在中国已经 _____ 了一种文化。

2. 中国南方很多地方都 _____ 茶叶。

3. 有的人非常 _____ 茶的香味、颜色、沏茶用的水、喝茶用的茶杯等等。
   _____，懂得喝茶常常也 _____ 一个人有文化。

Vocabulary

茶叶 cháyè   *n.*   tea leaves

B. 段落

Read the following passage and fill in each blank with the appropriate word or phrase from the given options.

方式   影响   之处   无论   特点

　　日本的"茶道"也是受了中国的 _____ 发展起来的。当然，日本人现在的"茶道"已经有了他们自己的 _____ 和他们自己的饮茶 _____，跟中国的茶文化不同 _____ 很多。但是 _____ 在中国、在日本、还是在美国，现在大家都认识到饮茶对身体有很多好处。所以，医生常常让大家少喝咖啡，多喝茶。

Vocabulary

茶道 chádào   *n.*   ways of drinking tea

2. **Verbs**   **Nouns**

1) 表示   a) 一些改變

2) 有   b) 什麼形狀

3) 受   c) 感謝

4) （不管）是   d) 氣候的影響

🎧 ✸ TASK 3. 填空 FILL IN THE BLANKS

A. 句子

Read the following sentences and fill in each blank with the appropriate word or phrase from the given options.

生產　　另外　　講究　　發展　　表示　　形成

1. 隨著幾千年來的 ＿＿＿＿＿＿＿＿，喝茶在中國已經 ＿＿＿＿＿＿＿＿ 了一種文化。

2. 中國南方很多地方都 ＿＿＿＿＿＿＿＿ 茶葉。

3. 有的人非常 ＿＿＿＿＿＿＿＿ 茶的香味、顏色、沏茶用的水、喝茶用的茶杯等等。
   ＿＿＿＿＿＿＿＿，懂得喝茶常常也 ＿＿＿＿＿＿＿＿ 一個人有文化。

Vocabulary

茶葉　cháyè　　　　　*n.*　　　tea leaves

B. 段落

Read the following passage and fill in each blank with the appropriate word or phrase from the given options.

方式　　影響　　之處　　無論　　特點

　　日本的"茶道"也是受了中國的 ＿＿＿＿＿＿＿＿ 發展起來的。當然，日本人現在的"茶道"已經有了他們自己的 ＿＿＿＿＿＿＿＿ 和他們自己的飲茶 ＿＿＿＿＿＿＿＿，跟中國的茶文化不同 ＿＿＿＿＿＿＿＿ 很多。但是 ＿＿＿＿＿＿＿＿ 在中國、在日本、還是在美國，現在大家都認識到飲茶對身體有很多好處。所以，醫生常常讓大家少喝咖啡，多喝茶。

Vocabulary

茶道　chádào　　　　　*n.*　　　ways of drinking tea

语法句型和练习
Grammar Structures and Exercises

I. The preposition 由于 (yóuyú): Because, due to

The preposition 由于 is often used in written language. It is placed at the beginning of a sentence to introduce a cause or reason and can be followed by a subject-predicate structure, a verb-object structure, or a noun phrase. When the phrase following 由于 is short, 的关系 can be attached to form the pattern 由于…的关系.

Sometimes the effect precedes the cause; in this case, 是由于(的关系) is used toward the end of the sentence to provide a reason. 由于 can be used in conjunction with 所以, 就, or 才 to make the cause and effect relationship more obvious.

1st clause (Cause)		2nd clause (Effect)	
由于	**Noun phrase,**	**Subject**	**Verb phrase**
由于	我女朋友的关系，	我	决定自己买一个房子。

I have decided to buy my own home because of my girlfriend.

由于	**Subject**	**Predicate,**	**Subject**	**Predicate**
由于	手机	既时髦又方便，	所以使用的人	越来越多。

Using cellular phones is not only convenient but also trendy, so more and more people are using them.

(Effect)		(Cause)	
Subject	**Verb Object**	是由于	**Verb phrase**
他暑期	打工	是由于	需要挣钱买新车。

He works in the summer because he wants to earn money to buy a new car.

Subject	**Verb Object**	是由于	**Noun phrase** 的关系
我	学中文	是由于	工作的关系。

I study Chinese because of my job.

🔲 PRACTICE

模仿造句

Make sentences of your own by following each of the examples given.

1. 由于讲究营养的关系，_____。

   (Example: 很多人都开始吃豆腐做的菜)

2. 现在中国速食店越来越多，是由于 _____。

   (Example: 受西方文化的影响)

語法句型和練習
Grammar Structures and Exercises

I. The preposition 由於 (yóuyú): Because, due to

The preposition 由於 is often used in written language. It is placed at the beginning of a sentence to introduce a cause or reason and can be followed by a subject-predicate structure, a verb-object structure, or a noun phrase. When the phrase following 由於 is short, 的關係 can be attached to form the pattern 由於…的關係.

   Sometimes the effect precedes the cause; in this case, 是由於(的關係) is used toward the end of the sentence to provide a reason. 由於 can be used in conjunction with 所以, 就, or 才 to make the cause and effect relationship more obvious.

1st clause (Cause)		2nd clause (Effect)	
由於	**Noun phrase,**	**Subject**	**Verb phrase**
由於	我女朋友的關係，	我	決定自己買一個房子。

I have decided to buy my own home because of my girlfriend.

由於	**Subject**	**Predicate,**	**Subject**	**Predicate**
由於	手機	既時髦又方便，	所以使用的人	越來越多。

Using cellular phones is not only convenient but also trendy, so more and more people are using them.

(Effect)		(Cause)	
Subject	**Verb Object**	**是由於**	**Verb phrase**
他暑期	打工	是由於	需要掙錢買新車。

He works in the summer because he wants to earn money to buy a new car.

Subject	**Verb Object**	**是由於**	**Noun phrase** 的關係
我	學中文	是由於	工作的關係。

I study Chinese because of my job.

🔲 PRACTICE

模仿造句

Make sentences of your own by following each of the examples given.

1. 由於講究營養的關係，_____。

   (Example: 很多人都開始吃豆腐做的菜)

2. 現在中國速食店越來越多，是由於_____。

   (Example: 受西方文化的影響)

3. 由于路远的关系 _____。

(Example: 他从来不去那家速食店买东西)

问答

Use the preposition 由于 to answer the following question.

为什么中国各地的饮食习惯都不一样？

翻译

Translate the following sentence into Chinese. Make sure your translation includes 由于 and 受…影响.

Because of the influence of Western culture, people's lifestyles and eating habits are different from what they were before.

II. 随着 (suízhe): Following the (event) of, along with

随着 can be used as a conjunction or a verb.

A. Used as a conjunction

As a preposition, it's often followed by a noun phrase indicating a certain event or action, after which something else happens. This structure shows how one situation affects another.

1st situation	2nd situation
随着 Noun phrase	Subject Predicate

随着天气的变化，   树上的叶子都黄了。
Following the change of the weather, all the leaves on the trees turned yellow.

随着历史的发展，   中国各地不同风味的菜慢慢地形成了多种菜系。
As history unfolded, different regional Chinese dishes gradually developed into various culinary systems.

B. Used as a verb

When 随着 functions as a verb, it's usually used in the second clause to indicate that one thing follows another. It is often used in conjunction with 也 or 就.

1st clause	2nd clause
Subject Verb phrase ，	Subject 也/就随着 Verb phrase

由于受到气候的影响，   他的饮食习惯也随着改变了。
Because of the influence of the climate, his eating habits have also changed.

前面的车往左拐，   后边的车就随着往左拐。
The car in front turned left, and the car in back turned left with it.

3. 由於路遠的關係 _____。

(Example: 他從來不去那家速食店買東西)

問答

Use the preposition 由於 to answer the following question.

為什麼中國各地的飲食習慣都不一樣？

翻譯

Translate the following sentence into Chinese. Make sure your translation includes 由於 and 受…影響.

Because of the influence of Western culture, people's lifestyles and eating habits are different from what they were before.

II. 隨著 (suízhe): Following the (event) of, along with

隨著 can be used as a conjunction or a verb.

A. Used as a conjunction

As a preposition, it's often followed by a noun phrase indicating a certain event or action, after which something else happens. This structure shows how one situation affects another.

1st situation	2nd situation
隨著 Noun phrase	Subject Predicate

隨著天氣的變化，　　　　　樹上的葉子都黃了。

Following the change of the weather, all the leaves on the trees turned yellow.

隨著歷史的發展，　　　　　中國各地不同風味的菜慢慢地形成了多種菜系。

As history unfolded, different regional Chinese dishes gradually developed into various culinary systems.

B. Used as a verb

When 隨著 functions as a verb, it's usually used in the second clause to indicate that one thing follows another. It is often used in conjunction with 也 or 就.

1st clause	2nd clause
Subject Verb phrase，	Subject 也/就隨著 Verb phrase

由於受到氣候的影響，　　　他的飲食習慣也隨著改變了。

Because of the influence of the climate, his eating habits have also changed.

前面的車往左拐，　　　　　後邊的車就隨著往左拐。

The car in front turned left, and the car in back turned left with it.

◩◪ PRACTICE

模仿造句

Make sentences of your own by following each of the examples given.

1. 随着人们饮食习惯的改变，很多饭馆 _____。
   (Example: 都开始注意讲究营养)

2. 随着 _____ 的改变，_____。
   (Example: 他学习习惯，他的中文一天比一天好)

3. 由于他要在美国工作几年，_____。
   (Example: 他的家人也就随着他到美国来了)

4. 大风一刮，_____。
   (Example: 随着来的就是大雨)

问答

Use 随着 to answer the following question.

中国的各种菜系是怎么形成的？

Steamed dumplings with meat filling are a popular snack food.

Andrew Buko

🔯 PRACTICE

模仿造句

Make sentences of your own by following each of the examples given.

1. 隨著人們飲食習慣的改變，很多飯館 _____。

   (Example: 都開始注意講究營養)

2. 隨著 _____ 的改變，_____。

   (Example: 他學習習慣，他的中文一天比一天好)

3. 由於他要在美國工作幾年，_____。

   (Example: 他的家人也就隨著他到美國來了)

4. 大風一刮，_____。

   (Example: 隨著來的就是大雨)

問答

Use 隨著 to answer the following question.

   中國的各種菜系是怎麼形成的？

Steamed dumplings with meat filling are a popular snack food.

翻译

Translate the following sentence into Chinese. Make sure your translation includes 随着 and 改变.

As eating habits change, some table manners are also changing.

III. 不管 (bùguǎn): No matter, regardless of, whether or not

The 不管 structure indicates that, no matter what the circumstance is, the result remains the same. 不管 is used in the first clause and must be followed by a question form using either an interrogative pronoun such as 谁, 什么, 哪, 哪儿, 怎么, 多少, 多, or an alternative, but never 吗. In the second clause (result), 都, 也, 还, 就, or 总 can be and are often placed before the verb phrase. 不管 is interchangeable with 不论 and 无论.

1st clause	2nd clause (result)
不管 Question form,	Subject 也/都/还/就/总 Verb phrase

这次考试不管分数多少，   我都不在乎。
This time, when I take the exam, I don't care what score I get, no matter what it is.

不论申请信用卡还是借记卡， 你总得填张表。
Regardless of whether you're applying for a credit or debit card, you always have to fill out a form.

一个人无论做什么事情，   都应当细心。
No matter what a person does, (s)he should pay attention to detail.

不管学生复习没复习，   老师今天就是要考试。
The teacher will give a test today no matter whether the students review or not.

❧ PRACTICE

改写句子

Use the 不管 structure to rewrite the following sentences.
1. 大家都喜欢吃中国菜。（Hint: 谁 or 还是）
2. 他虽然很忙还是每天锻炼。（Hint: 忙不忙 or 多）
3. 老师教了他很多次，他都学不会。（Hint: 多少 or 怎么）
4. 这家饭馆每一道菜的味道都很特别。（Hint: 哪）

问答

Use the 不管 structure to answer the following questions.

翻譯

Translate the following sentence into Chinese. Make sure your translation includes 隨著 and 改變.

As eating habits change, some table manners are also changing.

III. 不管 (bùguǎn): No matter, regardless of, whether or not

The 不管 structure indicates that, no matter what the circumstance is, the result remains the same. 不管 is used in the first clause and must be followed by a question form using either an interrogative pronoun such as 誰, 什麼, 哪, 哪兒, 怎麼, 多少, 多, or an alternative, but never 嗎. In the second clause (result), 都, 也, 還, 就, or 總 can be and are often placed before the verb phrase. 不管 is interchangeable with 不論 and 無論.

1st clause	2nd clause (result)
不管 Question form,	Subject 也/都/還/就/總 Verb phrase

這次考試不管分數多少，　　　我都不在乎。

This time, when I take the exam, I don't care what score I get, no matter what it is.

不論申請信用卡還是借記卡，　你總得填張表。

Regardless of whether you're applying for a credit or debit card, you always have to fill out a form.

一個人無論做什麼事情，　　　都應當細心。

No matter what a person does, (s)he should pay attention to detail.

不管學生復習沒復習，　　　　老師今天就是要考試。

The teacher will give a test today no matter whether the students review or not.

❀ PRACTICE

改寫句子

Use the 不管 structure to rewrite the following sentences.

1. 大家都喜歡吃中國菜。(Hint: 誰 or 還是)
2. 他雖然很忙還是每天鍛煉。(Hint: 忙不忙 or 多)
3. 老師教了他很多次，他都學不會。(Hint: 多少 or 怎麼)
4. 這家飯館每一道菜的味道都很特別。(Hint: 哪)

問答

Use the 不管 structure to answer the following questions.

1. 你想不想去看那个电影？

2. 这个周末你给我打电话，好吗？

造句

Use 不管 or 无论 with each of the following phrases to make sentences of your own.

1. 什么时候
2. 哪儿
3. 怎么样

翻译

Translate the following sentence into Chinese. Make sure your translation includes 无论 or 不管.

All types of Chinese cooking have one thing in common: whether the dishes are Northern or Southern, they all pay attention to color, smell, taste, and shape.

IV. 无论如何 (wúlùn rúhé): No matter what, at any rate

如何 is the formal version of "怎么样." 无论如何 is a set phrase, meaning "at any rate," often used with adverbs 也 and 都. It is also frequently used with auxiliary verbs such as 得 and 要. The subject can be placed before or after 无论如何.

Subject 无论如何	(Subject)	得/要Verb phrase
春节 无论如何		得回家一趟，因为我已经有三年没回家了。

This Spring Festival, no matter what, I have to return home because I haven't been home for three years.

无论如何	你	也要注意自己的身体，不要整天大吃大喝。

At any rate, you need to pay attention to your own health and stop overeating and drinking all day long.

1. 你想不想去看那個電影？

2. 這個週末你給我打電話，好嗎？

造句

Use 不管 or 無論 with each of the following phrases to make sentences of your own.

1. 什麼時候
2. 哪兒
3. 怎麼樣

翻譯

Translate the following sentence into Chinese. Make sure your translation includes 無論 or 不管.

　　All types of Chinese cooking have one thing in common: whether the dishes are Northern or Southern, they all pay attention to color, smell, taste, and shape.

IV. 無論如何 (wúlùn rúhé): No matter what, at any rate

如何 is the formal version of "怎麼樣." 無論如何 is a set phrase, meaning "at any rate," often used with adverbs 也 and 都. It is also frequently used with auxiliary verbs such as 得 and 要. The subject can be placed before or after 無論如何.

Subject 無論如何	(Subject)	得／要 Verb phrase
春節　無論如何		得回家一趟，因為我已經有三年沒回家了。

This Spring Festival, no matter what, I have to return home because I haven't been home for three years.

無論如何	你	也要注意自己的身體，不要整天大吃大喝。

At any rate, you need to pay attention to your own health and stop overeating and drinking all day long.

✀ PRACTICE

模仿造句

Make sentences of your own by following each of the examples given.

1. 请你无论如何要帮我这个忙，因为 _____。
   (Example: 我实在拿不动这些行李了)

2. 这个工作非常重要，我无论如何 _____。
   (Example: 得完成任务)

3. 你无论如何要_____，我从来就没 _____。

   (Example: 教我用电脑，用过电脑)

翻译

Translate the following sentence into Chinese. Make sure your translation includes 由于 and 无论如何.

Because he is a Southerner, he must have a little bit of rice every day no matter what.

V. 自从…以来 (zìcóng…yǐlái): Ever since…

This prepositional structure expresses the onset of an event in the past and is followed by a sentence about a situation that has continued from that time up to the present. 就 is frequently used in the second clause. 自从…以来 may also introduce a point in time in the past, but 自从 may be omitted in that case. E.g., (自从)2000年以来. A related pattern is time span + (以)来, meaning "for the past…(span of time)," e.g., …(以)来.

Subject 自从 Verb phrase 以来	(Subject) Verb phrase/predicate
他们自从认识以来，	就每天通电邮或电话。

Ever since meeting, they have sent e-mails or called each other every day.

自从学打太极拳以来，	他的身体就越来越健康。

Ever since he learned how to do tai chi, he's gotten healthier and healthier.

Time 以来	Subject Verb phrase
近几年来，	中国人也开始吃西餐，喝咖啡了。

In recent years, Chinese people have started to eat Western food and drink coffee.

❧ PRACTICE

模仿造句

Make sentences of your own by following each of the examples given.

1. 請你無論如何要幫我這個忙，因為 _____。

   (Example: 我實在拿不動這些行李了)

2. 這個工作非常重要，我無論如何 _____。

   (Example: 得完成任務)

3. 你無論如何要_____，我從來就沒 _____。

   (Example: 教我用電腦，用過電腦)

翻譯

Translate the following sentence into Chinese. Make sure your translation includes 由於 and 無論如何.

Because he is a Southerner, he must have a little bit of rice every day no matter what.

V. 自從…以來 (zìcóng...yǐlái): Ever since...

This prepositional structure expresses the onset of an event in the past and is followed by a sentence about a situation that has continued from that time up to the present. 就 is frequently used in the second clause. 自從…以來 may also introduce a point in time in the past, but 自從 may be omitted in that case. E.g., (自從) 2000年以來. A related pattern is time span + (以) 來, meaning "for the past...(span of time)," e.g., …(以) 來.

Subject 自從 Verb phrase 以來	(Subject) Verb phrase/predicate
他們自從認識以來，	就每天通電郵或電話。
Ever since meeting, they have sent e-mails or called each other every day.	
自從學打太極拳以來，	他的身體就越來越健康。
Ever since he learned how to do tai chi, he's gotten healthier and healthier.	

Time 以來	Subject Verb phrase
近幾年來，	中國人也開始吃西餐，喝咖啡了。
In recent years, Chinese people have started to eat Western food and drink coffee.	

⊞ PRACTICE

模仿造句

Make sentences of your own by following each of the examples given.

1. 他自从参加工作以来，＿＿＿＿＿＿＿＿＿＿＿＿＿＿＿＿＿＿＿＿＿。

   (Example: 就没有离开过他的单位)

2. 这几个月来，＿＿＿＿＿＿＿＿＿＿＿＿＿＿＿＿＿＿＿。

   (Example: 他一直在忙着搞翻译)

3. 自从他＿＿＿＿＿＿＿＿＿＿＿以来，就不再＿＿＿＿＿＿＿＿＿＿。

   (Example: 搬到南方，吃面食了)

问答

Use the prepositional structure 自从…以来 to answer the following questions.

你有什么特别的习惯？这个习惯是什么时候开始的？

翻译

Translate the following sentence into Chinese. Make sure your translation includes the 自从 structure.

Ever since we moved to the North, we have learned how to eat wheat products and have become accustomed to eating salty food.

VI. 按照… (ànzhào): According to, based on

This prepositional structure indicates the condition on which an action will be based. 按照 is often followed by a disyllabic noun, such as 习惯, 方法, 意见, etc., but NOT by a personal pronoun or a noun indicating a person, such as 他们, 老师, etc.

按照 Nominal phrase,	Subject Verb phrase
按照房间的大小，	旅馆决定每个房间应该是多少钱。

According to the size of the room, the hotel decides the price.

Subject 按照 Nominal phrase,	Verb phrase
学生按照老师教的方法，	用刚学的生词造了几个句子。

The students made sentences with the words they just learned in accordance with the teacher's instruction.

❀ PRACTICE

模仿造句

Make sentences of your own by following each of the examples given.

1. 他自從參加工作以來，_____。

　　(Example: 就沒有離開過他的單位)

2. 這幾個月來，_____。

　　(Example: 他一直在忙著搞翻譯)

3. 自從他 _____ 以來，就不再 _____。

　　(Example: 搬到南方，吃麵食了)

問答

Use the prepositional structure 自從⋯以來 to answer the following questions.

你有什麼特別的習慣？這個習慣是什麼時候開始的？

翻譯

Translate the following sentence into Chinese. Make sure your translation includes the 自從 structure.

Ever since we moved to the North, we have learned how to eat wheat products and have become accustomed to eating salty food.

VI. 按照⋯ (ànzhào): According to, based on

This prepositional structure indicates the condition on which an action will be based. 按照 is often followed by a disyllabic noun, such as 習慣, 方法, 意見, etc., but NOT by a personal pronoun or a noun indicating a person, such as 他們, 老師, etc.

按照 Nominal phrase,	Subject Verb phrase
按照房間的大小，	旅館決定每個房間應該是多少錢。

According to the size of the room, the hotel decides the price.

Subject 按照 Nominal phrase,	Verb phrase
學生按照老師教的方法，	用剛學的生詞造了幾個句子。

The students made sentences with the words they just learned in accordance with the teacher's instruction.

❧ PRACTICE

模仿造句

Make sentences of your own by following each of the examples given.

1. 按照老师教的方法，_____。

 (Example: 他做完了练习)

2. 我按照朋友的意思，_____。

 (Example: 也开始学着吃素了)

3. 按照他这次考试的成绩，我想 _____。

 (Example: 他去中国应该没有问题)

问答

Use the 按照 structure to answer the following questions.

1. 你是怎么回答这个问题的？

2. 你怎么给朋友介绍中国的饮食习惯？

3. 我怎么才能学会发电子邮件？

◈ PRACTICE

模仿造句

Make sentences of your own by following each of the examples given.

1. 按照老師教的方法，_____。
   (Example: 他做完了練習)

2. 我按照朋友的意思，_____。
   (Example: 也開始學著吃素了)

3. 按照他這次考試的成績，我想_____。
   (Example: 他去中國應該沒有問題)

問答

Use the 按照 structure to answer the following questions.

1. 你是怎麼回答這個問題的？

2. 你怎麼給朋友介紹中國的飲食習慣？

3. 我怎麼才能學會發電子郵件？

完成句子

Please complete each of the sentences below.

1. _____按照质量的好坏_____。

2. _____按照水平的高低_____。

3. _____按照时间的长短_____。

翻译

Translate the following sentences into Chinese. Make sure your translation includes 按照 and 无论如何.

According to Chinese customs, it is okay to make noise while eating, because it indicates that the food is delicious. However, at the dining table, no matter what, one cannot tap on a bowl with chopsticks.

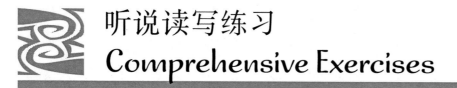

听说读写练习
Comprehensive Exercises

🎧📝 TASK 1. 听一听、选一选 LISTENING EXERCISES

A. Bingo

In this section, you will hear various Chinese phrases. Demonstrate your understanding of these phrases by numbering their English counterparts in the order in which you hear them.

to change eating habits	to love to eat Western food
no matter if it is staple or nonstaple food	Westernized
according to different shapes	to express thanks
to be influenced by the weather	workplace
special products from the South	all kinds of culinary systems
to produce rice	to care about nutrition
unique characteristics of the North	fast-food restaurant
table manners	half-cooked products

完成句子

Please complete each of the sentences below.

1. _____按照質量的好壞_____。

2. _____按照水平的高低_____。

3. _____按照時間的長短_____。

翻譯

Translate the following sentences into Chinese. Make sure your translation includes 按照 and 無論如何.

According to Chinese customs, it is okay to make noise while eating, because it indicates that the food is delicious. However, at the dining table, no matter what, one cannot tap on a bowl with chopsticks.

聽說讀寫練習
Comprehensive Exercises

🎧💬 TASK 1. 聽一聽、選一選 LISTENING EXERCISES

A. Bingo

In this section, you will hear various Chinese phrases. Demonstrate your understanding of these phrases by numbering their English counterparts in the order in which you hear them.

to change eating habits	to love to eat Western food
no matter if it is staple or nonstaple food	Westernized
according to different shapes	to express thanks
to be influenced by the weather	workplace
special products from the South	all kinds of culinary systems
to produce rice	to care about nutrition
unique characteristics of the North	fast-food restaurant
table manners	half-cooked products

B. Matching

Listen to the sentences in Chinese and number them in the order in which you hear them.

1. 这个餐馆的饭菜很讲究营养，跟速食店的东西没有什么相同之处。

2. 近几年来，很多中国人由于受到西方国家的影响也开始吃西餐了。

3. 随着历史的发展，中国人的菜慢慢地形成了不同的菜系。

4. 不管是什么菜，你都应该按照这种方式来做。

5. 到了北京以后，我每天无论如何都得吃面食。

6. 这个速食店的特点之一是主食很多，而且都是用南方特产做的。

7. 自从开放以来，中国人的饮食习惯有了很大的改变。

8. 你现在在中国应该按照中国人的方式吃饭。

9. 医生让我多吃中国饭，另外还让我少吃没有营养的速食。

C. Short Conversations

Listen to these short conversations. Select the correct answer for each question from the choices provided.

1. 是/不是

2. 常做/不常做

3. 有/没有

4. 有/没有

5. 想/不想

🎧 TASK 2. 听一听、说一说 SHORT PASSAGES

PASSAGE 1

Pre-Listening Activity

Before you begin, answer the following questions, which are designed to help you predict what will happen in the passage.

1. 你看中国饭馆的中文菜单觉得容易不容易？为什么？

2. 在美国的中餐馆的饭菜和在中国饭馆的饭菜一样不一样？为什么？

Listening Activity

Now listen to the passage and answer the questions that follow. Be sure to make a voice recording on the multimedia CD-ROM explaining each of your choices.

B. Matching

Listen to the sentences in Chinese and number them in the order in which you hear them.

1. 這個餐館的飯菜很講究營養，跟速食店的東西沒有什麼相同之處。

2. 近幾年來，很多中國人由於受到西方國家的影響也開始吃西餐了。

3. 隨著歷史的發展，中國人的菜慢慢地形成了不同的菜系。

4. 不管是什麼菜，你都應該按照這種方式來做。

5. 到了北京以後，我每天無論如何都得吃麵食。

6. 這個速食店的特點之一是主食很多，而且都是用南方特產做的。

7. 自從開放以來，中國人的飲食習慣有了很大的改變。

8. 你現在在中國應該按照中國人的方式吃飯。

9. 醫生讓我多吃中國飯，另外還讓我少吃沒有營養的速食。

C. Short Conversations

Listen to these short conversations. Select the correct answer for each question from the choices provided.

1. 是／不是

2. 常做／不常做

3. 有／沒有

4. 有／沒有

5. 想／不想

🎧 TASK 2. 聽一聽、說一說 SHORT PASSAGES

PASSAGE 1

Pre-Listening Activity

Before you begin, answer the following questions, which are designed to help you predict what will happen in the passage.

1. 你看中國飯館的中文菜單覺得容易不容易？為什麼？

2. 在美國的中餐館的飯菜和在中國飯館的飯菜一樣不一樣？為什麼？

Listening Activity

Now listen to the passage and answer the questions that follow. Be sure to make a voice recording on the multimedia CD-ROM explaining each of your choices.

A. Listening for the main idea

这段话主要谈的是什么？

a) 学生学了一、两年中文以后，看中国饭馆的中文菜单就不觉得难了。

b) 学中文的学生很难看懂中国饭馆的中文菜单。

c) 不管是中国学生还是外国学生，看中文菜单都会有困难。

d) 以上都不对。

B. Listening for details

1. 喜欢吃中国菜的外国学生点菜时，有没有困难？为什么？

   有/没有

2. 中国饭馆的菜和美国的中餐馆的菜是不是有很多相似之处？为什么？

   是/不是

3. 中国饭馆的菜单和美国中餐馆的中文菜单一样不一样？你怎么知道的？

   一样/不一样

Post-Listening Activity

Now state your opinion as you record your voice on the multimedia CD-ROM.

你同意不同意说话的人的看法？为什么？

PASSAGE 2

Pre-Listening Activity

Before you begin, answer the following questions, which are designed to help you predict what will happen in the passage.

1. 吃肉好还是吃蔬菜好？为什么？

2. 现在人们的饮食习惯跟二十几年前一样不一样？为什么？

Vocabulary

1. 大人   dàren   adult

2. 鸭   yā   duck

Listening Activity

Now listen to the passage and answer the questions that follow. Be sure to make a voice recording on the multimedia CD-ROM explaining each of your choices.

A. Listening for the main idea

這段話主要談的是什麼？

a) 學生學了一、兩年中文以後，看中國飯館的中文菜單就不覺得難了。

b) 學中文的學生很難看懂中國飯館的中文菜單。

c) 不管是中國學生還是外國學生，看中文菜單都會有困難。

d) 以上都不對。

B. Listening for details

1. 喜歡吃中國菜的外國學生點菜時，有沒有困難？為什麼？

   有/沒有

2. 中國飯館的菜和美國的中餐館的菜是不是有很多相似之處？為什麼？

   是/不是

3. 中國飯館的菜單和美國中餐館的中文菜單一樣不一樣？你怎麼知道的？

   一樣/不一樣

Post-Listening Activity

Now state your opinion as you record your voice on the multimedia CD-ROM.

   你同意不同意說話的人的看法？為什麼？

PASSAGE 2

Pre-Listening Activity

Before you begin, answer the following questions, which are designed to help you predict what will happen in the passage.

1. 吃肉好還是吃蔬菜好？為什麼？

2. 現在人們的飲食習慣跟二十幾年前一樣不一樣？為什麼？

Vocabulary

1. 大人   dàren   adult

2. 鴨   yā   duck

Listening Activity

Now listen to the passage and answer the questions that follow. Be sure to make a voice recording on the multimedia CD-ROM explaining each of your choices.

A. Listening for new words

Did you catch all the new words in the passage?

B. Listening for the main idea

这段短文主要谈的是什么？

a) 中国人觉得吃肉比吃菜好。

b) 现在请客人们都不会点素菜。

c) 中国人现在的饮食习惯跟以前不太一样了。

d) 以上都不对。

C. Listening for details

1. 二十年前中国人吃肉的机会多不多？你怎么知道的？
   多/不多

2. 过去请客人去饭馆，很少点素菜，对不对？为什么？
   对/不对

3. 现在人们有钱了，吃肉的人是不是越来越多了？为什么？
   是/不是

Post-Listening Activity

Now state your opinion as you record your voice on the multimedia CD-ROM.

你现在的饮食习惯跟小的时候一样不一样？你爸爸妈妈呢？

🎧 TASK 3. 看一看、说一说、写一写 SHORT VIDEO

Pre-Listening Activity

Before you begin, answer the following questions, which are designed to help you predict what will happen in the video.

1. 你知道四川人爱吃什么？为什么？

2. 山西人爱吃什么？为什么？

Vocabulary

1. 辣椒油	làjiāoyóu	*n.*	chili oil
2. 潮湿	cháoshī	*adj.*	moist, damp
3. 辣子	làzi	*n.*	cayenne pepper

A. Listening for new words

Did you catch all the new words in the passage?

B. Listening for the main idea

這段短文主要談的是什麼?

a) 中國人覺得吃肉比吃菜好。

b) 現在請客人們都不會點素菜。

c) 中國人現在的飲食習慣跟以前不太一樣了。

d) 以上都不對。

C. Listening for details

1. 二十年前中國人吃肉的機會多不多?你怎麼知道的?

   多/不多

2. 過去請客人去飯館,很少點素菜,對不對?為什麼?

   對/不對

3. 現在人們有錢了,吃肉的人是不是越來越多了?為什麼?

   是/不是

Post-Listening Activity

Now state your opinion as you record your voice on the multimedia CD-ROM.

你現在的飲食習慣跟小的時候一樣不一樣?你爸爸媽媽呢?

🎧 TASK 3. 看一看、説一説、寫一寫 SHORT VIDEO

Pre-Listening Activity

Before you begin, answer the following questions, which are designed to help you predict what will happen in the video.

1. 你知道四川人愛吃什麼?為什麼?

2. 山西人愛吃什麼?為什麼?

Vocabulary

1. 辣椒油	làjiāoyóu	*n.*	chili oil
2. 潮濕	cháoshī	*adj.*	moist, damp
3. 辣子	làzi	*n.*	cayenne pepper

4. 醋	cù	*n.*	vinegar
5. 碱	jiǎn	*n.*	alkali
6. 忌妒	jìdu	*adj.*	jealous of

Listening Activity

Now listen to the dialogue and then answer the questions that follow. Be sure to make a voice recording on the multimedia CD-ROM explaining each of your choices.

A. Listening for new words

Did you catch all the new words in the dialogue?

B. Listening for the main idea

在这段对话中，那两个人在说什么？

a) 四川人和山西人的饮食习惯。

b) 喝的水会影响到人们的饮食习惯。

c) 天气会影响到人们的饮食习惯。

d) 以上都对。

C. Listening for details

1. 说话的那个女的爱不爱吃酸的？为什么？

   爱／不爱

2. 山西人是不是很喜欢吃辣的？为什么？

   是／不是

3. "吃醋"有几个意思？是什么意思？

   一个／两个

Post-Listening Activity

Now state your opinion as you record your voice on the multimedia CD-ROM, and then write a summary of the dialogue.

请你用自己的话说一说这段对话都讲了些什么。

4. 醋	cù	*n.*	vinegar
5. 碱	jiǎn	*n.*	alkali
6. 忌妒	jìdu	*adj.*	jealous of

Listening Activity

Now listen to the dialogue and then answer the questions that follow. Be sure to make a voice recording on the multimedia CD-ROM explaining each of your choices.

A. Listening for new words

Did you catch all the new words in the dialogue?

B. Listening for the main idea

在這段對話中，那兩個人在說什麼？

a) 四川人和山西人的飲食習慣。

b) 喝的水會影響到人們的飲食習慣。

c) 天氣會影響到人們的飲食習慣。

d) 以上都對。

C. Listening for details

1. 說話的那個女的愛不愛吃酸的？為什麼？

   愛／不愛

2. 山西人是不是很喜歡吃辣的？為什麼？

   是／不是

3. "吃醋"有幾個意思？是什麼意思？

   一個／兩個

Post-Listening Activity

Now state your opinion as you record your voice on the multimedia CD-ROM, and then write a summary of the dialogue.

請你用自己的話說一說這段對話都講了些什麼。

🎧 📀 TASK 4. 读一读、写一写 READING EXERCISES

This section consists of two parts: Short Stories and Authentic Material.

A. Short Stories

After reading each of the two Chinese stories, respond in Chinese to the questions that follow.

成语故事：望梅止渴

中国古时候有一位有名的将军叫曹操，有一次，他带着他的士兵在路上走。天气太热了，士兵们走得满头大汗，又渴又累，由于找不到水喝，大家都走不动了。曹操虽然骑在马上，但是也是又热又渴，他看见他的士兵们渴得难受，心里很着急。突然曹操想出了一个好主意。他告诉大家说："这条路我熟悉。前面离这儿不远的地方有一大片梅树，树上长着很多大梅子，又甜又酸，吃了以后，马上就不觉得那么渴了。"士兵们听了以后，心里想着那些梅子，嘴里都流出了口水，马上就不觉得那么渴了，全身也有劲儿了，大家使劲地往前走。最后，他们走到了有水的地方。

Vocabulary

1. 望梅止渴	wàng méi zhǐ kě		
望	wàng	*v.*	to look into the distance
梅	méi	*n.*	plum (tree)
止	zhǐ	*v.*	to dissolve
2. 曹操	Cáo Cāo	*prop. n.*	famous general (from ancient times)
3. 士兵	shìbīng	*n.*	soldier
4. 难受	nánshòu	*adj.*	feeling bad
5. 主意	zhǔyì	*n*	idea
6. 片	piàn	*m. w.*	a piece, divided sections of a larger place, a slice
7. 梅子	méizi	*n.*	plum
8. 口水	kǒushuǐ	*n.*	saliva

Questions

1. 请用你自己的话讲一讲"望梅止渴"是什么意思？

2. 你觉得曹操聪明不聪明？为什么？

3. 在你所遇到的事情中，你能不能想出一个"望梅止渴"的故事？

🎧 🌀 TASK 4. 讀一讀、寫一寫 READING EXERCISES

This section consists of two parts: Short Stories and Authentic Material.

A. Short Stories

After reading each of the two Chinese stories, respond in Chinese to the questions that follow.

成語故事：望梅止渴

　　中國古時候有一位有名的將軍叫曹操，有一次，他帶著他的士兵在路上走。天氣太熱了，士兵們走得滿頭大汗，又渴又累，由於找不到水喝，大家都走不動了。曹操雖然騎在馬上，但是也是又熱又渴，他看見他的士兵們渴得難受，心裏很著急。突然曹操想出了一個好主意。他告訴大家說："這條路我熟悉。前面離這兒不遠的地方有一大片梅樹，樹上長著很多大梅子，又甜又酸，吃了以後，馬上就不覺得那麼渴了。"士兵們聽了以後，心裏想著那些梅子，嘴裏都流出了口水，馬上就不覺得那麼渴了，全身也有勁兒了，大家使勁地往前走。最後，他們走到了有水的地方。

Vocabulary

1.	望梅止渴	wàng méi zhǐ kě		
	望	wàng	*v.*	to look into the distance
	梅	méi	*n.*	plum (tree)
	止	zhǐ	*v.*	to dissolve
2.	曹操	Cáo Cāo	*prop. n.*	famous general (from ancient times)
3.	士兵	shìbīng	*n.*	soldier
4.	難受	nánshòu	*adj.*	feeling bad
5.	主意	zhǔyì	*n*	idea
6.	片	piàn	*m. w.*	a piece, divided sections of a larger place, a slice
7.	梅子	méizi	*n.*	plum
8.	口水	kǒushuǐ	*n.*	saliva

Questions

1. 請用你自己的話講一講"望梅止渴"是什麼意思？

2. 你覺得曹操聰明不聰明？為什麼？

3. 在你所遇到的事情中，你能不能想出一個"望梅止渴"的故事？

成语故事：画饼充饥

The phrase 画饼充饥 is a 成语 itself. However, the story below does not tell the origin of 画饼充饥. Instead, it is a popular legend.

　　从前有一家人。他们有一个儿子。这个儿子非常懒，什么事儿也不会做。有一次，他的爸爸妈妈要出门几天。他们怕这个懒儿子饿坏了，所以就给他做了一个非常大的饼，然后把饼挂在懒儿子的脖子上。这样，他们想他们的儿子什么时候饿了，张开嘴就有饭吃。爸爸妈妈出门以后，懒儿子每次饿了，就张开嘴吃他脖子上的大饼。但是两天以后，他嘴前边的饼都吃完了。他饿得不行，但是也不知道怎么办。最后，他在地上画了一个大饼。每次觉得饿得不行了，就看看大饼。几天以后，他的爸爸妈妈回来了，但是发现他们的懒儿子已经饿死了。

Vocabulary

1.	画饼充饥	huà bǐng chōng jī		
	充	chōng	*v.*	to fill
	饥	jī	*adj.*	hunger
2.	懒	lǎn	*adj.*	lazy
3.	饿坏	èhuài	*adj. comp.*	awfully hungry
4.	脖子	bózi	*n.*	neck
5.	张开	zhāngkāi	*v. comp.*	to open

Questions

1. 用你自己的话讲一讲"画饼充饥"是什么意思？
2. 你觉得那个懒儿子的爸爸妈妈想没想到他们的懒儿子会饿死？为什么？
3. 用你自己的话讲一个"画饼充饥"的故事？

B. Authentic Material

In this section, you will be exposed to some authentic materials used in China. Read the following list of the different culinary styles, and answer the questions.

Questions

1. 这八大菜系都是哪些地方的菜？
2. 在八大菜系中，哪些菜系比较辣？
3. 这八大菜系的代表菜中，你吃过哪些？

成語故事：畫餅充饑

The phrase 畫餅充饑 is a 成語 itself. However, the story below does not tell the origin of 畫餅充饑. Instead, it is a popular legend.

從前有一家人。他們有一個兒子。這個兒子非常懶，什麼事兒也不會做。有一次，他的爸爸媽媽要出門幾天。他們怕這個懶兒子餓壞了，所以就給他做了一個非常大的餅，然後把餅掛在懶兒子的脖子上。這樣，他們想他們的兒子什麼時候餓了，張開嘴就有飯吃。爸爸媽媽出門以後，懶兒子每次餓了，就張開嘴吃他脖子上的大餅。但是兩天以後，他嘴前邊的餅都吃完了。他餓得不行，但是也不知道怎麼辦。最後，他在地上畫了一個大餅。每次覺得餓得不行了，就看看大餅。幾天以後，他的爸爸媽媽回來了，但是發現他們的懶兒子已經餓死了。

Vocabulary

1. 畫餅充饑	huà bǐng chōng jī		
充	chōng	*v.*	to fill
饑	jī	*adj.*	hunger
2. 懶	lǎn	*adj.*	lazy
3. 餓壞	èhuài	*adj. comp.*	awfully hungry
4. 脖子	bózi	*n.*	neck
5. 張開	zhāngkāi	*v. comp.*	to open

Questions

1. 用你自己的話講一講 "畫餅充饑" 是什麼意思？
2. 你覺得那個懶兒子的爸爸媽媽想沒想到他們的懶兒子會餓死？為什麼？
3. 用你自己的話講一個 "畫餅充饑" 的故事？

B. Authentic Material

In this section, you will be exposed to some authentic materials used in China. Read the following list of the different culinary styles, and answer the questions.

Questions

1. 這八大菜系都是哪些地方的菜？
2. 在八大菜系中，哪些菜系比較辣？
3. 這八大菜系的代表菜中，你吃過哪些？

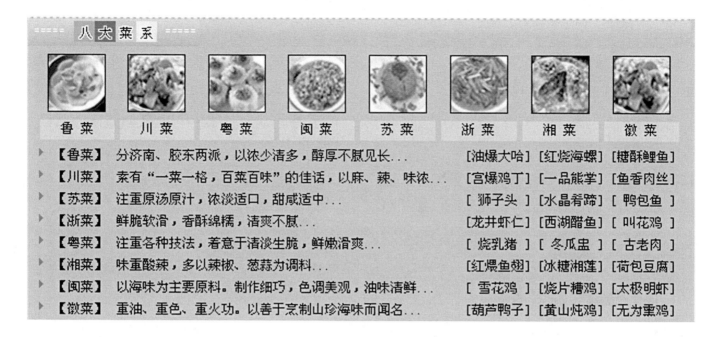

八大菜系

| 鲁 菜 | 川 菜 | 粤 菜 | 闽 菜 | 苏 菜 | 浙 菜 | 湘 菜 | 徽 菜 |

▶　【鲁菜】　分济南、胶东两派，以浓少清多，醇厚不腻见长...　　　[油爆大哈]　[红烧海螺]　[糖酥鲤鱼]

▶　【川菜】　素有"一菜一格，百菜百味"的佳话，以麻、辣、味浓...　　[宫爆鸡丁]　[一品熊掌]　[鱼香肉丝]

▶　【苏菜】　注重原汤原汁，浓淡适口，甜咸适中...　　　　　　　[狮子头]　[水晶肴蹄]　[鸭包鱼]

▶　【浙菜】　鲜脆软滑，香酥绵糯，清爽不腻...　　　　　　　　[龙井虾仁]　[西湖醋鱼]　[叫花鸡]

▶　【粤菜】　注重各种技法，着意于清淡生脆，鲜嫩滑爽...　　　[烧乳猪]　[冬瓜盅]　[古老肉]

▶　【湘菜】　味重酸辣，多以辣椒、葱蒜为调料...　　　　　　　[红煨鱼翅]　[冰糖湘莲]　[荷包豆腐]

▶　【闽菜】　以海味为主要原料。制作细巧，色调美观，油味清鲜...　[雪花鸡]　[烧片糟鸡]　[太极明虾]

▶　【徽菜】　重油、重色、重火功。以善于烹制山珍海味而闻名...　　[葫芦鸭子]　[黄山炖鸡]　[无为熏鸡]

🎧❦ TASK 5. 想一想、说一说 PRESENTATION

Please pick one of the following for your presentation.

A. Individual Presentation

Your Chinese friends treat you to your first meal at a Chinese restaurant. After returning to the dorm, you tell your roommate about this new experience, including a description of the following:
1) the restaurant;
2) how to order, what to order, and why;
3) how the dishes were presented and how this differs from Western customs;
4) which dish you like most and why;
5) Chinese etiquette during a meal.

B. Group Presentation

Setting: A Chinese restaurant
Cast: A waiter and two restaurant patrons
Situation: One patron is familiar with Chinese culture while the other is completely ignorant. The knowledgeable patron instructs his clueless friend on the food of various regions and how to act appropriately in a Chinese restaurant. Construct a dialogue of at least twelve sentences between the patrons. Make sure to include vocabulary and grammar structures learned in this lesson. And make sure the confused friend does not get laughed out of the restaurant!

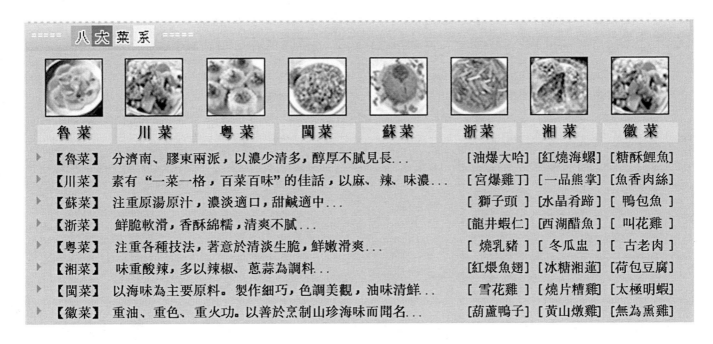

| 魯菜 | 川菜 | 粵菜 | 閩菜 | 蘇菜 | 浙菜 | 湘菜 | 徽菜 |

▸ 【魯菜】 分濟南、膠東兩派，以濃少清多，醇厚不膩見長…   ［油爆大哈］ ［紅燒海螺］ ［糖酥鯉魚］

▸ 【川菜】 素有 "一菜一格，百菜百味" 的佳話，以麻、辣、味濃…   ［宮爆雞丁］ ［一品熊掌］ ［魚香肉絲］

▸ 【蘇菜】 注重原湯原汁，濃淡適口，甜鹹適中…   ［ 獅子頭 ］ ［水晶肴蹄］ ［ 鴨包魚 ］

▸ 【浙菜】 鮮脆軟滑，香酥綿糯，清爽不膩…   ［龍井蝦仁］ ［西湖醋魚］ ［ 叫花雞 ］

▸ 【粵菜】 注重各種技法，著意於清淡生脆，鮮嫩滑爽…   ［ 燒乳豬 ］ ［ 冬瓜盅 ］ ［ 古老肉 ］

▸ 【湘菜】 味重酸辣，多以辣椒、蔥蒜為調料…   ［紅煨魚翅］ ［冰糖湘蓮］ ［荷包豆腐］

▸ 【閩菜】 以海味為主要原料。製作細巧，色調美觀，油味清鮮…   ［ 雪花雞 ］ ［燒片糟雞］ ［太極明蝦］

▸ 【徽菜】 重油、重色、重火功。以善於烹制山珍海味而聞名…   ［葫蘆鴨子］ ［黃山燉雞］ ［無為熏雞］

🎧 ✤ TASK 5. 想一想、說一說 PRESENTATION

Please pick one of the following for your presentation.

A. Individual Presentation

Your Chinese friends treat you to your first meal at a Chinese restaurant. After returning to the dorm, you tell your roommate about this new experience, including a description of the following:
1) the restaurant;
2) how to order, what to order, and why;
3) how the dishes were presented and how this differs from Western customs;
4) which dish you like most and why;
5) Chinese etiquette during a meal.

B. Group Presentation

Setting: A Chinese restaurant

Cast: A waiter and two restaurant patrons

Situation: One patron is familiar with Chinese culture while the other is completely ignorant. The knowledgeable patron instructs his clueless friend on the food of various regions and how to act appropriately in a Chinese restaurant. Construct a dialogue of at least twelve sentences between the patrons. Make sure to include vocabulary and grammar structures learned in this lesson. And make sure the confused friend does not get laughed out of the restaurant!

🎧 TASK 6. 想一想、写一写 COMPOSITION

Use http://chinese.yahoo.com or http://www.google.cn to research the similarities and differences between table manners in China and those in your own country. Ideas to address include but are not limited to the way in which food is served and why and when certain utensils should be used. Write a paragraph on this topic, using the vocabulary and grammar structures learned in this lesson.

⌁ TASK 6. 想一想、寫一寫 COMPOSITION

Use http://chinese.yahoo.com or http://www.google.cn to research the similarities and differences between table manners in China and those in your own country. Ideas to address include but are not limited to the way in which food is served and why and when certain utensils should be used. Write a paragraph on this topic, using the vocabulary and grammar structures learned in this lesson.

42
谈节庆
Chinese Holiday Celebrations

In this lesson you will:

■ Celebrate the major Chinese holidays and partake in their customs.

■ Present, describe, and discuss culturally accurate information about Chinese holidays.

■ Compare Chinese holidays with those of your own country.

　　中国的节日有两种：一种是按照公历计算的国家节日，重要的节日有五一"国际劳动节"、十月一日"国庆节"等等；另一种是按农历计算的民间传统节日，例如春节、中秋节、清明节、端午节等等。在所有的传统节日中，只有春节是国家法定的节日，其它的都没有假期。春节是农历的新年，有一点儿像西方的圣诞节，是一年之中最大的传统节日。在此之后，就是正月十五的元宵节，农历新年里的第一个月亮变圆的晚上。按照传统的习惯，很多中国人那天晚上都吃元宵。圆圆的月亮再加上圆圆的元宵，是全家人团圆的象征。元宵节之所以也叫灯节是因为那天晚上，街上、公园里到处都挂花灯，大家吃完了晚饭，就出去看灯。除此之外，还有清明节，一般在农历的二、

Year of the rooster celebration in a park in Beijing.

42

談節慶

Chinese Holiday Celebrations

In this lesson you will:

■ Celebrate the major Chinese holidays and partake in their customs.
■ Present, describe, and discuss culturally accurate information about Chinese holidays.
■ Compare Chinese holidays with those of your own country.

　　中國的節日有兩種，一種是按照公歷計算的國家節日。重要的節日有五一"國際勞動節"；十月一日"國慶日"等等。另一種是按農曆計算的民間傳統節日。例如春節、中秋節、清明節、端午節等等。在所有的傳統節日中，只有春節是國家法定的節日，其他的都沒有假期。春節是農曆的新年，有一點兒像西方的聖誕節，是一年之中最大的傳統節日。在此之後，就是正月十五的元宵節，農曆新年裏的第一個月亮變圓的晚上。按照傳統的習慣，很多中國人那天晚上都吃元宵。圓圓的月亮再加上圓圓的元宵，是全家人團圓的象徵。元宵節之所以也叫燈節是因為那天晚上，街上、公園裏到處都掛花燈，大家吃完了晚飯，就出去看燈。除此之外，還有清明節，一般在農曆的二、

Year of the rooster celebration in a park in Beijing.

三月之间，或公历的四月初。春天的绿色加上百花的香味，给人一种清亮明快的感觉，所以人们把这个节日叫作清明节。中国人习惯在这天去扫墓。农历五月初五[1]是端午节，也叫粽子节。据说人们在那天吃粽子是为了纪念怀才不遇[2]的楚国诗人屈原。中秋节是农历八月十五。按照农历，秋季是七月、八月和九月。八月是秋季中间的一个月，十五号又是八月中间的一天，因此人们把这个节日称之为[3]中秋节。为了庆祝中秋节，全家人团聚在一起，边赏月边吃月饼。中国古代有首名诗，诗中说"每逢佳节倍思亲[4]。""每逢佳节倍思亲"意思是每逢节日到来的时候，人们就更加想念自己的家人。很多传统节日的活动都可以看出人们希望跟家人团聚的愿望。一天，陈小云、李丽莉和吴文德谈起了中国的节庆活动。

Pyramid-shaped glutinous rice dumplings (zongzi) prepared for the Dragon Boat Festival.

（在李丽莉的宿舍。）

吴文德：中秋节快到了，我们去买一盒月饼尝尝吧。李丽莉，你在想什么？

李丽莉：我发现中国民间传统节日很多，可是没有任何宗教节日。

陈小云：中国虽然还没有正式的宗教节日，但是现在有宗教信仰的中国人也越来越多，所以，有的宗教节日也开始流行了，只不过还不太普及罢了。

李丽莉：美国最大的节日是圣诞节。以前圣诞节是一种宗教节日，但是现在世界上很多人都庆祝圣诞节。

陈小云：中国很多地方也开始庆祝圣诞节和其他一些西方节日，例如感恩节、万圣节、情人节等等。

三月之間，或西曆的四月初。春天的綠色加上百花的香味，給人一種清亮明快的感覺，所以人們把這個節日叫作清明節。中國人習慣在這天去掃墓。農曆五月初五[1]是端午節，也叫粽子節。據說人們在那天吃粽子是為了紀念懷才不遇[2]的楚國詩人屈原。中秋節是農曆八月十五。按照農曆，秋季是七月、八月和九月。八月是秋季中間的一個月，十五號又是八月中間的一天，因此人們把這個節日稱之為[3]中秋節。為了慶祝中秋節，全家人團聚在一起，邊賞月邊吃月餅。中國古代有首名詩，詩中說「每逢佳節倍思親[4]。」「每逢佳節倍思親」意思是每逢節日到來的時候，人們就更加想念自己的家人。很多傳統節日的活動都可以看出人們希望跟家人團聚的願望。一天，陳小雲、李麗莉和吳文德談起了中國的節慶活動。

Pyramid-shaped glutinous rice dumplings (zongzi) prepared for the Dragon Boat Festival.

（在李麗莉的宿舍。）

吳文德：中秋節快到了，我們去買一盒月餅嘗嘗吧。李麗莉，你在想什麼？

李麗莉：我發現中國民間傳統節日很多，可是沒有任何宗教節日。

陳小雲：中國雖然還沒有正式的宗教節日，但是現在有宗教信仰的中國人也越來越多，所以，有的宗教節日也開始流行了，只不過還不太普及罷了。

李麗莉：美國最大的節日是聖誕節。以前聖誕節是一種宗教節日，但是現在世界上很多人都慶祝聖誕節。

陳小雲：中國很多地方也開始慶祝聖誕節和其他一些西方節日，例如感恩節、萬聖節、情人節等等。

吴文德：中国人庆祝感恩节的时候，晚餐也吃火鸡吗？有花车游行吗？

陈小云：吃的东西中国应有尽有，火鸡、土豆泥、南瓜饼，要什么有什么。游行，只要美国有的，中国早晚都会有。因为节日是促销商品的好机会。

李丽莉：商人绝对不会放弃节日这种赚钱的好机会。去年过万圣节的时候，我看见大商店里什么奇怪的服装都有，一点儿也不比美国差。今年情人节卖花卖糖肯定也赚了不少钱。难怪，节日越多，商人就越高兴。

吴文德：节日越多，我也越高兴。因为吃的机会也越多。说到吃，我们赶快去买月饼吧，我都快馋死了。

A Spring Festival celebration.

Notes

1. 初五 (chūwǔ)

fifth day of the lunar month

2. 怀才不遇 (huái cái bú yù)

To have talents but no opportunity to show them to the world; (lit.) to have talents but not (the luck of) meeting (the right circumstances where one can put them to good use). For more information about this phrase, please see Task 4 in 听说读写练习.

3. 称之为 (chēng zhī wéi)

(formal) to be known as

称	b.f.	to call
之	pron.	the classical Chinese all-purpose pronoun for "they," "he/she," "it," etc.
为	b.f.	as

吳文德：中國人慶祝感恩節的時候，晚餐也吃火雞嗎？有花車遊行嗎？

陳小雲：吃的東西中國應有盡有，火雞、土豆泥、南瓜餅，要什麼有
什麼。遊行，只要美國有的，中國早晚都會有。因為節日是
促銷商品的好機會。

李麗莉：商人絕對不會放棄節日這種賺錢的好機會。去年過萬聖節的
時候，我看見大商店裏什麼奇怪的服裝都有，一點兒也不比
美國差。今年情人節賣花賣糖肯定也賺了不少錢。難怪，節
日越多，商人就越高興。

吳文德：節日越多，我也越高興。因為吃的機會也越多。說到吃，我
們趕快去買月餅吧，我都快饞死了。

A Spring Festival celebration.

Notes

1. 初五 (chūwǔ)
   fifth day of the lunar month

2. 懷才不遇 (huái cái bú yù)
   To have talents but no opportunity to show them to the world; (lit.) to have talents but not (the luck of) meeting (the right circumstances where one can put them to good use). For more information about this phrase, please see Task 4 in 聽說讀寫練習.

3. 稱之為 (chēng zhī wéi)
   (formal) to be known as

稱	*b.f.*	to call
之	*pron.*	the classical Chinese all-purpose pronoun for "they," "he/she," "it," etc.
為	*b.f.*	as

4. 每逢佳节倍思亲。 (Měi féng jiā jié bèi sī qīn.)
Every time a holiday comes, one misses one's family more than ever. For more information about this sentence, please see Task 4 in 听说读写练习.

课文问答 *Questions and Answers*

1. 中国都有哪些传统节日？人们怎么过这些节日？
2. 中国的中秋节和西方的感恩节有什么相同或不同的地方？
3. 节日跟商人有什么关系？在你的国家，商人会不会在节日的时候提高价格？
4. 你的国家有哪些节日？人们怎么庆祝这些节日？

Lauren Brown

Spring Festival celebration in Ditan Park, Beijing.

 ## 生词表 Vocabulary

Character	Pinyin	Part of Speech	English Definition
1. 节庆	jiéqìng	*n.*	holiday festivities, holiday celebrations

今年春节你们准备搞什么节庆活动？

2. 公历	gōnglì	*n.*	Western calendar; (lit.) public calendar

今年春节是公历的几月几号？

3. 计算	jìsuàn	*v.*	(formal) to calculate, to count

我们需要计算一下这个月我们花了多少钱。

		n.	calculation

这种计算方法很简单。

4. 每逢佳節倍思親。 (Měi féng jiā jié bèi sī qīn.)
   Every time a holiday comes, one misses one's family more than ever. For more information about this sentence, please see Task 4 in 聽說讀寫練習.

課文問答 *Questions and Answers*

1. 中國都有哪些傳統節日？人們怎麼過這些節日？
2. 中國的中秋節和西方的感恩節有什麼相同或不同的地方？
3. 節日跟商人有什麼關係？在你的國家，商人會不會在節日的時候提高價格？
4. 你的國家有哪些節日？人們怎麼慶祝這些節日？

Spring Festival celebration in Ditan Park, Beijing.

 生詞表
Vocabulary

Character	Pinyin	Part of Speech	English Definition
1. 節慶	jiéqìng	*n.*	holiday festivities, holiday celebrations

今年春節你們準備搞什麼節慶活動？

| 2. 公曆 | gōnglì | *n.* | Western calendar; (lit.) public calendar |

今年春節是公曆的幾月幾號？

| 3. 計算 | jìsuàn | *v.* | (formal) to calculate, to count |

我們需要計算一下這個月我們花了多少錢。

| | | *n.* | calculation |

這種計算方法很簡單。

4. 国家   guójiā   *n.*   country, nation, state
你去过那些国家吗?

5. 农历   nónglì   *n.*   traditional Chinese lunar calendar; (lit.) the
农历一月一号常常是在公历的二月。   agricultural calendar

6. 民间   mínjiān   *adj.*   folk, nongovernmental
这是一个中国民间节日。

7. 传统   chuántǒng   *n.*   tradition
在美国过春节已经成了我们家的一个传统。

传   *v.*   to pass on, to hand down, to circulate
统   *b.f.*   system

8. 法定   fǎdìng   *adj.*   determined by law, prescribed by law
中秋节在中国不是法定的节日。

9. 正月   zhēngyuè   *n.*   the first month of the traditional Chinese
正月初三是我爷爷的生日。   lunar calendar

10. 圆   yuán   *adj.*   (of shape) circular, round
月饼的形状是圆的。

11. 月亮   yuèliang   *n.*   the moon (See also vocabulary #26.
今天的月亮又大又圆,真好看。   [欣] 赏月亮=赏月.)

12. 团圆   tuányuán   *v.*   to have a family reunion; (lit.) to come
明天是家人团圆的时候,你怎么不回家呢?   together and form a circle

                                n.   reunion
家人团圆对中国人来说很重要。

团   *b.f.*   collective, group

13. 象征   xiàngzhēng   *n.*   symbol, sign
这是快乐的象征。

                                v.   to symbolize
那种花儿象征什么,我也不知道。

14. 除此之外   chú cǐ zhīwài   *conj.*   other than this/these, apart from this/these
月饼我都买好了,除此之外,我还在饭馆买了一些菜。

4. 國家   guójiā   *n.*   country, nation, state

你去過那些國家嗎？

5. 農曆   nónglì   *n.*   traditional Chinese lunar calendar; (lit.) the agricultural calendar

農曆一月一號常常是在公曆的二月。

6. 民間   mínjiān   *adj.*   folk, nongovernmental

這是一個中國民間節日。

7. 傳統   chuántǒng   *n.*   tradition

在美國過春節已經成了我們家的一個傳統。

傳   *v.*   to pass on, to hand down, to circulate

統   *b.f.*   system

8. 法定   fǎdìng   *adj.*   determined by law, prescribed by law

中秋節在中國不是法定的節日。

9. 正月   zhēngyuè   *n.*   the first month of the traditional Chinese lunar calendar

正月初三是我爺爺的生日。

10. 圓   yuán   *adj.*   (of shape) circular, round

月餅的形狀是圓的。

11. 月亮   yuèliang   *n.*   the moon (See also vocabulary #26. [欣] 賞月亮=賞月.)

今天的月亮又大又圓，真好看。

12. 團圓   tuányuán   *v.*   to have a family reunion; (lit.) to come together and form a circle

明天是家人團圓的時候，你怎麼不回家呢？

n.   reunion

家人團圓對中國人來說很重要。

團   *b.f.*   collective, group

13. 象徵   xiàngzhēng   *n.*   symbol, sign

這是快樂的象徵。

v.   to symbolize

那種花兒象徵什麼，我也不知道。

14. 除此之外   chú cǐ zhīwài   *conj.*   other than this/these, apart from this/these

月餅我都買好了，除此之外，我還在飯館買了一些菜。

除		*v.*	to take away, to divide
此		*prop.*	the Classical Chinese equivalent of 这/这些
之外		*b.f.*	outside of

15. 初　　　chū　　　*b.f.*　　　elementary, beginning, first part of, the first ten day period of a lunar month

初春的时候，天气还比较冷。

16. 清亮　　qīngliàng　*adj.*　　clear and bright

这首歌让人感到清亮快乐。

17. 明快　　míngkuài　　*adj.*　　bright and joyful

这也是非常明快的音乐。

18. 感觉　　gǎnjué　　*n.*　　feeling, sense

这个饭馆给我一种感觉，好像我在中国。

　　　　　　　　　　　v.　　to have the feeling

在这里我感觉很轻松。

19. 扫墓　　sǎo mù　　*v. obj.*　　to sweep graves, to go to one's ancestors' graves and pay respects

我今年去给我爷爷扫墓了。

　墓　　　　　　　　*n.*　　grave, tomb

20. 据说　　jùshuō　　*phr.*　　It is said...

据说很多人春节都来这儿吃饭。

　据　　　　　　　　*b.f.*　　according to, in accordance with

21. 纪念　　jìniàn　　*v.*　　to commemorate, to honor by remembering

这儿每年五月都有纪念这位作家的活动。

　　　　　　　　　　　n.　　commemoration, remembrance

我们在这儿照一张像留个纪念吧。

　纪　　　　　　　　*b.f.*　　to write down, to record
　念　　　　　　　　*b.f.*　　to constantly think of, to miss, to feel anxious about, to worry

22. 首　　　shǒu　　　*m.w.*　　measure word for songs or poems

她今晚一共唱了五首歌。

23. 诗　　　shī　　　*n.*　　poetry, poem

他写诗写得很好。

除   *v.*   to take away, to divide

此   *prop.*   the Classical Chinese equivalent of
這／這些

之外   *b.f.*   outside of

15. 初   chū   *b.f.*   elementary, beginning, first part of, the first
ten day period of a lunar month
初春的時候，天氣還比較冷。

16. 清亮   qīngliàng   *adj.*   clear and bright
這首歌讓人感到清亮快樂。

17. 明快   míngkuài   *adj.*   bright and joyful
這也是非常明快的音樂。

18. 感覺   gǎnjué   *n.*   feeling, sense
這個飯館給我一種感覺，好像我在中國。
                                       v.   to have the feeling
在這裏我感覺很輕鬆。

19. 掃墓   sǎo mù   *v. obj.*   to sweep graves, to go to one's ancestors'
graves and pay respects
我今年去給我爺爺掃墓了。

墓   *n.*   grave, tomb

20. 據說   jùshuō   *phr.*   It is said...
據說很多人春節都來這兒吃飯。

據   *b.f.*   according to, in accordance with

21. 紀念   jìniàn   *v.*   to commemorate, to honor by
remembering
這兒每年五月都有紀念這位作家的活動。
                                       n.   commemoration, remembrance
我們在這兒照一張像留個紀念吧。

紀   *b.f.*   to write down, to record

念   *b.f.*   to constantly think of, to miss, to feel
anxious about, to worry

22. 首   shǒu   *m.w.*   measure word for songs or poems
她今晚一共唱了五首歌。

23. 詩   shī   *n.*   poetry, poem
他寫詩寫得很好。

24. 因此   yīncǐ   *conj.*   therefore
今年春节是二月十九号，学校已经开学了，因此，我们家不准备回中国过年了。

25. 团聚   tuánjù   *v.*   to have a reunion; (lit.) (of a group) to come together and gather in one place
今年春节我们家只能在美国团聚。

26. 赏月   shǎngyuè   *v.*   to appreciate or admire the moon ([欣]赏月亮＝赏月)
秋天是赏月最好的时候。

27. 古代   gǔdài   *n.*   ancient times
中国古代有很多非常伟大的诗人。
代   *n.*   generation, dynasty, era

28. 每逢   měi féng   *adv.*   each/every time one encounters somebody or something
每逢春节他都去看他爸爸妈妈。
逢   *v.*   to come upon, to encounter

29. 更加   gèngjiā   *adv.*   (formal) even more
我希望明年的节庆活动能搞得更加热闹。

30. 想念   xiǎngniàn   *v.*   (formal) to feel a longing for
这位诗人虽然住在美国，但是他非常想念自己的国家。
    n.   longing
他对家人的想念是别人无法理解的。

31. 愿望   yuànwàng   *n.*   wish, deeply-felt desire
你今年怎么没有想回家的愿望？

32. 盒   hé   *m. w.*   box
这是一盒送你爸爸妈妈的礼物。

33. 宗教   zōngjiào   *n.*   religion
我以后想去研究中国古代的宗教。
宗   *n.*   ancestor

34. 信仰   xìnyǎng   *n.*   belief, faith
一个人应该有自己的信仰。
    v.   to believe in (a religion)
你信仰什么宗教？
信   *v.*   to believe, to trust
仰   *v.*   to look up to, to admire, to adore

24. 因此   yīncǐ   *conj.*   therefore

今年春節是二月十九號，學校已經開學了，因此，我們家不準備回中國過年了。

25. 團聚   tuánjù   *v.*   to have a reunion; (lit.) (of a group) to come together and gather in one place

今年春節我們家只能在美國團聚。

26. 賞月   shǎngyuè   *v.*   to appreciate or admire the moon ([欣]賞月亮=賞月)

秋天是賞月最好的時候。

27. 古代   gǔdài   *n.*   ancient times

中國古代有很多非常偉大的詩人。

代   *n.*   generation, dynasty, era

28. 每逢   měi féng   *adv.*   each/every time one encounters somebody or something

每逢春節他都去看他爸爸媽媽。

逢   *v.*   to come upon, to encounter

29. 更加   gèngjiā   *adv.*   (formal) even more

我希望明年的節慶活動能搞得更加熱鬧。

30. 想念   xiǎngniàn   *v.*   (formal) to feel a longing for

這位詩人雖然住在美國，但是他非常想念自己的國家。

    n.   longing

他對家人的想念是別人無法理解的。

31. 願望   yuànwàng   *n.*   wish, deeply-felt desire

你今年怎麼沒有想回家的願望？

32. 盒   hé   *m. w.*   box

這是一盒送你爸爸媽媽的禮物。

33. 宗教   zōngjiào   *n.*   religion

我以後想去研究中國古代的宗教。

宗   *n.*   ancestor

34. 信仰   xìnyǎng   *n.*   belief, faith

一個人應該有自己的信仰。

    v.   to believe in (a religion)

你信仰什麼宗教？

信   *v.*   to believe, to trust

仰   *v.*   to look up to, to admire, to adore

35. 流行   liúxíng   *v.*   to be popular, to be in vogue; (lit.) to circulate in a flow

中国现在也流行这种样式。

                     adj.   popular, fashionable, in vogue

这首歌现在很流行。

36. 普及   pǔjí   *adj.*   widespread, far-reaching

中文在我们这儿很普及。

普   *b.f.*   common, ubiquitous, pervasive

及   *b.f.*   to reach, to extend

37. 世界   shìjiè   *n.*   the world, (Buddhist) the cosmos

世界上现在有多少人说中文，你知道吗？

38. 游行   yóuxíng   *n.*   parade, demonstration

明天你去参加游行吗？

39. 应有尽有   yīng yǒu jìn yǒu   *phr.*   to have everything needed; (lit.) Whatever one should have, one has it all.

你们家的年货真是应有尽有！

40. 商品   shāngpǐn   *n.*   merchandise, goods, commodity

我们商店不卖那种商品。

41. 绝对   juéduì   *adv.*   absolutely, definitely

今年春节我绝对不想自己一个人过。

绝   *b.f.*   extreme, end

42. 放弃   fàngqì   *v.*   to give up; (lit.) to let go and abandon

你不应该放弃这么好的机会。

弃   *v.*   to abandon

43. 难怪   nánguài   *conj.*   no wonder; (lit.) difficult to blame

难怪他不想让我去，他想自己去。

44. 馋   chán   *adj.*   gluttonous, drooling over (food), making (somebody) drool over (food)

别老说这个菜好，那个菜好的，快馋死我了。

食品名称 Names of Foods

1. 粽子   zòngzi   glutinous rice cake wrapped with large bamboo leaves

2. 月饼   yuèbǐng   mooncake

35. 流行   liúxíng   v.   to be popular, to be in vogue; (lit.) to circulate in a flow

中國現在也流行這種樣式。

                                              adj.   popular, fashionable, in vogue

這首歌現在很流行。

36. 普及   pǔjí   adj.   widespread, far-reaching

中文在我們這兒很普及。

普   b.f.   common, ubiquitous, pervasive

及   b.f.   to reach, to extend

37. 世界   shìjiè   n.   the world, (Buddhist) the cosmos

世界上現在有多少人說中文，你知道嗎？

38. 遊行   yóuxíng   n.   parade, demonstration

明天你去參加遊行嗎？

39. 應有盡有   yīng yǒu jìn yǒu   phr.   to have everything needed; (lit.) Whatever one should have, one has it all.

你們家的年貨真是應有盡有！

40. 商品   shāngpǐn   n.   merchandise, goods, commodity

我們商店不賣那種商品。

41. 絕對   juéduì   adv.   absolutely, definitely

今年春節我絕對不想自己一個人過。

絕   b.f.   extreme, end

42. 放棄   fàngqì   v.   to give up; (lit.) to let go and abandon

你不應該放棄這麼好的機會。

棄   v.   to abandon

43. 難怪   nánguài   conj.   no wonder; (lit.) difficult to blame

難怪他不想讓我去，他想自己去。

44. 饞   chán   adj.   gluttonous, drooling over (food), making (somebody) drool over (food)

別老說這個菜好，那個菜好的，快饞死我了。

食品名稱 Names of Foods

1. 粽子   zòngzi   glutinous rice cake wrapped with large bamboo leaves

2. 月餅   yuèbǐng   mooncake

3. 火鸡	huǒjī	turkey
4. 土豆泥	tǔdòu ní	mashed potatoes
5. 南瓜饼	nánguā bǐng	pumpkin pie

中国节日 Names of Chinese Holidays

1. 国际劳动节	Guójì Láodòngjié	International Labor Day (May 1)
2. 国庆节	Guóqìngjié	National Day; (lit.) national celebration holiday
3. 中秋节	Zhōngqiūjié	Mid-Autumn Festival
4. 清明节	Qīngmíngjié	Pure and Bright Festival (approximately April 5, for paying respect to one's ancestors who have passed away)
5. 端午节	Duānwǔjié	Dragon Boat Festival (fifth day of the fifth lunar month)
6. 元宵节	Yuánxiāojié	Lantern Festival (fifteenth of the first lunar month); (lit.) sweet dumplings holiday
7. 灯节	Dēngjié	Lantern Festival; the same as 元宵节

西方节日 Names of Western Holidays

1. 圣诞节	Shèngdànjié	Christmas; (lit.) the saint's birth holiday
2. 感恩节	Gǎn'ēnjié	Thanksgiving Day; (lit.) feeling gratitude holiday
3. 万圣节	Wànshèngjié	Halloween; (lit.) ten thousand saints holiday
4. 情人节	Qíngrénjié	Valentine's Day; (lit.) lover's holiday
5. 元旦	Yuándàn	New Year's Day; (lit.) the first dawn

专有名词 Proper Nouns

| 1. 楚国 | Chǔguó | Chu, an ancient state in China |
| 2. 屈原 | Qū Yuán | Qū Yuán (ca 340–278 BC, considered one of China's first great poets) |

3. 火雞   huǒjī   turkey

4. 土豆泥   tǔdòu ní   mashed potatoes

5. 南瓜餅   nánguā bǐng   pumpkin pie

中國節日 Names of Chinese Holidays

1. 國際勞動節   Guójì Láodòngjié   International Labor Day (May 1)

2. 國慶日   Guóqìngjié   National Day; (lit.) national celebration holiday

3. 中秋節   Zhōngqiūjié   Mid-Autumn Festival

4. 清明節   Qīngmíngjié   Pure and Bright Festival (approximately April 5, for paying respect to one's ancestors who have passed away)

5. 端午節   Duānwǔjié   Dragon Boat Festival (fifth day of the fifth lunar month)

6. 元宵節   Yuánxiāojié   Lantern Festival (fifteenth of the first lunar month); (lit.) sweet dumplings holiday

7. 燈節   Dēngjié   Lantern Festival; the same as 元宵節

西方節日 Names of Western Holidays

1. 聖誕節   Shèngdànjié   Christmas; (lit.) the saint's birth holiday

2. 感恩節   Gǎn'ēnjié   Thanksgiving Day; (lit.) feeling gratitude holiday

3. 萬聖節   Wànshèngjié   Halloween; (lit.) ten thousand saints holiday

4. 情人節   Qíngrénjié   Valentine's Day; (lit.) lover's holiday

5. 元旦   Yuándàn   New Year's Day; (lit.) the first dawn

專有名詞 Proper Nouns

1. 楚國   Chǔguó   Chu, an ancient state in China

2. 屈原   Qū Yuán   Qū Yuán (ca 340–278 BC, considered one of China's first great poets)

书面语 *vs.* 口语 Written Form vs. Spoken Form

In Chinese, the "written form" preserves a lot of words and expressions from Classical Chinese and is therefore more concise and formal. As its name implies, the "written form" is used primarily in writing, but it does occur frequently in speech as well.

书面语	口语
1. 按	按照
2. 一年之中	一年里
3. 在此之后	在这个以后
4. 除此之外	除了这(个)以外
5. 称之为	把…叫作
6. 名诗	有名的诗
7. 每逢	每次到了
8. 晚餐	晚饭
9. 应有尽有	应该有的都有了

词汇注解 Featured Vocabulary

1. 其他 (qítā) vs. 别的 (biéde) vs. 另外 (lìngwài)

其他(的)	*pron.*	the rest, other (的 is optional.)
其他的学生 其他老师		the rest of the students other teachers

别的	*pron.*	(all) other (的 cannot be omitted.)
别的老师		other teachers

另外	*adj.*	(the) other (must be followed by a number or a specifier plus a measure word)
另外那位老师 另外两位老师		the other teacher the other two teachers

2. 感觉 (gǎnjué) vs. 觉得 (juéde)

感觉	*n.*	feeling

我有一种很奇怪的感觉。
I have a very strange feeling.

書面語 *vs.* 口語 Written Form vs. Spoken Form

In Chinese, the "written form" preserves a lot of words and expressions from Classical Chinese and is therefore more concise and formal. As its name implies, the "written form" is used primarily in writing, but it does occur frequently in speech as well.

書面語	口語
1. 按	按照
2. 一年之中	一年裏
3. 在此之後	在這個以後
4. 除此之外	除了這（個）以外
5. 稱之為	把…叫作
6. 名詩	有名的詩
7. 每逢	每次到了
8. 晚餐	晚飯
9. 應有盡有	應該有的都有了

辭彙注解 Featured Vocabulary

1. 其他 (qítā) vs. 別的 (biéde) vs. 另外 (lìngwài)

其他(的)	*pron.*	the rest, other (的 is optional.)
其他的學生		the rest of the students
其他老師		other teachers

別的	*pron.*	(all) other (的 cannot be omitted.)
別的老師		other teachers

另外	*adj.*	(the) other (must be followed by a number or a specifier plus a measure word)
另外那位老師		the other teacher
另外兩位老師		the other two teachers

2. 感覺 (gǎnjué) vs. 覺得 (juéde)

感覺	*n.*	feeling

我有一種很奇怪的感覺。
I have a very strange feeling.

感觉	*v.*	to feel (often used together with 到)

我感觉到身体很累。
I feel that my body is very tired.

觉得	*v.*	to feel (more colloquial than the verb 感觉)

我觉得很累。
I feel very tired.

觉得	*v.*	to think that

我觉得昨天的电影很好看。
I think that yesterday's movie was very good.

3. 据说 (jushuō) vs. 听说 (tīngshuō)

据说	*phr.*	It is said…, (usually occurs at the beginning of a sentence)

据说那个学校的老师都很棒。
It is said that the teachers in that school are very good.

听说	*phr.*	hear (somebody/others) say

Sometimes a personal noun can be placed before 听 or inserted between 听 and 说.

我听说老师病了。
I have heard that the teacher is sick.

我听老师说明天有考试。
I heard from the teacher that there is a test tomorrow.

4. 团圆 (tuányuán) vs. 团聚 (tuánjù)

团圆	*n.*	reunion (usually used to indicate a family member get-together)

家人团圆
family reunion

团聚	*v.*	to reunite (used to indicate a get-together by family or friends)

朋友团聚在一起
a get-together with friends

5. 愿望 (yuànwang) vs. 希望 (xīwàng)

愿望	*n.*	desire, wish, aspiration

他的愿望是当一个医生。
He wants to be a doctor.

希望	*n.*	hope

他爸爸妈妈对他的希望很高。
His parents have high hopes for him.

| 感覺 | *v.* | to feel (often used together with 到) |

我感覺到身體很累。
I feel that my body is very tired.

| 覺得 | *v.* | to feel (more colloquial than the verb 感觉) |

我覺得很累。
I feel very tired.

| 覺得 | *v.* | to think that |

我覺得昨天的電影很好看。
I think that yesterday's movie was very good.

3. 據說 (jushuō) vs. 聽說 (tīngshuō)

| 據說 | *phr.* | It is said..., (usually occurs at the beginning of a sentence) |

據說那個學校的老師都很棒。
It is said that the teachers in that school are very good.

| 聽說 | *phr.* | hear (somebody/others) say |

Sometimes a personal noun can be placed before 聽 or inserted between 聽 and 說.

我聽說老師病了。
I have heard that the teacher is sick.

我聽老師說明天有考試。
I heard from the teacher that there is a test tomorrow.

4. 團圓 (tuányuán) vs. 團聚 (tuánjù)

| 團圓 | *n.* | reunion (usually used to indicate a family member get-together) |

家人團圓
family reunion

| 團聚 | *v.* | to reunite (used to indicate a get-together by family or friends) |

朋友團聚在一起
a get-together with friends

5. 願望 (yuànwang) vs. 希望 (xīwàng)

| 願望 | *n.* | desire, wish, aspiration |

他的願望是當一個醫生。
He wants to be a doctor.

| 希望 | *n.* | hope |

他爸爸媽媽對他的希望很高。
His parents have high hopes for him.

希望	*v.*	to wish, to hope

他希望能当医生。
He hopes that he could be a doctor.

6. 不过 (búguò)

不过	*adv.*	only

不过 can be emphasized by 只 and it is frequently used with 罢了 to form the pattern 只不过…罢了.

他只不过是没有钱罢了。
It's just that he does not have money.

不过	*conj.*	but

他很聪明，不过他学习不太认真。
He is very smart, but he does not study hard.

7. 早晚 (zǎowǎn) vs. 早/晚 (zǎo/wǎn)

早晚	*adv.*	sooner or later (frequently used with aux. verb 会)

他早晚会来。
He will come sooner or later.

早/晚	*adj.*	early/late

他今天来得很早/晚。
He came very early/late today.

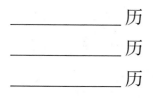

词汇练习
Vocabulary Exercises

🎧 🌀 TASK 1. 组词 WORD AND PHRASE COMPOSITION

Use the given word or phrase on the left as a guide to help you think of other, similar compound words. Feel free to use a dictionary when needed. Then write down the English definition of each of the compound words you've created.

1. 历 (calendar): 农历   lunar calendar

_____历

_____历

_____历

| 希望 | *v.* | to wish, to hope |

他希望能當醫生。

He hopes that he could be a doctor.

6. 不過 (búguò)

| 不過 | *adv.* | only |

不過 can be emphasized by 只 and it is frequently used with 罷了 to form the pattern 只不過…罷了.

他只不過是沒有錢罷了。

It's just that he does not have money.

| 不過 | *conj.* | but |

他很聰明，不過他學習不太認真。

He is very smart, but he does not study hard.

7. 早晚 (zǎowǎn) vs. 早/晚 (zǎo/wǎn)

| 早晚 | *adv.* | sooner or later (frequently used with aux. verb 會) |

他早晚會來。

He will come sooner or later.

| 早/晚 | *adj.* | early/late |

他今天來得很早/晚。

He came very early/late today.

辭彙練習
Vocabulary Exercises

🎧 🔊 TASK 1. 組詞 WORD AND PHRASE COMPOSITION

Use the given word or phrase on the left as a guide to help you think of other, similar compound words. Feel free to use a dictionary when needed. Then write down the English definition of each of the compound words you've created.

1. 曆 (calendar): 農曆   lunar calendar

   _____曆

   _____曆

   _____曆

2. 庆 (to celebrate): 节庆   holiday celebration

_____庆

_____庆

_____庆

3. 代 (period): 古代   ancient times

_____代

_____代

_____代

4. 教 (religion): 宗教   religion

_____教

_____教

_____教

5. 团 (group): 团圆   reunion

团_____

团_____

团_____

🎧 TASK 2. 搭配 MATCHING

A. 近义词

Match synonyms from among the following words and phrases.

1) 团圆	a) 思念
2) 象征	b) 普及
3) 感觉	c) 根本
4) 想念	d) 觉得
5) 流行	e) 表示
6) 绝对	f) 团聚

2. 慶 (to celebrate): 節慶   holiday celebration

   _____慶

   _____慶

   _____慶

3. 代 (period): 古代   ancient times

   _____代

   _____代

   _____代

4. 教 (religion): 宗教   religion

   _____教

   _____教

   _____教

5. 團 (group): 團圓   reunion

   團_____

   團_____

   團_____

🎧 ✐ TASK 2. 搭配 MATCHING

A. 近義詞

Match synonyms from among the following words and phrases.

1) 團圓   a) 思念

2) 象徵   b) 普及

3) 感覺   c) 根本

4) 想念   d) 覺得

5) 流行   e) 表示

6) 絕對   f) 團聚

B. 动宾词组

Match verbs in the left column with nouns in the right column to form phrases.

Verbs	Nouns
1) 放弃	a) 日期
2) 信仰	b) 家人
3) 称之为	c) 宗教
4) 想念	d) 这个好机会
5) 计算	e) 圣诞节

🎧 TASK 3. 填空 FILL IN THE BLANKS

A. 句子

Read the following sentences and fill in each blank with the appropriate word or phrase from the given options.

1. 尽早　　　只不过　　　早晚　　　不过

   a) 你应该 ＿＿＿＿＿＿＿＿ 准备年货。

   b) 你 ＿＿＿＿＿＿＿＿ 得去买年货。我们今天一起去吧。

   c) 今天的月亮真漂亮，我们应该去赏月，＿＿＿＿＿＿＿＿＿ 我还有这么多功课没有做。

   d) 这些商人也不是坏人，＿＿＿＿＿＿＿＿ 想赚几个钱罢了。

2. 愿望　　　另外　　　团圆　　　团聚　　　希望　　　其他

   a) 感恩节只有我和小张留在宿舍，＿＿＿＿＿＿＿＿ 的人都回家跟家人团聚去了。

   b) 感恩节的时候，我们宿舍不回家过节的学生只有两个，一个是我，＿＿＿＿＿＿ 一个是小张。

   c) 我爸爸 ＿＿＿＿＿＿ 我能回家跟他们一起过年。当然那也是我自己的 ＿＿＿＿＿＿ 。

   d) 中国的很多节日都是为了庆祝家人 ＿＿＿＿＿＿＿＿ 。

   e) 每逢节日大家都希望能跟自己家人 ＿＿＿＿＿＿＿＿ 在一起。

B. 動賓詞組

Match verbs in the left column with nouns in the right column to form phrases.

Verbs　　　　　　　　**Nouns**

1) 放棄　　　　　　　　a) 日期

2) 信仰　　　　　　　　b) 家人

3) 稱之為　　　　　　　c) 宗教

4) 想念　　　　　　　　d) 這個好機會

5) 計算　　　　　　　　e) 聖誕節

🎧 TASK 3. 填空 FILL IN THE BLANKS

A. 句子

Read the following sentences and fill in each blank with the appropriate word or phrase from the given options.

1. 儘早　　　只不過　　　早晚　　　　不過

   a) 你應該 ＿＿＿＿＿＿ 準備年貨。

   b) 你 ＿＿＿＿＿＿ 得去買年貨。我們今天一起去吧。

   c) 今天的月亮真漂亮，我們應該去賞月，＿＿＿＿＿＿＿ 我還有這麼多功課沒有做。

   d) 這些商人也不是壞人，＿＿＿＿＿＿ 想賺幾個錢罷了。

2. 願望　　　另外　　　團圓　　　團聚　　　希望　　　其他

   a) 感恩節只有我和小張留在宿舍，＿＿＿＿＿＿ 的人都回家跟家人團聚去了。

   b) 感恩節的時候，我們宿舍不回家過節的學生只有兩個，一個是我，＿＿＿＿＿ 一個是小張。

   c) 我爸爸 ＿＿＿＿ 我能回家跟他們一起過年。當然那也是我自己的 ＿＿＿＿＿。

   d) 中國的很多節日都是為了慶祝家人 ＿＿＿＿＿＿。

   e) 每逢節日大家都希望能跟自己家人 ＿＿＿＿＿＿ 在一起。

B. 段落

Read the following passage and fill in each blank with the appropriate word or phrase from the given options.

放弃   其他   象征   纪念

　　清明节和中国 _____ 的节日不太一样。这一天不是为了吃，也不是为了玩儿，是为了 _____ 家里已经去世的老人。这一天很多人会 _____ 自己的休息时间去扫墓，有的人还会带着自己的小孩子去。这也是一种家人团圆的 _____ 吧。

Vocabulary

去世 qù shì   *v.*   to pass away

语法句型和练习
Grammar Structures and Exercises

I. 在…中 (zài...zhōng): In the middle of, in the process of, among

The 在…中 structure often functions as an adverbial phrase, indicating a location, process, or range. It must be placed before the main verb or at the beginning of the sentence. The elements inserted within 在…中 may be either noun or verb phrases.

Subject	在 Noun 中	Verb	Object
老师	在作业中	加了	一些语法练习。

The teacher added a few grammar exercises to the homework assignments.

在 Noun 中		Subject	Predicate
在全班同学中，他的听力理解考试成绩			最高。

Of the students in the class, his grade in listening comprehension is the highest.

Subject	在 Verb 中	Verb	Object
学生	在学习中	经常遇到	很多困难。

Students frequently come across many difficulties while studying.

导游	在介绍中	讲了	很多有意思的故事。

The tour guide told many interesting stories while giving his introduction.

B. 段落

Read the following passage and fill in each blank with the appropriate word or phrase from the given options.

放棄　　　其他　　　象徵　　　紀念

　　清明節和中國 _____ 的節日不太一樣。這一天不是為了吃，也不是為了玩兒，是為了 _____ 家裏已經去世的老人。這一天很多人會 _____ 自己的休息時間去掃墓，有的人還會帶著自己的小孩子去。這也是一種家人團圓的 _____ 吧。

Vocabulary

去世　qù shì　　　*v.*　　　to pass away

語法句型和練習
Grammar Structures and Exercises

I. 在⋯中 (zài...zhōng): In the middle of, in the process of, among

The 在⋯中 structure often functions as an adverbial phrase, indicating a location, process, or range. It must be placed before the main verb or at the beginning of the sentence. The elements inserted within 在⋯中 may be either noun or verb phrases.

Subject	在 Noun 中	Verb	Object
老師	在作業中	加了	一些語法練習。

The teacher added a few grammar exercises to the homework assignments.

在 Noun 中		Subject	Predicate
在全班同學中，		他的聽力理解考試成績	最高。

Of the students in the class, his grade in listening comprehension is the highest.

Subject	在 Verb 中	Verb	Object
學生	在學習中	經常遇到	很多困難。

Students frequently come across many difficulties while studying.

| 導遊 | 在介紹中 | 講了 | 很多有意思的故事。 |

The tour guide told many interesting stories while giving his introduction.

Note

There are two similar structures: 在…上 means "in a certain respect" and 在…下 indicates a certain condition. You will learn more about these two structures in future lessons.

❧ PRACTICE

模仿造句

Make sentences of your own by following each of the examples given.

1. 在 _____ 中，我学到了很多 _____。
   (Example: 学习，新知识)

2. 在 _____ 中，_____ 帮了我很大的忙。
   (Example: 工作，我的同事)

3. 在 _____ 中，他 _____。
   (Example: 过去的一年，交了一些新朋友)

❧ PRACTICE

完成句子

Complete each of the sentences below.

1. 在节庆活动中，_____。

2. 在招聘广告中，_____。

3. 在工作单位中，_____。

4. _____ 在 _____ 的发展中，_____。

5. _____ 在 _____ 的对话中，_____。

6. _____ 在 _____ 的课文中，_____。

翻译

Translate the following sentence into Chinese. Make sure your translation includes 在…中.

   Due to the influence of his British friend, whenever he drinks tea he adds milk to it.

Note

There are two similar structures: 在…上 means "in a certain respect" and 在…下 indicates a certain condition. You will learn more about these two structures in future lessons.

🔲 PRACTICE

模仿造句

Make sentences of your own by following each of the examples given.

1. 在 _____ 中，我學到了很多 _____ 。
   (Example: 學習，新知識)

2. 在 _____ 中，_____ 幫了我很大的忙。
   (Example: 工作，我的同事)

3. 在 _____ 中，他 _____ 。
   (Example: 過去的一年，交了一些新朋友)

🔲 PRACTICE

完成句子

Complete each of the sentences below.

1. 在節慶活動中，_____ 。
2. 在招聘廣告中，_____ 。
3. 在工作單位中，_____ 。
4. _____ 在 _____ 的發展中，_____ 。
5. _____ 在 _____ 的對話中，_____ 。
6. _____ 在 _____ 的課文中，_____ 。

翻譯

Translate the following sentence into Chinese. Make sure your translation includes 在…中.

Due to the influence of his British friend, whenever he drinks tea he adds milk to it.

II. 之所以…是因为…(zhī suǒyǐ… shì yīnwéi…): The reason why..., is because...

In Lesson 31 you learned the conjunction 因为…所以, which indicates cause and effect. In this lesson you will learn the similar but more formal structure 之所以…是因为. 之所以 is used after the subject of the first clause, which provides a result or conclusion. The second clause starts with the pattern 是因为 to emphasize the reason behind the first clause.

1st clause (Effect)	2nd clause (Cause)
Subject 之所以 Verb phrase,	是因为 Subject Verb phrase

我之所以参加汉语水平考试，   是因为想得到中国政府发的考试证书。

The reason I participated in the HSK test is because I want to obtain the certificate given by the Chinese government.

中国旅馆之所以每个房间都准备纯净水，是因为房间里的自来水不能喝。

Every Chinese hotel room has spring water because the tap water is not drinkable.

❈ PRACTICE

模仿造句

Make sentences of your own by following each of the examples given.

1. _____ 之所以越来越普及，是因为 _____ 。

   (Example: 速食店，大家忙得没有时间做饭)

2. _____ 之所以 _____ ，是因为这 _____ 。

   (Example: 中秋节人们，吃月饼，象征着家人团圆)

3. 我之所以对 _____ 感兴趣，是因为 _____ 。

   (Example: 中文，我将来想去中国工作)

问答

Use the sentence pattern 之所以…是因为 to answer the following questions.

1. 为什么每逢过节，商人就特别高兴？

II. 之所以⋯是因為⋯(zhī suǒyǐ... shì yīnwéi...):
The reason why..., is because...

In Lesson 31 you learned the conjunction 因為⋯所以, which indicates cause and effect. In this lesson you will learn the similar but more formal structure 之所以⋯是因為. 之所以 is used after the subject of the first clause, which provides a result or conclusion. The second clause starts with the pattern 是因為 to emphasize the reason behind the first clause.

1st clause (Effect)	2nd clause (Cause)
Subject 之所以 Verb phrase,	是因為 **Subject Verb phrase**

我之所以參加漢語水平考試，   是因為想得到中國政府發的考試證書。

The reason I participated in the HSK test is because I want to obtain the certificate given by the Chinese government.

中國旅館之所以每個房間都準備純淨水，是因為房間裏的自來水不能喝。

Every Chinese hotel room has spring water because the tap water is not drinkable.

🕉 PRACTICE

模仿造句

Make sentences of your own by following each of the examples given.

1. _____之所以越來越普及，是因為 _____ 。

   (Example: 速食店，大家忙得沒有時間做飯)

2. _____之所以 _____，是因為這 _____ 。

   (Example: 中秋節人們，吃月餅，象徵著家人團圓)

3. 我之所以對 _____ 感興趣，是因為_____ 。

   (Example: 中文，我將來想去中國工作)

問答

Use the sentence pattern 之所以⋯是因為 to answer the following questions.

1. 為什麼每逢過節，商人就特別高興？

2. 为什么很多美国人都喜欢吃中国饭呢？

翻译

Translate the following sentences into Chinese. Make sure your translation includes 按照 and 之所以…是因为.

According to traditional customs, everyone eats *zòngzi* on the fifth of May of the lunar calendar. It is said that people eat *zòngzi* that day to commemorate an ancient Chinese poet.

III. 为了 (wèile): In order to

In Lesson 21 you learned the preposition 为, "for." 为了 has a similar function as 为, but the two are grammatically different. 为了 introduces the purpose or reason for the action indicated in the main clause of the sentence. Sometimes the main action is stated first, followed by the purpose or reason stated in the second clause, which begins with 是为了.

1st clause (Purpose/Cause)	2nd clause (Action)
为了方便，	他出去旅游的时候，总是只带一点儿行李。

For convenience, whenever he travels, he brings very little luggage.

为了记住生词，	他每天早上五点钟就起床做词汇练习。

In order to remember new words, he gets out of bed at five o'clock each morning to do vocabulary practice.

1st clause (Action)	2nd clause (Purpose/Cause)
他每天帮助妈妈做晚饭，	是为了不让妈妈太辛苦。

In order to ease his mother's workload, he helps her make dinner every day.

❀ PRACTICE

模仿造句

Make sentences of your own by following each of the examples given.

1. 为了庆祝 _____，人们 _____。

  (Example: 感恩节，那天晚上都吃火鸡)

2. 為什麼很多美國人都喜歡吃中國飯呢？

翻譯

Translate the following sentences into Chinese. Make sure your translation includes 按照 and 之所以…是因為.

According to traditional customs, everyone eats *zòngzi* on the fifth of May of the lunar calendar. It is said that people eat *zòngzi* that day to commemorate an ancient Chinese poet.

III. 為了 (wèile): In order to

In Lesson 21 you learned the preposition 為, "for." 為了 has a similar function as 為, but the two are grammatically different. 為了 introduces the purpose or reason for the action indicated in the main clause of the sentence. Sometimes the main action is stated first, followed by the purpose or reason stated in the second clause, which begins with 是為了.

1st clause (Purpose/Cause)	2nd clause (Action)
為了方便，	他出去旅遊的時候，總是只帶一點兒行李。

For convenience, whenever he travels, he brings very little luggage.

| 為了記住生詞， | 他每天早上五點鐘就起床做辭彙練習。 |

In order to remember new words, he gets out of bed at five o'clock each morning to do vocabulary practice.

1st clause (Action)	2nd clause (Purpose/Cause)
他每天幫助媽媽做晚飯，	是為了不讓媽媽太辛苦。

In order to ease his mother's workload, he helps her make dinner every day.

❧ PRACTICE

模仿造句

Make sentences of your own by following each of the examples given.

1. 為了慶祝 _____，人們 _____。
   (Example: 感恩節，那天晚上都吃火雞)

2. 为了纪念 _____，大家都 _____ 。

    (Example: 中国诗人屈原，在端午节那天吃粽子)

3. 学生 _____ 是为了表示 _____ 。

    (Example: 给他送礼物，对他的感谢)

问答

Use the preposition 为了 to answer the following questions.

1. 你为什么学中文？

2. 你每天锻炼身体吗？为什么？

3. 你今年圣诞节的时候有什么计划？为什么？

翻译

Translate the following sentence into Chinese. Make sure your translation includes 为了 and 无论如何.

    In order to reunite with family members, for this year's Spring Festival I will go home to celebrate the holidays no matter what.

IV. 除此以外 (chú cǐ yǐ wài): In addition to this

In Lesson 39 you learned the structure "除了···以外," (in addition to...). In this lesson you will learn the related set phrase 除此以外 (in addition to this). "This" (此) usually refers to a fact that has just been mentioned by the speaker. The set phrase 除此以外 is always placed between two clauses and is usually followed by 还, 也, or 再.

2. 為了紀念 ＿＿＿＿＿＿＿＿＿＿＿＿＿＿＿＿ ，大家都 ＿＿＿＿＿＿＿＿＿＿＿＿＿＿＿＿＿＿＿ 。

(Example: 中國詩人屈原，在端午節那天吃粽子)

3. 學生 ＿＿＿＿＿＿＿＿＿＿＿＿＿＿＿ 是為了表示 ＿＿＿＿＿＿＿＿＿＿＿＿＿＿＿＿＿＿＿ 。

(Example: 給他送禮物，對他的感謝)

问答

Use the preposition 為了 to answer the following questions.

1. 你為什麼學中文？

2. 你每天鍛煉身體嗎？為什麼？

3. 你今年聖誕節的時候有什麼計畫？為什麼？

翻譯

Translate the following sentence into Chinese. Make sure your translation includes 為了 and 無論如何.

In order to reunite with family members, for this year's Spring Festival I will go home to celebrate the holidays no matter what.

IV. 除此以外 (chú cǐ yǐ wài): In addition to this

In Lesson 39 you learned the structure "除了…以外," (in addition to…). In this lesson you will learn the related set phrase 除此以外 (in addition to this). "This" (此) usually refers to a fact that has just been mentioned by the speaker. The set phrase 除此以外 is always placed between two clauses and is usually followed by 還, 也, or 再.

1st clause	2nd clause
Subject Verb phrase,	除此以外 **(Subject)** 还/也/再 **Verb phrase**

手机用起来很方便，　　　　　　　除此以外还有很多别的好处。

The cellular phone is very convenient to use; besides, it also has a lot of other advantages.

在中国乘火车可以选硬座、硬卧，除此以外也有软座和软卧。

When taking the train in China, one can choose hard seats or hard beds, as well as soft seats or soft beds.

他只存了一万块钱，　　　　　　　除此以外，他再也拿不出更多的钱交买房订金了。

He only managed to save ten thousand dollars. Beyond that, he could not come up with any more of the deposit for the new house.

Note

此外 is a short form of 除此以外, and it is more formal than 除此以外. It can also be used between paragraphs.

❑❑ PRACTICE

模仿造句

Make sentences of your own by following each of the examples given.

1. _____ 有很多传统节日，除此以外 _____。

   (Example: 中国，还有一些国家法定的节日)

A typical Spring Festival decoration.

1st clause	2nd clause
Subject Verb phrase,	除此以外 **(Subject)** 還／也／再 **Verb phrase**

手機用起來很方便，　　　　　　除此以外還有很多別的好處

The cellular phone is very convenient to use; besides, it also has a lot of other advantages.

在中國乘火車可以選硬座、硬臥，除此以外也有軟座和軟臥。

When taking the train in China, one can choose hard seats or hard beds, as well as soft seats or soft beds.

他只存了一萬塊錢，　　　　　　除此以外，他再也拿不出更多的錢交買房訂金了。

He only managed to save ten thousand dollars. Beyond that, he could not come up with any more of the deposit for the new house.

Note

此外 is a short form of 除此以外, and it is more formal than 除此以外. It can also be used between paragraphs.

❀ PRACTICE

模仿造句

Make sentences of your own by following each of the examples given.

1. ＿＿＿＿＿＿＿＿＿＿ 有很多傳統節日，除此以外 ＿＿＿＿＿＿＿＿＿＿＿＿＿＿＿＿。

   (Example: 中國，還有一些國家法定的節日)

A typical Spring Festival decoration.

Xueying Wang.

2. _____ 除此以外，我什么 _____ 都 _____ 。

(Example: 星期天我只在家休息，地方，没有去)

3. _____ 改变了很多。此外 _____ 。

(Example: 中国人的饮食习惯，人们也慢慢开始庆祝西方的节日)

问答

Use the phrase 除此以外 to answer the following questions.

1. 你放假的时候，都做了些什么？

2. 你的家庭怎么庆祝感恩节？

翻译

Translate the following sentences into Chinese. Make sure your translation includes 不论···还是··· and 此外.

Chinese people, whether it be their style of eating and drinking or their way of celebrating holidays, are becoming more and more Westernized. Also, there are more and more people who practice Western religions.

V. 因此 (yīncǐ): Hence, therefore

The conjunction 因此 is used in a complex sentence involving cause and effect. 因此 precedes the clause stating the effect. It must have an antecedent clause. The 此 of 因此 refers back to the first clause. Sometimes 由于 can be used in the first clause. 因此 can also be used between paragraphs.

1st clause	2nd clause (Effect)	
Subject Predicate,	因此	Subject Verb phrase
他的基础很好，	因此	汉语提高得很快。

His foundation is very good, so his Chinese improved very quickly.

2. _____ 除此以外，我什麼 _____ 都 _____。

(Example: 星期天我只在家休息，地方，沒有去)

3. _____ 改變了很多。此外 _____。

(Example: 中國人的飲食習慣，人們也慢慢開始慶祝西方的節日)

問答

Use the phrase 除此以外 to answer the following questions.

1. 你放假的時候，都做了些什麼？

2. 你的家庭怎麼慶祝感恩節？

翻譯

Translate the following sentences into Chinese. Make sure your translation includes 不論···還是··· and 此外.

Chinese people, whether it be their style of eating and drinking or their way of celebrating holidays, are becoming more and more Westernized. Also, there are more and more people who practice Western religions.

V. 因此 (yīncǐ): Hence, therefore

The conjunction 因此 is used in a complex sentence involving cause and effect. 因此 precedes the clause stating the effect. It must have an antecedent clause. The 此 of 因此 refers back to the first clause. Sometimes 由於 can be used in the first clause. 因此 can also be used between paragraphs.

1st clause	2nd clause (Effect)	
Subject Predicate,	因此	**Subject Verb phrase**
他的基礎很好，	因此	漢語提高得很快。

His foundation is very good, so his Chinese improved very quickly.

Subject 由于 Predicate,	因此	Subject Predicate
这位运动员由于怯场，	因此	比赛成绩很差。

This athlete had stage fright, so his competition scores are very bad.

PRACTICE

模仿造句

Make sentences of your own by following each of the examples given.

1. _____ ，因此人们把 _____ 称之为 _____ 。

   (Example: 这个季节常常给人一种清亮明快的感觉，这个节日，清明节)

2. 据说 _____ ，因此 _____ 。

   (Example: 屈原是一位非常有名的诗人，很多中学生都知道他)

3. 由于_____ ，因此 _____ 。

   (Example: 近几年来中国受西方文化影响很大，有的中国人也开始庆祝西方的节日了)

问答

Use the conjunction 因此 to answer the following question.

近几年来，为什么有这么多的人都想到中国去？

翻译

Translate the following sentence into Chinese. Make sure your translation includes 由于 and 因此.

Because more and more people are interested in Western culture, more and more people in the world are now celebrating Christmas.

Subject 由於 Predicate,	因此	Subject Predicate
這位運動員由於怯場，	因此	比賽成績很差。

This athlete had stage fright, so his competition scores are very bad.

🔳 PRACTICE

模仿造句

Make sentences of your own by following each of the examples given.

1. _____ ，因此人們把 _____稱之為 _____ 。

   (Example: 這個季節常常給人一種清亮明快的感覺，這個節日，清明節)

2. 據說 _____ ，因此 _____ 。

   (Example: 屈原是一位非常有名的詩人，很多中學生都知道他)

3. 由於_____ ，因此 _____ 。

   (Example: 近幾年來中國受西方文化影響很大，有的中國人也開始慶祝西方的節日了)

問答

Use the conjunction 因此 to answer the following question.

　　近幾年來，為什麼有這麼多的人都想到中國去？

翻譯

Translate the following sentence into Chinese. Make sure your translation includes 由於 and 因此.

　　Because more and more people are interested in Western culture, more and more people in the world are now celebrating Christmas.

VI. 每（逢/到）…都 (měi[féng/dào]...dōu): Every...always

每逢 or 每到 is followed by a verb phrase and functions as an adverbial phrase to mean "every time when something happens." It is often used in conjunction with 都/就/总. The subject can be used before or after the 每逢 or 每到 verb phrase.

每(逢/到)Verb phrase,	Subject 都/就/总 Verb Verb phrase
每逢/到过年，	她都回北京和她的爸爸妈妈团聚。

She always goes home to Beijing to reunite with her parents for the Chinese New Year.

每逢数学课，   他就睡觉。
Whenever it's time for math class, he falls asleep.

每到一个新的地方，   我总要找个最好的饭馆去吃饭。
Every time I go to a new place, I have to go to the best restaurant to eat.

❂ PRACTICE

模仿造句

Make sentences of your own by following each of the examples given.

1. 每逢 _____ ，我们这儿就有 _____ 。
   (Example: 感恩节，花车游行)

2. 每到 _____ 的时候，这儿到处都 _____ 。
   (Example: 过元宵节，挂着花灯)

3. 我每到 _____ ，总是 _____ 。
   (Example: 一家服装店，要买很多新衣服)

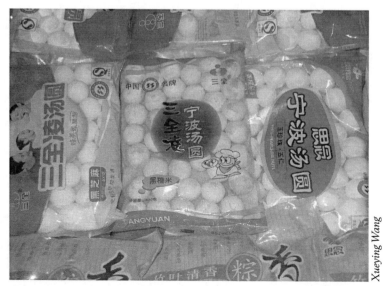

Sweet glutinous rice dumplings traditionally eaten on the Lantern Festival.

VI. 每(逢/到)…都 (měi[féng/dào]...dōu): Every...always

每逢 or 每到 is followed by a verb phrase and functions as an adverbial phrase to mean "every time when something happens." It is often used in conjunction with 都/就/總. The subject can be used before or after the 每逢 or 每到 verb phrase.

每(逢/到)Verb phrase,	Subject 都/就/總 Verb Verb phrase
每逢/到過年，	她都回北京和她的爸爸媽媽團聚。

She always goes home to Beijing to reunite with her parents for the Chinese New Year.

每逢數學課，　　　　　　　　他就睡覺。

Whenever it's time for math class, he falls asleep.

每到一個新的地方，　　　　我總要找個最好的飯館去吃飯。

Every time I go to a new place, I have to go to the best restaurant to eat.

❖ PRACTICE

模仿造句

Make sentences of your own by following each of the examples given.

1. 每逢 _____ ，我們這兒就有 _____ 。

   (Example: 感恩節，花車遊行)

2. 每到 _____ 的時候，這兒到處都 _____ 。

   (Example: 過元宵節，掛著花燈)

3. 我每到 _____ ，總是 _____ 。

   (Example: 一家服裝店，要買很多新衣服)

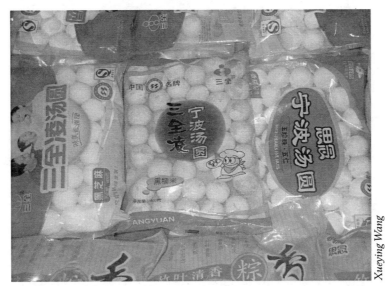

Sweet glutinous rice dumplings traditionally eaten on the Lantern Festival.

问答

Use the pattern 每（逢/到）…都 to answer the following question.

请你说一说你什么时候觉得：紧张、高兴、难过、激动、糊涂、或者不好意思？

翻译

Translate the following sentence into Chinese. Make sure your translation includes 每（逢/到）.

Whenever a Western holiday comes around, merchants make use of the opportunity to make money.

VII. 难怪 (nánguài): No wonder

In Lesson 33 you learned 怪不得, which indicates that the speaker understands the reason for an action or behavior. It is interchangeable with 难怪 but more colloquial than 难怪. 难怪 also implies that the speaker has reached a new level of understanding regarding an issue. It is placed at the beginning of the clause containing the action or behavior. The clause that explains the reason can precede or follow it. Sometimes 原来 can be used in front of the clause with the reason.

1st clause (Cause)	2nd clause (Fact)
Subject Verb phrase,	难怪 **Subject Verb phrase**

他们来这儿换了三次公共汽车，难怪迟到了。

No wonder they're late. They had to transfer buses three times to get here.

1st clause	2nd clause (Cause)
难怪 **Subject Predicate,**	原来 **Subject Verb phrase**

难怪街上到处都很拥挤，   原来大家都在忙着买年货准备过年。

No wonder it's crowded everywhere on the street — it turns out that everyone is busy buying goods for the Chinese New Year.

問答

Use the pattern 每（逢/到）…都 to answer the following question.

請你說一說你什麼時候覺得：緊張、高興、難過、激動、糊塗、或者不好意思？

翻譯

Translate the following sentence into Chinese. Make sure your translation includes 每（逢/到）.

Whenever a Western holiday comes around, merchants make use of the opportunity to make money.

VII. 難怪 (nánguài): No wonder

In Lesson 33 you learned 怪不得, which indicates that the speaker understands the reason for an action or behavior. It is interchangeable with 難怪 but more colloquial than 難怪. 難怪 also implies that the speaker has reached a new level of understanding regarding an issue. It is placed at the beginning of the clause containing the action or behavior. The clause that explains the reason can precede or follow it. Sometimes 原來 can be used in front of the clause with the reason.

1st clause (Cause)	2nd clause (Fact)
Subject Verb phrase,	難怪 **Subject Verb phrase**

他們來這兒換了三次公共汽車，難怪遲到了。
No wonder they're late. They had to transfer buses three times to get here.

1st clause	2nd clause (Cause)
難怪 **Subject Predicate,**	原來 **Subject Verb phrase**

難怪街上到處都很擁擠，　　　　原來大家都在忙著買年貨準備過年。
No wonder it's crowded everywhere on the street — it turns out that everyone is busy buying goods for the Chinese New Year.

❧ PRACTICE

模仿造句

Make a sentence of your own by following each of the examples given.

1. _____ ，难怪 _____ 放弃了。

   (Example: 数学太难学了，他)

2. 难怪 _____ ，原来是受 _____ 的影响。

   (Example: 这个孩子爱吃西餐，他爸爸)

3. _____ ，难怪他 _____ 。

   (Example: 这个东西又好看又便宜，想买)

4. 难怪_____ ，原来 _____ 变了。

   (Example: 这个教室里没有人，上课时间)

❧ PRACTICE

完成对话

After reading each statement, come up with a response to it using 难怪…原来….

Example:

Statement: (我买的是软卧票，他买的是硬座票。)

Response: 难怪你的票比他的贵，原来你买的是软卧。

1. Statement: (我是四川人。)

   Response: 难怪…原来…

2. Statement: (大家都在吃月饼呢。)

   Response: 难怪…原来…

翻译

Translate the following sentences into Chinese. Make sure your translation includes 难怪 and 原来.

   No wonder the moon is so big and round; it turns out that the Mid-Autumn Festival has arrived. Let's all go out and eat mooncakes and admire the moon.

🟥 PRACTICE

模仿造句

Make a sentence of your own by following each of the examples given.

1. _____ ，難怪 _____ 放棄了。

   (Example: 數學太難學了，他)

2. 難怪 _____ ，原來是受 _____ 的影響。

   (Example: 這個孩子愛吃西餐，他爸爸)

3. _____ ，難怪他 _____ 。

   (Example: 這個東西又好看又便宜，想買)

4. 難怪_____ ，原來 _____ 變了。

   (Example: 這個教室裏沒有人，上課時間)

🟥 PRACTICE

完成對話

After reading each statement, come up with a response to it using 難怪…原來….

Example:

Statement: (我買的是軟臥票，他買的是硬座票。)

Response: 難怪你的票比他的貴，原來你買的是軟臥。

1. Statement: (我是四川人。)

   Response: 難怪…原來…

2. Statement: (大家都在吃月餅呢。)

   Response: 難怪…原來…

翻譯

Translate the following sentences into Chinese. Make sure your translation includes 難怪 and 原來.

No wonder the moon is so big and round; it turns out that the Mid-Autumn Festival has arrived. Let's all go out and eat mooncakes and admire the moon.

听说读写练习
Comprehensive Exercises

🎧📝 TASK 1. 听一听、选一选 LISTENING EXERCISES

A. Bingo

In this section, you will hear various Chinese phrases. Demonstrate your understanding of these phrases by numbering their English counterparts in the order in which you hear them.

to calculate according to the lunar calendar

the symbol of family reunion

a very good feeling

other religions and faiths

folk tradition

festooned car parade

the round moon

a large box of mooncakes

to miss family members even more

to commemorate an ancient poet

no wonder he's drooling (over the food)

very popular merchandise

to give up this wish

absolutely impossible

in the world

government-designated holiday

B. Matching

Listen to the sentences in Chinese and number them in the order in which you hear them.

1. 中国的民间传统节日都是按农历定的。

2. 据说人们在端午节吃粽子是为了纪念一位有名的诗人。

3. 除此之外，现在中国人很多也庆祝其它国家的节日。

4. 八月在秋季中间，十五号是八月中间的一天，因此这一天被称之为中秋节。

5. 在外国的节日中，我只喜欢过圣诞节。

6. 他之所以信仰宗教是因为受了他妈妈的影响。

7. 今天是中秋节，难怪月亮又圆又亮。

8. 每逢清明节，他都要去给他爸爸扫墓。

9. 他去参加感恩节游行只不过是为了让他女朋友高兴罢了。

聽說讀寫練習
Comprehensive Exercises

🎧 TASK 1. 聽一聽、選一選 LISTENING EXERCISES

A. Bingo

In this section, you will hear various Chinese phrases. Demonstrate your understanding of these phrases by numbering their English counterparts in the order in which you hear them.

to calculate according to the lunar calendar	to miss family members even more
the symbol of family reunion	to commemorate an ancient poet
a very good feeling	no wonder he's drooling (over the food)
other religions and faiths	very popular merchandise
folk tradition	to give up this wish
festooned car parade	absolutely impossible
the round moon	in the world
a large box of mooncakes	government-designated holiday

B. Matching

Listen to the sentences in Chinese and number them in the order in which you hear them.

1. 中國的民間傳統節日都是按農曆定的。

2. 據說人們在端午節吃粽子是為了紀念一位有名的詩人。

3. 除此之外，現在中國人很多也慶祝其它國家的節日。

4. 八月在秋季中間，十五號是八月中間的一天，因此這一天被稱之為中秋節。

5. 在外國的節日中，我只喜歡過聖誕節。

6. 他之所以信仰宗教是因為受了他媽媽的影響。

7. 今天是中秋節，難怪月亮又圓又亮。

8. 每逢清明節，他都要去給他爸爸掃墓。

9. 他去參加感恩節游行只不過是為了讓他女朋友高興罷了。

C. Short Conversations

Listen to these short conversations. Select the correct answer for each question from the choices provided.

1. 过/不过

2. 是/不是

3. 男的/女的

4. 是/不是

5. 知道/不知道

🎧 TASK 2. 听一听、说一说 SHORT PASSAGES

PASSAGE 1

Pre-Listening Activity

Before you begin, answer the following questions, which are designed to help you predict what will happen in the passage.

1. 你们国家都庆祝什么节日？

2. 你了解中国的节日吗？

Vocabulary

| 长假 | cháng jià | long vacation |

Listening Activity

Now listen to the passage and answer the questions that follow. Be sure to make a voice recording on the multimedia CD-ROM explaining each of your choices.

A. Listening for new words

Did you catch all the new words in the passage?

B. Listening for the main idea

这段短文主要谈的是什么？

a) 中国的传统节日。

b) 中国人庆祝的国家节日。

c) 中国人庆祝的所有的节日。

d) 以上都不对。

C. *Short Conversations*

Listen to these short conversations. Select the correct answer for each question from the choices provided.

1. 過/不過

2. 是/不是

3. 男的/女的

4. 是/不是

5. 知道/不知道

🎧💠 TASK 2. 聽一聽、說一說 SHORT PASSAGES

PASSAGE 1

Pre-Listening Activity

Before you begin, answer the following questions, which are designed to help you predict what will happen in the passage.

1. 你們國家都慶祝什麼節日？

2. 你瞭解中國的節日嗎？

Vocabulary

長假   cháng jià   long vacation

Listening Activity

Now listen to the passage and answer the questions that follow. Be sure to make a voice recording on the multimedia CD-ROM explaining each of your choices.

A. Listening for new words

Did you catch all the new words in the passage?

B. Listening for the main idea

這段短文主要談的是什麼？

a) 中國的傳統節日。

b) 中國人慶祝的國家節日。

c) 中國人慶祝的所有的節日。

d) 以上都不對。

C. Listening for details

1. 在中国哪个节日放假？你怎么知道的？

   国庆节/中秋节

2. 中国人庆祝不庆祝外国节日？为什么？

   庆祝/不庆祝

3. 说话的人认为中国的商人和美国的商人有没有相同之处？你怎么知道的？

   有/没有

Post-Listening Activity

Now state your opinion as you record your voice on the multimedia CD-ROM.

你最喜欢的节日是什么？为什么？

PASSAGE 2

Pre-Listening Activity

Before you begin, answer the following questions, which are designed to help you predict what will happen in the passage.

1. 你喜欢不喜欢过节？为什么？

2. 你觉得谁最喜欢过节？为什么？

Vocabulary

1. 聚会	jùhuì	*n.*	party
2. 甚至	shènzhì	*adv.*	even to the point of...
3. 平常	píngcháng	*adv.*	usually

Listening Activity

Now listen to the passage and answer the questions that follow. Be sure to make a voice recording on the multimedia CD-ROM explaining each of your choices.

A. Listening for new words

Did you catch all the new words in the passage?

C. Listening for details

1. 在中國哪個節日放假？你怎麼知道的？

   國慶日/中秋節

2. 中國人慶祝不慶祝外國節日？為什麼？

   慶祝/不慶祝

3. 說話的人認為中國的商人和美國的商人有沒有相同之處？你怎麼知道的？

   有/沒有

Post-Listening Activity

Now state your opinion as you record your voice on the multimedia CD-ROM.

你最喜歡的節日是什麼？為什麼？

PASSAGE 2

Pre-Listening Activity

Before you begin, answer the following questions, which are designed to help you predict what will happen in the passage.

1. 你喜歡不喜歡過節？為什麼？
2. 你覺得誰最喜歡過節？為什麼？

Vocabulary

1. 聚會	jùhuì	*n.*	party
2. 甚至	shènzhì	*adv.*	even to the point of...
3. 平常	píngcháng	*adv.*	usually

Listening Activity

Now listen to the passage and answer the questions that follow. Be sure to make a voice recording on the multimedia CD-ROM explaining each of your choices.

A. Listening for new words

Did you catch all the new words in the passage?

B. Listening for the main idea

谁过节最高兴？为什么？

a) 小孩

b) 商人

c) 大人

d) 以上都不对

C. Listening for details

1. 过节的时候，人们花的钱常常比平时多还是少？为什么？

   多／少

2. 过节的时候，商品比平常贵还是便宜？为什么？

   贵／便宜

3. 过节是商人赚钱的好机会，是不是？为什么？

   是／不是

Post-Listening Activity

Now state your opinion as you record your voice on the multimedia CD-ROM.

你觉得说话人说的对不对？为什么？

🎧 TASK 3. 看一看、说一说、写一写 SHORT VIDEO

Pre-Listening Activity

Before you begin, answer the following questions, which are designed to help you predict what will happen in the video.

1. 你知道中国人怎么庆祝中秋节吗？

2. 你在中国人家里庆祝过中秋节吗？

Vocabulary

1. 在···当中	zài...dāngzhōng	*phr.*	among, in the middle of
2. 做客	zuò kè	*v. obj.*	to be a guest
3. 空手	kōngshǒu	*adv.*	empty-handed

B. Listening for the main idea

誰過節最高興？為什麼？

a) 小孩

b) 商人

c) 大人

d) 以上都不對

C. Listening for details

1. 過節的時候，人們花的錢常常比平時多還是少？為什麼？

   多/少

2. 過節的時候，商品比平常貴還是便宜？為什麼？

   貴/便宜

3. 過節是商人賺錢的好機會，是不是？為什麼？

   是/不是

Post-Listening Activity

Now state your opinion as you record your voice on the multimedia CD-ROM.

你覺得說話人說的對不對？為什麼？

🎧❊ TASK 3. 看一看、說一說、寫一寫 SHORT VIDEO

Pre-Listening Activity

Before you begin, answer the following questions, which are designed to help you predict what will happen in the video.

1. 你知道中國人怎麼慶祝中秋節嗎？

2. 你在中國人家裏慶祝過中秋節嗎？

Vocabulary

1. 在⋯當中	zài...dāngzhōng	*phr.*	among, in the middle of
2. 做客	zuò kè	*v. obj.*	to be a guest
3. 空手	kōngshǒu	*adv.*	empty-handed

Listening Activity

Now listen to the dialogue and answer the questions that follow. Be sure to make a voice recording on the multimedia CD-ROM explaining each of your choices.

A. Listening for new words

Did you catch all the new words in the dialogue?

B. Listening for the main idea

这段对话主要讲的是什么？

a) 怎么庆祝中秋节？

b) 怎么买月饼？

c) 怎么招待客人？

d) 以上都不对。

C. Listening for details

1. 说话的这两个人也排队买月饼了吗？为什么？

   买／没买

2. 过中秋节是不是只吃月饼？为什么？

   是／不是

3. 谁的爷爷奶奶请客人吃饭？为什么请客？

   女的／男的

Post-Listening Activity

Now state your opinion as you record your voice on the multimedia CD-ROM, and then write a summary of the dialogue.

请用自己的话讲一讲这段对话都说了些什么？

Listening Activity

Now listen to the dialogue and answer the questions that follow. Be sure to make a voice recording on the multimedia CD-ROM explaining each of your choices.

A. Listening for new words

Did you catch all the new words in the dialogue?

B. Listening for the main idea

這段對話主要講的是什麼？

a) 怎麼慶祝中秋節？

b) 怎麼買月餅？

c) 怎麼招待客人？

d) 以上都不對。

C. Listening for details

1. 說話的這兩個人也排隊買月餅了嗎？為什麼？
   買／沒買

2. 過中秋節是不是只吃月餅？為什麼？
   是／不是

3. 誰的爺爺奶奶請客人吃飯？為什麼請客？
   女的／男的

Post-Listening Activity

Now state your opinion as you record your voice on the multimedia CD-ROM, and then write a summary of the dialogue.

請用自己的話講一講這段對話都說了些什麼？

🎧 ❧ TASK 4. 读一读、写一写 READING EXERCISES

This section consists of two parts: Short Stories and Authentic Material.

A. *Short Stories*

成语故事：怀才不遇

　　古时候楚国有一个诗人叫屈原。他非常有才，过去一直帮助楚国的国王管理国家。但是，楚国国王身边的很多人都不喜欢屈原，还有一些人老在楚国国王面前说他的坏话，所以，国王就不再让屈原参加讨论国家的大事，叫他到很远很远的地方去工作。一天，楚国被打败了。屈原心里感到非常难过，就跳江自杀了。据说，大家听说屈原跳江的事以后，为了不让鱼吃掉他的身体，就用树叶包上大米，（也就是现在我们吃的粽子，）扔到江里喂鱼。后来常常用"怀才不遇"这个成语来形容屈原的一生。就是说，他有才，但是没有人欣赏他。

Vocabulary

1. 怀才不遇	huái cái bù yù		
怀	huái	*v.*	to have in one's bosom, to be pregnant with
才	cái	*n.*	talent
遇	yù	*v.*	to meet
2. 管理	guǎnlǐ	*v.*	to manage
3. 讨论	tǎolùn	*v.*	to discuss
4. 败	bài	*b.f.*	defeated
5. 跳江自杀	tiào jiāng zì shā	*phr.*	to commit suicide by jumping into the river
6. 扔	rēng	*v.*	to throw
7. 喂	wèi	*v.*	to feed
8. 形容	xíngróng	*v.*	to describe
9. 一生	yī shēng	*n.*	a lifetime

Questions

1. 请用自己的话讲一讲"怀才不遇"是什么意思。

2. 如果你是屈原，你会不会自杀？为什么？

3. 写一个你所知道的"怀才不遇"的人的故事。别忘了写一写这个人有什么才，后来怎么样了？

🎧🖌 TASK 4. 讀一讀、寫一寫 READING EXERCISES

This section consists of two parts: Short Stories and Authentic Material.

A. Short Stories

成語故事：懷才不遇

　　古時候楚國有一個詩人叫屈原。他非常有才，過去一直幫助楚國的國王管理國家。但是，楚國國王身邊的很多人都不喜歡屈原，還有一些人老在楚國國王面前說他的壞話，所以，國王就不再讓屈原參加討論國家的大事，叫他到很遠很遠的地方去工作。一天，楚國被打敗了。屈原心裏感到非常難過，就跳江自殺了。據說，大家聽說屈原跳江的事以後，為了不讓魚吃掉他的身體，就用樹葉包上大米，（也就是現在我們吃的粽子，）扔到江裏喂魚。後來常常用"懷才不遇"這個成語來形容屈原的一生。就是說，他有才，但是沒有人欣賞他。

Vocabulary

1. 懷才不遇	huái cái bù yù		
懷	huái	*v.*	to have in one's bosom, to be pregnant with
才	cái	*n.*	talent
遇	yù	*v.*	to meet
2. 管理	guǎnlǐ	*v.*	to manage
3. 討論	tǎolùn	*v.*	to discuss
4. 敗	bài	*b.f.*	defeated
5. 跳江自殺	tiào jiāng zì shā	*phr.*	to commit suicide by jumping into the river
6. 扔	rēng	*v.*	to throw
7. 喂	wèi	*v.*	to feed
8. 形容	xíngróng	*v.*	to describe
9. 一生	yī shēng	*n.*	a lifetime

Questions

1. 請用自己的話講一講"懷才不遇"是什麼意思。

2. 如果你是屈原，你會不會自殺？為什麼？

3. 寫一個你所知道的"懷才不遇"的人的故事。別忘了寫一寫這個人有什麼才，後來怎麼樣了？

古诗：每逢佳节倍思亲

　　"每逢佳节倍思亲"是一句王维的古诗。王维是中国一位非常有名的诗人、书法家和画家。他很小的时候就开始写诗。这首诗是他十七岁的时候写的。中国农历的九月九号在古时候是重阳节。据说，这一天人们都去爬山，采一种叫茱萸的草，用来做成一个小包，带在身上辟邪。王维写这首诗的时候，他在离家很远的地方。那时候，他虽然和他的家人不在一起。但是他知道他的兄弟们一定都会去采茱萸，在他们爬到山上的时候，一定会发现他们中间少了一个人。所以他在诗里说他自己一个人在一个很远很远的地方，每次一到过年过节的时候，他就更加想念亲人。

Vocabulary

1. 每逢佳节倍思亲。 Měi féng jiājié bèi sīqīn.

佳	jiā	*adj.*	lovely, happy
节	jié	*n.*	holidays
倍	bèi	*adv.*	double, fold, many times
思	sī	*v.*	to miss (someone)
亲	qīn	*n.*	family
2. 书法	shūfǎ	*n.*	calligraphy
3. 首	shǒu	*m.w.*	for poems and songs
4. 重阳节	Chóngyángjié	*prop. n.*	Double Ninth Festival, the ninth of the ninth lunar month
5. 爬	pá	*v.*	to climb
6. 采	cǎi	*v.*	to pick
7. 茱萸	zhūyú	*n.*	fruit of medicinal cornel (dogwood)
8. 辟邪	bìxié	*v. obj.*	to exorcise evil spirits

Questions

1. 请用你自己的话来讲一讲"每逢佳节倍思亲"的意思。

2. 写一个"每逢佳节倍思亲"的故事。

3. 你觉得"每逢佳节倍思亲"这句话说得对不对？为什么？

古诗：每逢佳節倍思親

　　"每逢佳節倍思親"是一句王維的古詩。王維是中國一位非常有名的詩人、書法家和畫家。他很小的時候就開始寫詩。這首詩是他十七歲的時候寫的。中國農曆的九月九號在古時候是重陽節。據說，這一天人們都去爬山，採一種叫茱萸的草，用來做成一個小包，帶在身上辟邪。王維寫這首詩的時候，他在離家很遠的地方。那時候，他雖然和他的家人不在一起。但是他知道他的兄弟們一定都會去採茱萸，在他們爬到山上的時候，一定會發現他們中間少了一個人。所以他在詩裏說他自己一個人在一個很遠很遠的地方，每次一到過年過節的時候，他就更加想念親人。

Vocabulary

1. 每逢佳節倍思親。 *Měi féng jiājié bèi sīqīn.*

佳	jiā	*adj.*	lovely, happy
節	jié	*n.*	holidays
倍	bèi	*adv.*	double, fold, many times
思	sī	*v.*	to miss (someone)
親	qīn	*n.*	family

2. 書法　　　shūfǎ　　　*n.*　　　calligraphy

3. 首　　　shǒu　　　*m.w.*　　　for poems and songs

4. 重陽節　　　Chóngyángjié　　　*prop. n.*　　　Double Ninth Festival, the ninth of the ninth lunar month

5. 爬　　　pá　　　*v.*　　　to climb

6. 采　　　cǎi　　　*v.*　　　to pick

7. 茱萸　　　zhūyú　　　*n.*　　　fruit of medicinal cornel (dogwood)

8. 辟邪　　　bìxié　　　*v. obj.*　　　to exorcise evil spirits

Questions

1. 請用你自己的話來講一講"每逢佳節倍思親"的意思。

2. 寫一個"每逢佳節倍思親"的故事。

3. 你覺得"每逢佳節倍思親"這句話說得對不對？為什麼？

B. Authentic Material

In this section, you will be exposed to some authentic materials used in China. Read the following newspaper article about New Year festivities and answer the questions.

8   经济生活

又是一年春节到！吃饺子、逛庙会、放烟花、看大戏……一样都不能少！但要想把年过得有滋有味、与众不同、还不得不动动心思。编者搜罗了几个点子，希望能帮您将这个大年过得热热闹闹、红红火火……

春节点子多　过年花样新

点子一　花样翻新年夜饭

一说起过年，最该做的一件事恐怕就是吃饺子了。但如果还是像平常一样，猪肉大葱、鸡蛋韭菜的清水煮饺，那可就太没"年味儿"了。其实，只要稍稍动一点心思，你就可以将过年的饺子吃得有声有色、与众不同了。

点子二　庙会里面见绝活

庙会是许多城市年景儿中的一个亮点。不过如果仍旧像往年一样随大流儿得拥来挤去的话，恐怕还会落得个白搭工夫空费力。所以建议你不妨先将春节各大庙会了解个底儿掉，然后心明眼亮地去搜索自己的心仪目标吧。

点子三　寻芳觅艳赏春花

春节赏花早就成了一大批人过大年时的不变选择。在吃爽了，玩好了以后，不妨再搜些养眼的东西绚烂一下自己的心情。其实，这时候，山野中迎风傲雪的腊梅大棚中火热绽放的桃花，温室中素淡优雅的水仙、兰花都是寻方觅艳的理想目标。

点子四　房车组成旅游团

初二到初五，上海张先生率领的由10辆豪华房车组成的旅游团，将沿高速公路向山西驶去，到晋商风火节上领略一份时尚和民俗的节日风情。

点子五　到村里头过大年

杀猪、宰鸡、磨豆腐、贴春联、做花灯的热闹劲儿是刚筋水泥的丛林里永远看不到的。正因为如此，越来越多的城市里人选择到村子里去过年。

热点连线

1. 这篇文章讲的是什么节日？
2. 这篇文章讲到五个"点子"。"点子"是什么意思？
3. 这五个"点子"都是什么？

B. *Authentic Material*

In this section, you will be exposed to some authentic materials used in China. Read the following newspaper article about New Year festivities and answer the questions.

1. 這篇文章講的是什麼節日？
2. 這篇文章講到五個"點子"。"點子"是什麼意思？
3. 這五個"點子"都是什麼？

◯◖ TASK 5. 想一想、说一说 PRESENTATION

Please pick one of the following for your presentation.

A. Individual Presentation

1. During the Mid-Autumn Festival you are invited to have dinner with a Chinese family. They ask you if you celebrate anything similar in the U.S. Tell them about the similarities and differences between Thanksgiving and the Mid-Autumn Festival. Also compare and contrast New Year's celebrations in each country.

2. Your Chinese friend asks you which Chinese festivals or holidays are your favorites. Choose two or three of them and, referring to the text, explain why you like them. Also, choose your least favorite holiday and explain why it's your least favorite.

B. Group Presentation

Setting: At a Chinese home
Cast: As many people (Chinese and American) as you want.
Situation: Pick any Chinese holiday. Create a scene and give a performance illustrating how the Chinese celebrate that holiday. Make it culturally appropriate and festive!

◯◖ TASK 6. 想一想、写一写 COMPOSITION

Search the Internet and find information about your favorite holiday. Then write a paragraph describing the holiday — please include a description of the holiday's origins, its meaning, how people celebrate it, the associated traditional foods and clothes, etc.

🎧📖 TASK 5. 想一想、説一説 PRESENTATION

Please pick one of the following for your presentation.

A. Individual Presentation

1. During the Mid-Autumn Festival you are invited to have dinner with a Chinese family. They ask you if you celebrate anything similar in the U.S. Tell them about the similarities and differences between Thanksgiving and the Mid-Autumn Festival. Also compare and contrast New Year's celebrations in each country.

2. Your Chinese friend asks you which Chinese festivals or holidays are your favorites. Choose two or three of them and, referring to the text, explain why you like them. Also, choose your least favorite holiday and explain why it's your least favorite.

B. Group Presentation

Setting: At a Chinese home
Cast: As many people (Chinese and American) as you want.
Situation: Pick any Chinese holiday. Create a scene and give a performance illustrating how the Chinese celebrate that holiday. Make it culturally appropriate and festive!

🎧📖 TASK 6. 想一想、寫一寫 COMPOSITION

Search the Internet and find information about your favorite holiday. Then write a paragraph describing the holiday — please include a description of the holiday's origins, its meaning, how people celebrate it, the associated traditional foods and clothes, etc.

43
休闲

Leisure and Entertainment

In this lesson you will:

■ Describe how the Chinese spend their spare time.
■ Present information about Chinese entertainment.
■ Talk about and debate the differences between Chinese entertainment and entertainment in your own country.

　　中国人利用休闲时间去串门聊天是很常见的事。常常在去之前，也不打招呼，想去就去。敲门以后，家里有人就进，没人以后再去。除此以外，不同年龄的人，休闲方式也不太一样。大学生与美国学生相似，喜欢活动，常常跳舞、打乒乓球、游泳、等等。但是大学毕业或者工作以后，中国人与美国人相比，就不太注意利用休闲时间去锻炼身体。在街上、茶馆、家中、常常能看到打牌、打麻将、下棋的人，而在户外跑步，锻炼身体的人却比较少。近几年来，随着人们的生活条件的提高，打高尔夫或打保龄球在中国也非常流行。但是，这种高消费的活动，并不是为了锻炼身体，而是为了赶时髦，或是为了交际。中国的退休老人在锻炼身体这方面与美国人相反，公园里和一些安静的地方常能看见老人打太极拳、练气功、做操、散步等等。

Lauren Brown

Practicing sword exercises in a park in Hangzhou.

43
休閒

Leisure and Entertainment

In this lesson you will:

- Describe how the Chinese spend their spare time.
- Present information about Chinese entertainment.
- Talk about and debate the differences between Chinese entertainment and entertainment in your own country.

　　中國人利用休閒時間去串門聊天是很常見的事。常常在去之前，也不打招呼，想去就去。敲門以後，家裏有人就進，沒人以後再去。除此以外，不同年齡的人，休閒方式也不太一樣。大學生與美國學生相似，喜歡活動，常常跳舞、打乒乓球、游泳、等等。但是大學畢業或者工作以後，中國人與美國人相比，就不太注意利用休閒時間去鍛煉身體。在街上、茶館、家中、常常能看到打牌、打麻將、下棋的人，而在戶外跑步，鍛煉身體的人卻比較少。近幾年來，隨著人們的生活條件的提高，打高爾夫或打保齡球在中國也非常流行。但是，這種高消費的活動，並不是為了鍛煉身體，而是為了趕時髦，或是為了交際。中國的退休老人在鍛煉身體這方面與美國人相反，公園裏和一些安靜的地方常能看見老人打太極拳、練氣功、做操、散步等等。

Practicing sword exercises in a park in Hangzhou.

133

　　随着社会的发展，休闲时间的娱乐活动也越来越多。中国过去很时兴的一些传统节目，例如京剧和一些地方戏剧等在逐渐地消失。一般人对这些传统的节目一方面不了解，另一方面也不感兴趣，结果，观众越来越少。然而，电视、现代流行歌曲、相声、小品、卡拉OK等却越来越时兴。中国的电视台是由国家控制的。中央、各个省市都有自己的电视台，但是没有私立或民间的电视台。中国的电影虽然没有电视流行，但是美国好莱坞的电影一向在中国都很受欢迎。不过，凡是外国的电影都必须经过政府的审查。一个星期五的下午，李丽莉、陈小云和吴文德几个人谈起了中国人休闲活动的习惯。

（在学校图书馆。）

李丽莉：我最近发现中国人打牌、打麻将成风，常常打到深夜。

陈小云：打牌、打麻将很上瘾，能使人把社会上、工作中、家庭里的烦恼都忘得干干净净，所以在中国一直是一种很时兴的休闲活动。

李丽莉：这真是文化的不同。我觉得休闲的时候应该去户外跑步、爬山、滑雪、滑冰、或者去健身房攀岩、举重、锻炼身体什么的，那才是乐在其中[1]呢。坐在牌桌上打几个小时的牌，实在是不可理解。

吴文德：在玩儿的方面，我比你有经验。我在美国的时候，一玩起电脑游戏来常常一夜不睡。这就叫乐此不疲[2]。说起休闲，今天是星期五，我们晚上干什么呢？

李丽莉：我们上网进聊天室聊聊天儿或者玩网上游戏吧，这可是中国大学生在休闲的时候，最喜欢做的事。咱们就入乡随俗吧。

A game of mahjongg.

Xueying Wang

　　隨著社會的發展，休閒時間的娛樂活動也越來越多。中國過去很時興的一些傳統節目，例如京劇和一些地方戲劇等在逐漸地消失。一般人對這些傳統的節目一方面不瞭解，另一方面也不感興趣，結果，觀眾越來越少。然而，電視、現代流行歌曲、相聲、小品、卡拉OK等卻越來越時興。中國的電視臺是由國家控制的。中央、各個省市都有自己的電視臺，但是沒有私立或民間的電視臺。中國的電影雖然沒有電視流行，但是美國好萊塢的電影一向在中國都很受歡迎。不過，凡是外國的電影都必須經過政府的審查。一個星期五的下午，李麗莉、陳小雲和吳文德幾個人談起了中國人休閒活動的習慣。

（在學校圖書館。）

李麗莉：我最近發現中國人打牌、打麻將成風，常常打到深夜。

陳小雲：打牌、打麻將很上癮，能使人把社會上、工作中、家庭裏的煩惱都忘得乾乾淨淨，所以在中國一直是一種很時興的休閒活動。

李麗莉：這真是文化的不同。我覺得休閒的時候應該去戶外跑步、爬山、滑雪、滑冰、或者去健身房攀岩、舉重、鍛煉身體什麼的，那才是樂在其中[1]呢。坐在牌桌上打幾個小時的牌，實在是不可理解。

吳文德：在玩兒的方面，我比你有經驗。我在美國的時候，一玩起電腦遊戲來常常一夜不睡。這就叫樂此不疲[2]。說起休閒，今天是星期五，我們晚上幹什麼呢？

李麗莉：我們上網進聊天室聊聊天兒或者玩網上遊戲吧，這可是中國大學生在休閒的時候，最喜歡做的事。咱們就入鄉隨俗吧。

A game of mahjongg.

Xueying Wang

吴文德：啊呀，上网又要动脑子，怎么能放松？我们还是听相声或看
小品吧！

陈小云：我上午在中央电视台的电视节目预告网页上看过今晚的电视
节目里没有小品，但是新浪网可能会有相声。……果然，我
猜对了，这个网页上有很多相声，其中还有不少有名的相
声。

（……陈小云手机响了。）

陈小云：我的几个朋友叫我们今天晚上去唱卡拉OK，怎么样想不想去
凑凑热闹？

吴文德：当然去啦。唱卡拉OK比听相声要好玩多了。

A traditional Chinese music ensemble.

Notes

1. 乐在其中 (lè zài qí zhōng)

   To find joy in what one does; (Lit.) The joy lies within (an activity). For more information about this phrase, please see Task 4 in 听说读写练习.

2. 乐此不疲 (lè cǐ bù pí)

   When one enjoys doing something, one does not feel tired. For more information about this phrase, please see Task 4 in 听说读写练习.

课文问答 *Questions and Answers*

1. 中国什么休闲活动最流行？不同年龄的人的休闲方式有什么不同？

2. 中国人的娱乐活动与过去相比有什么改变？

吳文德：啊呀，上網又要動腦子，怎麼能放鬆？我們還是聽相聲或看
　　　　小品吧！

陳小雲：我上午在中央電視臺的電視節目預告網頁上看過今晚的電視
　　　　節目裏沒有小品，但是新浪網可能會有相聲。……果然，我
　　　　猜對了，這個網頁上有很多相聲，其中還有不少有名的相
　　　　聲。

（……陳小雲手機響了。）

陳小雲：我的幾個朋友叫我們今天晚上去唱卡拉OK，怎麼樣想不想去
　　　　湊湊熱鬧？

吳文德：當然去啦。唱卡拉OK比聽相聲要好玩多了。

A traditional Chinese music ensemble.

Notes

1. **樂在其中** (lè zài qí zhōng)

   To find joy in what one does; (Lit.) The joy lies within (an activity). For more information about this phrase, please see Task 4 in 聽說讀寫練習.

2. **樂此不疲** (lè cǐ bù pí)

   When one enjoys doing something, one does not feel tired. For more information about this phrase, please see Task 4 in 聽說讀寫練習.

課文問答 *Questions and Answers*

1. 中國什麼休閒活動最流行？不同年齡的人的休閒方式有什麼不同？
2. 中國人的娛樂活動與過去相比有什麼改變？

3. 李丽莉喜欢什么休闲活动？你呢？

4. 这个星期五晚上李丽莉想干什么？吴文德呢？最后他们决定干什么？

Learning traditional Chinese dance.

生词表
Vocabulary

Character	Pinyin	Part of Speech	English Definition
1. 休闲	xiūxián	*n.*	leisure
你休闲时间常常做什么？			
闲		*b.f.*	idle, leisurely
2. 利用	lìyòng	*v.*	to make use of, to utilize (negative connotation), to take advantage of (somebody, opportunity, etc.)
我想利用这个暑假去中国好好地玩一玩儿。			
3. （打）招呼	(dǎ) zhāohu	*v.*	to say hello
你在跟谁打招呼呢？			
招		*v.*	to wave (hands)
呼		*v.*	to call out
4. 与···相似	yǔ...xiāngsì	*phr.*	to be similar to, to bear resemblance to
这本书与（跟）那本很相似。			

3. 李麗莉喜歡什麼休閒活動？你呢？

4. 這個星期五晚上李麗莉想幹什麼？吳文德呢？最後他們決定幹什麼？

Learning traditional Chinese dance.

生詞表
Vocabulary

Character	Pinyin	Part of Speech	English Definition
1. 休閒	xiūxián	*n.*	leisure
你休閒時間常常做什麼？			
閒		*b.f.*	idle, leisurely
2. 利用	lìyòng	*v.*	to make use of, to utilize (negative connotation), to take advantage of (somebody, opportunity, etc.)
我想利用這個暑假去中國好好地玩一玩兒。			
3. (打)招呼	(dǎ) zhāohu	*v.*	to say hello
你在跟誰打招呼呢？			
招		*v.*	to wave (hands)
呼		*v.*	to call out
4. 與···相似	yǔ...xiāngsì	*phr.*	to be similar to, to bear resemblance to
這本書與(跟)那本很相似。			

| 与 | | *prep.* | (formal) with |
| 相似 | | *adj.* | similar |

5. 与···相比   yǔ...xiāngbǐ   *phr.*   in comparison to, comparing with
这个电影与(跟)那个相比，你更喜欢哪个？

| 相比 | | *v.* | to compare with each other |

6. 毕业   bìyè   *v. obj.*   to graduate; (lit.) to complete one's study
你什么时候大学毕业？

| 业 | | *b.f.* | career, profession, study |

7. 却   què   *adv.*   on the contrary, in contrast to what one would expect
我大学一毕业就工作了，可是我的室友却还没有
开始找工作。

8. 户外   hùwài   *n.*   outdoors
我喜欢户外活动。

9. 生活   shēnghuó   *n.*   life
她现在的生活很快乐。

| | | *v.* | to live |

他们在那儿生活得非常好。

10. 条件   tiáojiàn   *n.*   condition, requirement
现在的生活条件比以前好多了。

11. 消费   xiāofèi   *n.*   expenditure, (of money) spending, consumption
在北京生活消费太高，我们还是去西安吧。

| 消 | | *b.f.* | to reduce, to diminish |

12. 并不是···而是   bìng búshì...érshì   *conj.*   contrary to what one would expect, it is not true that..., it is however true that...
我并不是不想去，而是没有时间去。

13. 交际   jiāojì   *v. obj.*   to socialize with others
他这个人很会交际。

| 交 | | *v.* | (of two things) to cross, to interact, to meet (new friends), to hand over, to deliver |
| 际 | | *n.* | boundary, border |

14. 退休   tuìxiū   *v.*   to retire
你爸爸是什么时候退休的？

| 與 | | *prep.* | (formal) with |
| 相似 | | *adj.* | similar |

5. 與···相比   yǔ...xiāngbǐ   *phr.*   in comparison to, comparing with

這個電影與（跟）那個相比，你更喜歡哪個？

| 相比 | | *v.* | to compare with each other |

6. 畢業   bìyè   *v. obj.*   to graduate; (lit.) to complete one's study

你什麼時候大學畢業？

| 業 | | *b.f.* | career, profession, study |

7. 卻   què   *adv.*   on the contrary, in contrast to what one would expect

我大學一畢業就工作了，可是我的室友卻還沒有開始找工作。

8. 戶外   hùwài   *n.*   outdoors

我喜歡戶外活動。

9. 生活   shēnghuó   *n.*   life

她現在的生活很快樂。

     v.   to live

他們在那兒生活得非常好。

10. 條件   tiáojiàn   *n.*   condition, requirement

現在的生活條件比以前好多了。

11. 消費   xiāofèi   *n.*   expenditure, (of money) spending, consumption

在北京生活消費太高，我們還是去西安吧。

| 消 | | *b.f.* | to reduce, to diminish |

12. 並不是···而是   bìng búshì...érshì   *conj.*   contrary to what one would expect, it is not true that..., it is however true that...

我並不是不想去，而是沒有時間去。

13. 交際   jiāojì   *v. obj.*   to socialize with others

他這個人很會交際。

| 交 | | *v.* | (of two things) to cross, to interact, to meet (new friends), to hand over, to deliver |
| 際 | | *n.* | boundary, border |

14. 退休   tuìxiū   *v.*   to retire

你爸爸是什麼時候退休的？

| | | *n.* | retirement |

我退休以后，准备到世界各地去旅行。

| 休 | | *v.* | to stop, to rest |

| 15. 方面 | fāngmiàn | *n.* | aspect, side |

在工作方面我没有你有经验。

| 16. 相反 | xiāngfǎn | *adj.* | opposite |

我想的和你想的正好相反。

| 17. 安静 | ānjìng | *adj.* | quiet, tranquil |

请你们安静一点，好吗？

| 18. 社会 | shèhuì | *n.* | society |

我现在还不了解中国的社会。

| 19. 娱乐 | yúlè | *n.* | entertainment, recreation |

你每个星期都应该有一些娱乐活动。

| 20. 过去 | guòqù | *n.* | the past |

过去的事儿就让它过去吧。

| | | *v. comp.* | to pass by; to go over |

你过去看看吧。

| 21. 时兴 | shíxīng | *adj.* | to be in vogue, to be in fashion, to consider (something) fashionable |

现在这样的样式已经不时兴了。

| 22. 节目 | jiémù | *n.* | program |

今天晚上有什么好看的电视节目？

| 23. 逐渐 | zhújiàn | *adv.* | gradually |

到了中国以后，你会逐渐地习惯使用筷子。

| 逐 | | *b.f.* | one by one, in succession |
| 渐 | | *b.f.* | gradually |

| 24. 消失 | xiāoshī | *v.* | (formal) to disappear, to vanish |

现在北京的老房子正在逐渐消失。

| 失 | | *b.f.* | to lose, to miss, to fail |

| 25. 结果 | jiéguǒ | *conj.* | as a result |

他不想出门，结果我们在旅馆的房间看了一个晚上的电视。

| | | | n. | retirement |

我退休以後，準備到世界各地去旅行。

| | 休 | | v. | to stop, to rest |
| 15. | 方面 | fāngmiàn | n. | aspect, side |

在工作方面我沒有你有經驗。

| 16. | 相反 | xiāngfǎn | adj. | opposite |

我想的和你想的正好相反。

| 17. | 安靜 | ānjìng | adj. | quiet, tranquil |

請你們安靜一點，好嗎？

| 18. | 社會 | shèhuì | n. | society |

我現在還不瞭解中國的社會。

| 19. | 娛樂 | yúlè | n. | entertainment, recreation |

你每個星期都應該有一些娛樂活動。

| 20. | 過去 | guòqù | n. | the past |

過去的事兒就讓它過去吧。

| | | | v. comp. | to pass by; to go over |

你過去看看吧。

| 21. | 時興 | shíxīng | adj. | to be in vogue, to be in fashion, to consider (something) fashionable |

現在這樣的樣式已經不時興了。

| 22. | 節目 | jiémù | n. | program |

今天晚上有什麼好看的電視節目？

| 23. | 逐漸 | zhújiàn | adv. | gradually |

到了中國以後，你會逐漸地習慣使用筷子。

	逐		b.f.	one by one, in succession
	漸		b.f.	gradually
24.	消失	xiāoshī	v.	(formal) to disappear, to vanish

現在北京的老房子正在逐漸消失。

| | 失 | | b.f. | to lose, to miss, to fail |
| 25. | 結果 | jiéguǒ | conj. | as a result |

他不想出門，結果我們在旅館的房間看了一個晚上的電視。

| | | *n.* | result, consequence |

这样做是不会有结果的。

| 26. 然而 | rán' ér | *conj.* | (formal) (in spite of the fact that...) yet, nevertheless (indicating a contrast to what one would expect) |

现在我们这儿的饭馆越来越多，然而可口的却越来越少。

| 27. 现代 | xiàndài | *n.* | modern times, modern age |

现代的中国社会人多，消费多。

| 28. 歌曲 | gēqǔ | *n.* | (formal) song |

这个电影歌曲现在在中国很流行。

| 29. 电视台 | diànshì tái | *n.* | TV station, TV channel |

你看看北京电视台今天有什么节目？

| 30. 控制 | kòngzhì | *v.* | to control, to supervise |

你这辆车怎么这么不好控制？

| | | *n.* | control, supervision |

这个学校对学生休息时间有很多控制。

| 31. 中央 | zhōngyāng | *n.* | center, central authorities |

我们看看中央(电视)一台，怎么样？

| 32. 私立 | sīlì | *adj.* | privately owned; (lit.) privately established |

中国现在有没有私立电视台？

| 33. 一向 | yīxiàng | *adv.* | unwaveringly, steadfastly; (lit.) (constant) in one direction |

他一向喜欢看中国电影。

| 34. 经过 | jīngguò | *v.* | to pass through (an area), to go through (an experience) |

经过这次旅游，我比以前更了解北京了。

| | | *n.* | process |

请你把这件事情的经过说一说。

| 35. 审查 | shěnchá | *n.* | investigation, careful examination |

经过审查，他们决定出版这本书。

| | | *v.* | to investigate, to carefully examine |

他们正在审查这本书的内容。

| 审 | | *b.f.* | to examine |

| | | *n.* | result, consequence |

這樣做是不會有結果的。

| 26. 然而 | rán'ér | *conj.* | (formal) (in spite of the fact that...) yet, nevertheless (indicating a contrast to what one would expect) |

現在我們這兒的飯館越來越多，然而可口的卻越來越少。

| 27. 現代 | xiàndài | *n.* | modern times, modern age |

現代的中國社會人多，消費多。

| 28. 歌曲 | gēqǔ | *n.* | (formal) song |

这个电影歌曲现在在中国很流行。

| 29. 電視臺 | diànshì tái | *n.* | TV station, TV channel |

你看看北京電視臺今天有什麼節目？

| 30. 控制 | kòngzhì | *v.* | to control, to supervise |

你這輛車怎麼這麼不好控制？

| | | *n.* | control, supervision |

這個學校對學生休息時間有很多控制。

| 31. 中央 | zhōngyāng | *n.* | center, central authorities |

我們看看中央（電視）一台，怎麼樣？

| 32. 私立 | sīlì | *adj.* | privately owned; (lit.) privately established |

中國現在有沒有私立電視臺？

| 33. 一向 | yīxiàng | *adv.* | unwaveringly, steadfastly; (lit.) (constant) in one direction |

他一向喜歡看中國電影。

| 34. 經過 | jīngguò | *v.* | to pass through (an area), to go through (an experience) |

經過這次旅遊，我比以前更瞭解北京了。

| | | *n.* | process |

請你把這件事情的經過說一說。

| 35. 審查 | shěnchá | *n.* | investigation, careful examination |

經過審查，他們決定出版這本書。

| | | *v.* | to investigate, to carefully examine |

他們正在審查這本書的內容。

| 審 | | *b.f.* | to examine |

36. 使   shǐ   v.   to cause, to make or let (somebody do
    他唱的歌儿使我想起了一件事儿。   something), to send, to dispatch

37. 家庭   jiātíng   n.   (formal) family, household
    现代社会的家庭和过去的很不一样。

38. 烦恼   fánnǎo   n.   trouble, vexation
    他的工作给他带来了很多烦恼。

                            adj.   troublesome, vexing
    你应该少想烦恼的事儿，多想高兴的事儿。
    烦   v.   to irritate, to bother
    恼   v.   to anger, to annoy

39. 健身房   jiànshēnfáng   n.   gymnasium
    你每个星期去几次健身房？
    健身   v. obj.   to strengthen the body, to improve health

40. 聚会   jùhuì   n.   get-together, party
    这个星期六我们有一个聚会，你来不来？
    聚   v.   to gather together

41. 游戏   yóuxì   n.   game, play, recreation
    我们玩儿游戏吧。我教你们一个新的。

42. 预告   yùgào   n.   advance notification, forecast
    电视预告说今天晚上北京电视一台有一个美国电影。

43. 网页   wǎngyè   n.   Web page
    我去那个网页查一查。
    页   n.   page

44. 果然   guǒrán   conj.   as expected, just as one would expect
    我跟我妈妈说他今天可能不会来，果然他真的没有来。

45. 其中   qízhōng   phr.   (in) the midst (of something); (lit.) its
    我有不少中文书，其中有很多都是我在中国学习的   midst
    时候买的。

46. 响   xiǎng   v.   to echo, to ring, to produce a sound
    你的电话铃响了，一定又是你妈妈。

36. 使　　　　shǐ　　　　*v.*　　　　to cause, to make or let (somebody do something), to send, to dispatch

他唱的歌兒使我想起了一件事兒。

37. 家庭　　　　jiātíng　　　　*n.*　　　　(formal) family, household

現代社會的家庭和過去的很不一樣。

38. 煩惱　　　　fánnǎo　　　　*n.*　　　　trouble, vexation

他的工作給他帶來了很多煩惱。

　　　　　　　　　　　　　　　adj.　　　　troublesome, vexing

你應該少想煩惱的事兒，多想高興的事兒。

煩　　　　　　　　　　*v.*　　　　to irritate, to bother
惱　　　　　　　　　　*v.*　　　　to anger, to annoy

39. 健身房　　　　jiànshēnfáng　　　　n.　　　　gymnasium

你每個星期去幾次健身房？

健身　　　　　　　　*v. obj.*　　　　to strengthen the body, to improve health

40. 聚會　　　　jùhuì　　　　*n.*　　　　get-together, party

這個星期六我們有一個聚會，你來不來？

聚　　　　　　　　　*v.*　　　　to gather together

41. 遊戲　　　　yóuxì　　　　*n.*　　　　game, play, recreation

我們玩兒遊戲吧。我教你們一個新的。

42. 預告　　　　yùgào　　　　*n.*　　　　advance notification, forecast

電視預告說今天晚上北京電視一台有一個美國電影。

43. 網頁　　　　wǎngyè　　　　*n.*　　　　Web page

我去那個網頁查一查。

頁　　　　　　　　　*n.*　　　　page

44. 果然　　　　guǒrán　　　　*conj.*　　　　as expected, just as one would expect

我跟我媽媽說他今天可能不會來，果然他真的沒有來。

45. 其中　　　　qízhōng　　　　*phr.*　　　　(in) the midst (of something); (lit.) its midst

我有不少中文書。其中有很多都是我在中國學習的時候買的。

46. 響　　　　xiǎng　　　　*v.*　　　　to echo, to ring, to produce a sound

你的電話鈴響了，一定又是你媽媽。

体育名称 Names of Sports

1. 乒乓球	pīngpāng qiú	*n.*	Ping-Pong; (lit.) ping-pong ball
2. 高尔夫(球)	gāo'erfū (qiú)	*n.*	golf
3. 保龄球	bǎolíng qiú	*n.*	bowling; (lit.) bowling ball
4. 练气功	liàn qìgōng	*v. obj.*	to practice qigong
气功		*n.*	(lit.) qi cultivation
5. 做操	zuò cāo	*v. obj.*	to do calisthenics
6. 散步	sàn bù	*v. obj.*	to take a walk, to take a casual stroll
7. 爬山	pá shān	*v. obj.*	to climb a mountain
8. 滑雪	huá xuě	*v. obj.*	to ski (in snow); (lit.) to slide on snow
9. 滑冰	huá bīng	*v. obj.*	to skate (on ice); (lit.) to slide on ice
10. 攀岩	pān yán	*v. obj*	to climb rocks
11. 举重	jǔzhòng	*v. obj.*	to lift weights

游戏名称 Names of Games

1. 打牌	dǎ pái	*v. obj.*	to play cards
牌		*n.*	cards
2. 打麻将	dǎ májiàng	*v. obj.*	to play mahjongg
3. 下棋	xià qí	*v. obj.*	to play chess

娱乐名称 Names of Types of Entertainment

1. 京剧	jīngjù	*n.*	Beijing Opera
2. 戏剧	xìjù	*n.*	musical drama
3. 相声	xiàngsheng	*n.*	"cross talk," comic dialogue show
4. 小品	xiǎopǐn	*n.*	a short theatrical piece
5. 卡拉OK	kǎlā OK	*n.*	karaoke

體育名稱 Names of Sports

1. 乒乓球	pīngpāng qiú	*n.*	Ping-Pong; (lit.) ping-pong ball
2. 高爾夫(球)	gāo'erfū (qiú)	*n.*	golf
3. 保齡球	bǎolíng qiú	*n.*	bowling; (lit.) bowling ball
4. 練氣功	liàn qìgōng	*v. obj.*	to practice qigong
氣功		*n.*	(lit.) qi cultivation
5. 做操	zuò cāo	*v. obj.*	to do calisthenics
6. 散步	sàn bù	*v. obj.*	to take a walk, to take a casual stroll
7. 爬山	pá shān	*v. obj.*	to climb a mountain
8. 滑雪	huá xuě	*v. obj.*	to ski (in snow); (lit.) to slide on snow
9. 滑冰	huá bīng	*v. obj.*	to skate (on ice); (lit.) to slide on ice
10. 攀岩	pān yán	*v. obj*	to climb rocks
11. 舉重	jǔzhòng	*v. obj.*	to lift weights

遊戲名稱 Names of Games

1. 打牌	dǎ pái	*v. obj.*	to play cards
牌		*n.*	cards
2. 打麻將	dǎ májiàng	*v. obj.*	to play mahjongg
3. 下棋	xià qí	*v. obj.*	to play chess

娛樂名稱 Names of Types of Entertainment

1. 京劇	jīngjù	*n.*	Beijing Opera
2. 戲劇	xìjù	*n.*	musical drama
3. 相聲	xiàngsheng	*n.*	"cross talk," comic dialogue show
4. 小品	xiǎopǐn	*n.*	a short theatrical piece
5. 卡拉OK	kǎlā OK	*n.*	karaoke

专有名词 Proper Nouns

1.	好莱坞	Hǎoláiwū	Hollywood
2.	中央电视台	Zhōngyāng Diànshìtái	China Central Television (CCTV)
3.	新浪网	Xīnlàng wǎng	http://www.sina.com

口头用语 Spoken Expressions

1.	上瘾	shàng yǐn	to get addicted to, to get hooked on
2.	什么的	shénmede	etc., and so forth
3.	动脑子	dòng nǎozi	to think; (lit.) to move one's brain

书面语 vs. 口语 Written Form vs. Spoken Form

In Chinese, the "written form" preserves a lot of words and expressions from Classical Chinese and is therefore more concise and formal. As its name implies, the "written form" is used primarily in writing, but it occurs frequently in speech as well.

书面语	口语
1. 常见	常常看见
2. 与	和
3. 相似	差不多一样
4. 相比	互相比较
5. 家中	家里
6. 户外	房子外边
7. 却	可是，但是
8. 逐渐	渐渐，慢慢
9. 成风	变成风气，流行
10. 不可理解	不容易懂

專有名詞 Proper Nouns

1.	好萊塢	Hǎoláiwū	Hollywood
2.	中央電視臺	Zhōngyāng Diànshìtái	China Central Television (CCTV)
3.	新浪網	Xīnlàng wǎng	http://www.sina.com

口頭用語 Spoken Expressions

1.	上癮	shàng yǐn	to get addicted to, to get hooked on
2.	什麼的	shénmede	etc., and so forth
3.	動腦子	dòng nǎozi	to think; (lit.) to move one's brain

書面語 *vs.* 口語 Written Form vs. Spoken Form

In Chinese, the "written form" preserves a lot of words and expressions from Classical Chinese and is therefore more concise and formal. As its name implies, the "written form" is used primarily in writing, but it occurs frequently in speech as well.

書面語	口語
1. 常見	常常看見
2. 與	和
3. 相似	差不多一樣
4. 相比	互相比較
5. 家中	家裏
6. 戶外	房子外邊
7. 卻	可是，但是
8. 逐漸	漸漸，慢慢
9. 成風	變成風氣，流行
10. 不可理解	不容易懂

词汇注解 Featured Vocabulary

1. 利用 (lìyòng) vs. 用 (yòng)

利用	*v.*	to take advantage of

他常常利用暑期的时间打工挣钱。
He often takes advantage of summer vacation to make some money.

(When the object of 利用 is people, this phrase has negative connotations.)

他很会利用人。
He is very skilled at using people.

用	*v.*	to use

我用一下儿你的电脑，好吗？
May I use your computer for a few minutes?

2. 感兴趣 (gǎn xìngqu) vs. 有意思 (yǒu yìsi)

感兴趣	*v. obj.*	to be interested in

我对学中文很感兴趣。
I am interested in learning Chinese.

有意思	*adj.*	interesting

那本书很有意思。
That is very interesting.

3. 一向 (yīxiàng) vs. 一直 (yīzhí): Always

Both 一向 and 一直 are frequently used with other adverbs, such as 都 or 就. In addition, when the adjective is monosyllabic, an adverb, such as 很/非常, etc., must be used.

一向	*adv.*	a consistent situation or action up to the present

这家饭馆的菜一向都很贵。
Food in this restaurant is always expensive.

一直	*adv.*	a continuous situation or action taking place within a given time frame

自从感冒以后，他一直发烧、咳嗽。
Ever since he caught a cold, he has had a fever and cough.

4. 受欢迎 (shòu huānyíng) vs. 欢迎 (huānyíng)

受欢迎	*v. obj.*	to be popular (受欢迎 functions as an adjective.)

那个电影很受欢迎。
That movie is very popular.

辭彙注解 Featured Vocabulary

1. 利用 (lìyòng) vs. 用 (yòng)

利用	v.	to take advantage of

他常常利用暑期的時間打工掙錢。

He often takes advantage of summer vacation to make some money.

(When the object of 利用 is people, this phrase has negative connotations.)

他很會利用人。

He is very skilled at using people.

用	v.	to use

我用一下兒你的電腦，好嗎？

May I use your computer for a few minutes?

2. 感興趣 (gǎn xìngqu) vs. 有意思 (yǒu yìsi)

感興趣	v. obj.	to be interested in

我對學中文很感興趣。

I am interested in learning Chinese.

有意思	adj.	interesting

那本書很有意思。

That is very interesting.

3. 一向 (yīxiàng) vs. 一直 (yīzhí): Always

Both 一向 and 一直 are frequently used with other adverbs, such as 都 or 就. In addition, when the adjective is monosyllabic, an adverb, such as 很/非常, etc., must be used.

一向	adv.	a consistent situation or action up to the present

這家飯館的菜一向都很貴。

Food in this restaurant is always expensive.

一直	adv.	a continuous situation or action taking place within a given time frame

自從感冒以後，他一直發燒、咳嗽。

Ever since he caught a cold, he has had a fever and cough.

4. 受歡迎 (shòu huānyíng) vs. 歡迎 (huānyíng)

受歡迎	v. obj.	to be popular (受歡迎 functions as an adjective.)

那個電影很受歡迎。

That movie is very popular.

欢迎	*v.*	to welcome

欢迎你常来。
You are welcome to come here often.

5. 使 (shǐ) vs. 让 (ràng)

使	*v.*	to cause, to enable (formal)

This is a pivotal verb and is frequently followed by a noun or personal noun that functions as the subject of the clause.

这次去中国使我更加认识到要想学好中文就必须了解中国文化。
My last trip to China made me realize that to learn the Chinese language well one must also understand the culture.

让	*v.*	to cause, to enable (less formal than 使)

This is also a pivotal verb.

这件事让我非常高兴。
This makes me very happy.

让	*v.*	to ask somebody to do something

我朋友让我今天晚上给他打电话。
My friend asked me to call him tonight.

让	*v.*	to allow

他妈妈不让他喝酒。
His mother does not allow him to drink alcohol.

词汇练习
Vocabulary Exercises

🎧 🖋 TASK 1. 组词 WORD AND PHRASE COMPOSITION

Use the given word or phrase on the left as a guide to help you think of other similar compound words. Feel free to use a dictionary when needed. Then write down the English definition of each of the compound words you've created.

1. 交 (to interact with): 交际   to socialize with others

    交 _____

    交 _____

    交 _____

歡迎	*v.*	to welcome

歡迎你常來。

You are welcome to come here often.

5. 使 (shǐ) vs. 讓 (ràng)

使	*v.*	to cause, to enable (formal)

This is a pivotal verb and is frequently followed by a noun or personal noun that functions as the subject of the clause.

這次去中國使我更加認識到要想學好中文就必須瞭解中國文化。

My last trip to China made me realize that to learn the Chinese language well one must also understand the culture.

讓	*v.*	to cause, to enable (less formal than 使)

This is also a pivotal verb.

這件事讓我非常高興。

This makes me very happy.

讓	*v.*	to ask somebody to do something

我朋友讓我今天晚上給他打電話。

My friend asked me to call him tonight.

讓	*v.*	to allow

他媽媽不讓他喝酒。

His mother does not allow him to drink alcohol.

辭彙練習
Vocabulary Exercises

 TASK 1. 組詞 WORD AND PHRASE COMPOSITION

Use the given word or phrase on the left as a guide to help you think of other similar compound words. Feel free to use a dictionary when needed. Then write down the English definition of each of the compound words you've created.

1. 交 (to interact with): 交際   to socialize with others

   交 _____

   交 _____

   交 _____

2. 退 (to move backward): 退休   to retire
    退 _____
    退 _____
    退 _____

3. 相 (mutually): 相比   to compare with each other
    相 _____
    相 _____
    相 _____

4. 节 (section): 节目   program
    节 _____
    节 _____
    节 _____

5. 游 (to wander): 游戏   game, play, recreation
    游 _____
    游 _____
    游 _____

6. 预 (in advance): 预告   advance notification, forecast
    预 _____
    预 _____
    预 _____

🎧 ✿ TASK 2. 搭配 MATCHING

A. 反义词

Match antonyms from among the following words and phrases.

1.

1) 休闲   a) 过时
2) 安静   b) 公立
3) 现代   c) 热闹
4) 私立   d) 工作
5) 时兴   e) 古代

2. 退 (to move backward): 退休   to retire
   退 _____
   退 _____
   退 _____

3. 相 (mutually): 相比   to compare with each other
   相 _____
   相 _____
   相 _____

4. 節 (section): 節目   program
   節 _____
   節 _____
   節 _____

5. 遊 (to wander): 遊戲   game, play, recreation
   遊 _____
   遊 _____
   遊 _____

6. 預 (in advance): 預告   advance notification, forecast
   預 _____
   預 _____
   預 _____

🎧❀ TASK 2. 搭配 MATCHING

A. 反義詞

Match antonyms from among the following words and phrases.

1.

1) 休閒   a) 過時
2) 安靜   b) 公立
3) 現代   c) 熱鬧
4) 私立   d) 工作
5) 時興   e) 古代

2.

1) 退休	a) 现在
2) 社会	b) 民间
3) 政府	c) 上班
4) 过去	d) 个人

B. 动宾词组

Match verbs in the left column with nouns in the right column to form phrases.

1. Verbs   **Nouns**

1) 利用	a) 审查
2) 经过	b) 聚会
3) 带来	c) 时间
4) 参加	d) 烦恼

2. Verbs   **Nouns**

1) 玩	a) 烦恼
2) 受	b) 高尔夫球
3) 使人	c) 游戏
4) 时兴	d) 控制

🎧 🐌 TASK 3. 填空 FILL IN THE BLANKS

A. 句子

Read the following sentences and fill in each blank with the appropriate word or phrase from the options given.

1. 感兴趣   一直   一向   有意思

a) 他 _____ 的娱乐活动很多，例如打牌、下棋、爬山、跑步、还有唱卡拉OK.

b) 他除了工作以外还参加很多社会活动，所以生活得很 _____。

c) 他过去 _____ 喜欢看电视，怎么现在也开始喜欢户外活动了？

d) 她的爸爸妈妈 _____ 不喜欢现代社会的娱乐方式。

2.

1) 退休	a) 現在
2) 社會	b) 民間
3) 政府	c) 上班
4) 過去	d) 個人

B. 動賓詞組

Match verbs in the left column with nouns in the right column to form phrases.

1. Verbs   **Nouns**

1) 利用	a) 審查
2) 經過	b) 聚會
3) 帶來	c) 時間
4) 參加	d) 煩惱

2. Verbs   **Nouns**

1) 玩	a) 煩惱
2) 受	b) 高爾夫球
3) 使人	c) 遊戲
4) 時興	d) 控制

🎧 ⚘ TASK 3. 填空 FILL IN THE BLANKS

A. 句子

Read the following sentences and fill in each blank with the appropriate word or phrase from the options given.

1. 感興趣   一直   一向   有意思

a) 他 _____ 的娛樂活動很多，例如打牌、下棋、爬山、跑步、還有唱卡拉OK.

b) 他除了工作以外還參加很多社會活動，所以生活得很 _____。

c) 他過去 _____ 喜歡看電視，怎麼現在也開始喜歡戶外活動了？

d) 她的爸爸媽媽 _____ 不喜歡現代社會的娛樂方式。

The Summer Palace in Beijing.

2. 欢迎　　利用　　用　　让　　受欢迎　　使

a) 在中国，除夕的春节联欢晚会是最 _____ 的电视节目之一。

b) 他们正在 _____ 新来的学生。

c) 他的不健康的饮食方式 _____ 他变得越来越胖。

d) 为了复习考试，他妈妈不 _____ 他参加任何娱乐活动。

e) 很多学生都会 _____ 暑假打工。

f) 这种中文软件很好 _____。

B. 段落

Read the following passages and fill in each blank with the appropriate word or phrase from the options given.

1. 另一方面　　感兴趣　　并不是　　利用

　　有人说现代社会的人 _____ 工作太紧张，没有时间休息，而是对休息根本不 _____。一方面大家都觉得上班很累，但是 _____ 很多人工作以后也不去放松，还要 _____ 休闲时间去健身房或做户外运动。

2. 聚会　　使　　安静　　相比

　　与现代社会 _____，中国传统的休闲方式虽然不是很多，但是能真正 _____ 人放松。比方说去茶馆，你可以去跟朋友 _____、聊天、下棋。你也可以自己找一个 _____ 的地方坐下来看书、写信。

The Summer Palace in Beijing.

2. 歡迎　　利用　　用　　讓　　受歡迎　　使

a) 在中國，除夕的春節聯歡晚會是最 ＿＿＿＿＿＿ 的電視節目之一。

b) 他們正在 ＿＿＿＿＿＿ 新來的學生。

c) 他的不健康的飲食方式 ＿＿＿＿＿＿ 他變得越來越胖。

d) 為了復習考試，他媽媽不 ＿＿＿＿＿＿ 他參加任何娛樂活動。

e) 很多學生都會 ＿＿＿＿＿＿ 暑假打工。

f) 這種中文軟件很好 ＿＿＿＿＿＿。

B. 段落

Read the following passages and fill in each blank with the appropriate word or phrase from the options given.

1. 另一方面　　感興趣　　並不是　　利用

　　有人說現代社會的人 ＿＿＿＿＿＿ 工作太緊張，沒有時間休息，而是對休息根本不 ＿＿＿＿＿＿。一方面大家都覺得上班很累，但是 ＿＿＿＿＿＿ 很多人工作以後也不去放鬆，還要 ＿＿＿＿＿＿ 休閒時間去健身房或做戶外運動。

2. 聚會　　使　　安靜　　相比

　　與現代社會 ＿＿＿＿＿＿＿＿，中國傳統的休閒方式雖然不是很多，但是能真正 ＿＿＿＿＿＿＿ 人放鬆。比方說去茶館，你可以去跟朋友 ＿＿＿＿＿＿ 、聊天、下棋。你也可以自己找一個 ＿＿＿＿＿＿ 的地方坐下來看書、寫信。

3. 相似   欢迎   难怪   相反   消费

除此以外，现代的休闲活动的 _____ 都比较高。传统的休闲活动与现代的休闲活动 _____，常常很便宜，比如中国的茶馆，与法国的咖啡馆 _____，你去茶馆买了一杯茶以后，你可以在里边喝一天。_____ 现在很多地方茶馆很受 _____。

语法句型和练习
Grammar Structures and Exercises

I. 与…相比 (yǔ...xiāngbǐ): To compare with

与 is basically the same as 跟, but it carries a literary flavor. When 与 indicates comparison, there must be 相比, 相似, 相反, 相同, or 不同 to go with it. The element inserted in 与…相比 can be a noun or noun phrase. The subject is usually placed after 与…相比, but it can also be placed before 与…相比. 相比 is the abbreviation of 互相比较.

与 Noun/Noun phrase	相比,	Subject Predicate/Verb Object
与去年的考题	相比，	今年的考题更难了。
This year's exam questions were harder than last year's.		
与十年前	相比，	他现在更有经验了。
Compared to ten years ago, he is now more experienced.		

PRACTICE
模仿造句

Make sentences of your own by following each of the examples given.

1. 与中国学生相比，_____学生_____。
   (Example: 美国，更喜欢户外活动)

2. _____ 与 _____ 相反，他们比较 _____。
   (Example: 老人，年轻人，注意锻炼身体)

3. 与_____相似，_____。
   (Example: 美国人庆祝情人节的方式，中国人也买花买糖送朋友)

4. _____ 与 _____ 不同，_____。
   (Example: 南方人的饮食口味，北方人的，南方人常常吃米饭)

3. 相似　　歡迎　　難怪　　相反　　消費

　　除此以外，現代的休閒活動的 ＿＿＿＿＿＿ 都比較高。傳統的休閒活動與現代的休閒活動 ＿＿＿＿＿＿，常常很便宜。比如中國的茶館，與法國的咖啡館 ＿＿＿＿＿＿，你去茶館買了一杯茶以後，你可以在裏邊喝一天。＿＿＿＿＿＿ 現在很多地方茶館很受 ＿＿＿＿＿＿。

語法句型和練習
Grammar Structures and Exercises

I. 與…相比 (yǔ…xiāngbǐ): To compare with

與 is basically the same as 跟, but it carries a literary flavor. When 與 indicates comparison, there must be 相比, 相似, 相反, 相同, or 不同 to go with it. The element inserted in 與…相比 can be a noun or noun phrase. The subject is usually placed after 與…相比, but it can also be placed before 與…相比. 相比 is the abbreviation of 互相比較.

與 Noun/Noun phrase	相比,	Subject Predicate/Verb Object
與去年的考題，	相比，	今年的考題更難了。
This year's exam questions were harder than last year's.		
與十年前	相比，	他現在更有經驗了。
Compared to ten years ago, he is now more experienced.		

PRACTICE

模仿造句

Make sentences of your own by following each of the examples given.

1. 與中國學生相比，＿＿＿＿＿＿＿＿＿＿＿＿＿學生 ＿＿＿＿＿＿＿＿＿＿＿＿＿。
   (Example: 美國，更喜歡戶外活動)

2. ＿＿＿＿＿＿＿＿＿與 ＿＿＿＿＿＿＿＿ 相反，他們比較 ＿＿＿＿＿＿＿＿＿＿＿＿。
   (Example: 老人，年輕人，注意鍛煉身體)

3. 與＿＿＿＿＿＿＿＿＿＿＿＿＿＿相似，＿＿＿＿＿＿＿＿＿＿＿＿＿＿＿＿＿。
   (Example: 美國人慶祝情人節的方式，中國人也買花買糖送朋友)

4. ＿＿＿＿＿＿＿＿＿＿＿與 ＿＿＿＿＿＿＿＿＿＿ 不同，＿＿＿＿＿＿＿＿＿＿＿。
   (Example: 南方人的飲食口味，北方人的，南方人常常吃米飯)

问答

Use the pattern 与…相比 to answer the following question.

周末的时候，美国家庭和中国家庭在休闲活动方面有什么相同之处或是不同之处？

翻译

Translate the following sentences into Chinese. Make sure your translation includes 与…相比 and 此外.

Compared to Americans, Chinese people don't much like to spend their leisure time exercising. They like to stop by and visit people for casual chats. In addition, they like to play cards or mahjongg.

II. 却 (què): But, however

The adverb 却 is often used in written Chinese. It indicates a contrast or something unexpected, and it must be placed immediately before the verb phrase in the second clause (i.e., after the subject if there is a subject). 却 can be used with conjunctions such as 可是, 但是, 然而, 而, and 不过 to intensify the contrast. 却 can also be used together with conjunctions of concession, such as 虽然 or 尽管.

1st clause	2nd clause
Subject Verb phrase,	**(然而/不过/但是) Subject 却 Verb phrase**

我要跟售货员讲价钱，   然而他却说价钱已经定了，不能改变了。
I wanted to bargain with the salesperson, but he said that the price was fixed and couldn't be changed.

老师知道应该改变考试的方式，   不过却想不出一个好的办法。
The teacher knows (s)he should change the testing methods, but (s)he cannot think of a good way to do so.

虽然他的朋友都很热心地帮他找对象，   但是他自己却一点儿也不着急。
All of his friends are enthusiastically trying to find a girlfriend for him, but he himself is not the least bit anxious about it.

✴ PRACTICE

连句子

Use 却, 可是, 但是, 然而, 而, or 不过, whichever is most appropriate for connecting each pair to form a grammatically correct sentence. In some cases, 虽然 may also be inserted in the first clause.

問答

Use the pattern 與…相比 to answer the following question.

週末的時候，美國家庭和中國家庭在休閒活動方面有什麼相同之處或是不同之處？

翻譯

Translate the following sentences into Chinese. Make sure your translation includes 與…相比 and 此外.

Compared to Americans, Chinese people don't much like to spend their leisure time exercising. They like to stop by and visit people for casual chats. In addition, they like to play cards or mahjongg.

II. 卻 (què): But, however

The adverb 卻 is often used in written Chinese. It indicates a contrast or something unexpected, and it must be placed immediately before the verb phrase in the second clause (i.e., after the subject if there is a subject). 卻 can be used with conjunctions such as 可是, 但是, 然而, 而, and 不過 to intensify the contrast. 卻 can also be used together with conjunctions of concession, such as 雖然 or 儘管.

1st clause	2nd clause
Subject Verb phrase,	**(然而/不過/但是) Subject 卻 Verb phrase**

我要跟售貨員講價錢，　　　　　　　然而他卻說價錢已經定了，不能改變了。

I wanted to bargain with the salesperson, but he said that the price was fixed and couldn't be changed.

老師知道應該改變考試的方式，　　　不過卻想不出一個好的辦法。

The teacher knows (s)he should change the testing methods, but (s)he cannot think of a good way to do so.

雖然他的朋友都很熱心地幫他找對象，但是他自己卻一點兒也不著急。

All of his friends are enthusiastically trying to find a girlfriend for him, but he himself is not the least bit anxious about it.

❧ PRACTICE

連句子

Use 卻, 可是, 但是, 然而, 而, or 不過, whichever is most appropriate for connecting each pair to form a grammatically correct sentence. In some cases, 雖然 may also be inserted in the first clause.

1. 他对中国古诗很感兴趣；他没有认真地研究过中国古诗。
2. 中国很多地方都庆祝圣诞节；他一向不过圣诞节。
3. 传统节目过去很受欢迎；现在在逐渐消失。
4. 他打牌打了很多年；总也打不好。
5. 上网聊天或玩网上游戏很有意思；要动脑子，不能放松。

翻译

Translate the following sentences into Chinese. Make sure your translation includes 是为了, 却, and 难怪.

Most people use the Internet to look for information or to socialize, but he is addicted to the Internet and is on the Web all day chatting and playing games. No wonder his parents are worried.

III. 并不(是)…而(是)…(bìng bú[shì]...er[shi]...): ...Not...but...

The conjunction 而 usually connects two elements that have opposite or contrary meanings. The adverb 并 is placed before a negative form to indicate that the fact is not as one may expect. This structure 并不…而 is superimposed on two verb phrases or clauses, implying a contrast. The subject is always placed at the beginning of the sentence.

1st clause	2nd clause
Subject 并不是 Verb phrase,	**而是 Verb phrase**

我并不是不想买房子，   而是还没有足够的钱来买。
It's not that I don't want to purchase a house; I just don't have enough money.

他今天迟到，并不是因为起得太晚，而是坐错了车。
He's late, not because he overslept, but because he got on the wrong bus.

❧ PRACTICE

完成句子

Please complete each of the sentences below using 并不(是)…而(是)…. Upon completion, make a sentence of your own.

1. 他的休闲活动 _____。

   (Suggested phrases: 在家打麻将，去户外活动)

1. 他對中國古詩很感興趣；他沒有認真地研究過中國古詩。
2. 中國很多地方都慶祝聖誕節；他一向不過聖誕節。
3. 傳統節目過去很受歡迎；現在在逐漸消失。
4. 他打牌打了很多年；總也打不好。
5. 上網聊天或玩網上遊戲很有意思；要動腦子，不能放鬆。

翻譯

Translate the following sentences into Chinese. Make sure your translation includes 是為了, 卻, and 難怪.

Most people use the Internet to look for information or to socialize, but he is addicted to the Internet and is on the Web all day chatting and playing games. No wonder his parents are worried.

III. 並不(是)…而(是)…(bìng bú[shì]...er[shi]...): ...Not...but...

The conjunction 而 usually connects two elements that have opposite or contrary meanings. The adverb 並 is placed before a negative form to indicate that the fact is not as one may expect. This structure 並不…而 is superimposed on two verb phrases or clauses, implying a contrast. The subject is always placed at the beginning of the sentence.

1st clause	2nd clause
Subject 並不是 Verb phrase,	而是 Verb phrase

我並不是不想買房子，   而是還沒有足夠的錢來買。
It's not that I don't want to purchase a house; I just don't have enough money.

他今天遲到，並不是因為起得太晚，而是坐錯了車。
He's late, not because he overslept, but because he got on the wrong bus.

❀❀ PRACTICE

完成句子

Please complete each of the sentences below using 並不(是)…而(是)…. Upon completion, make a sentence of your own.

1. 他的休閒活動 _____。

   (Suggested phrases: 在家打麻將，去戶外活動)

2. 信仰宗教 _____。

   (Suggested phrases: 为了赶时髦，为了忘掉烦恼)

3. 每天上网 _____。

   (Suggested phrases: 浪费时间，对学习有帮助)

4. 讲究营养的人 _____。

   (Suggested phrases: 常去饭馆吃饭，在家自己做饭)

5. 速食店流行 _____。

   (Suggested phrases: 因为味道好，因为又便宜又方便)

翻译

Translate the following sentences into Chinese. Make sure your translation includes 与…相比 and 并不(是)…而(是)….

   Chinese people's leisurely activities, as compared with those in past years, have increased in number. This is not necessarily because people have more leisure time but because of the influence of Western culture.

IV. 在…方面 (zài…fāngmiàn): In this respect

方面 means "aspect." It has many different usages. In this section, you will learn two of them.

A. 在…方面

This can be used with 在 and forms an adverbial phrase. 在…方面 is usually placed before or after the subject. 在…方面 can also be used as an attributive. In this case, sometimes 在 is omitted.

	Adverbial phrase	
Subject	在 **Noun/Verb phrase** 方面	**Verb Object**
各国	在庆祝节日方面	都有很多不同的习俗和方式。

Every country has different traditions and ways of celebrating holidays.

Adverbial phrase	
在 **Noun/Verb phrase** 方面	**Subject Predicate**
在谈恋爱方面，	王业的经验更丰富些。

Wang Ye has more experience when it comes to romantic relationships.

2. 信仰宗教 _____。

   (Suggested phrases: 為了趕時髦，為了忘掉煩惱)

3. 每天上網 _____。

   (Suggested phrases: 浪費時間，對學習有幫助)

4. 講究營養的人 _____。

   (Suggested phrases: 常去飯館吃飯，在家自己做飯)

5. 速食店流行 _____。

   (Suggested phrases: 因為味道好，因為又便宜又方便)

翻譯

Translate the following sentences into Chinese. Make sure your translation includes 與…相比 and 並不 (是)…而 (是)….

Chinese people's leisurely activities, as compared with those in past years, have increased in number. This is not necessarily because people have more leisure time but because of the influence of Western culture.

IV. 在…方面 (zài…fāngmiàn): In this respect

方面 means "aspect." It has many different usages. In this section, you will learn two of them.

A. 在…方面

This can be used with 在 and forms an adverbial phrase. 在…方面 is usually placed before or after the subject. 在…方面 can also be used as an attributive. In this case, sometimes 在 is omitted.

	Adverbial phrase	
Subject	**在 Noun/Verb phrase 方面**	**Verb Object**
各國	在慶祝節日方面	都有很多不同的習俗和方式。

Every country has different traditions and ways of celebrating holidays.

Adverbial phrase

在 Noun/Verb phrase 方面	**Subject Predicate**
在談戀愛方面，	王業的經驗更豐富些。

Wang Ye has more experience when it comes to romantic relationships.

Subject Verb	Attributive Noun/Verb phrase 方面的	Object
他给我介绍了很多	旅游方面的	知识。

He provided me with a lot of knowledge about traveling.

B. 一方面…，另一方面…

一方面…, 另一方面… is used to compare two verb phrases or clauses. It is translated as: "on the one hand...on the other hand."

他一方面忙，另一方面又没有钱，所以不常出外旅游。
One thing is that he's busy; another is that he doesn't have money, so he doesn't often go out and travel.

我夏天去中国，一方面是为了看朋友，另一方面也想去玩儿玩儿。
I went to China this summer — for one thing to visit friends, and for another to go around and sightsee.

❀ PRACTICE

完成句子

Complete the sentences below.

1. _____ 在工作方面 _____。

2. _____ 在谈对象方面 _____。

3. _____ 在音乐方面 _____。

4. _____ 一方面 _____ 另一方面 _____。

问答

Use either 在…方面 or 一方面…另一方面… to answer the questions below.

1. 中国人在饮食方面有什么特点？

2. 毕业以后，你打算做什么？

3. 这个节目里你最喜爱的地方是什么？

	Attributive	
Subject Verb	**Noun/Verb phrase 方面的**	**Object**
他給我介紹了很多	旅遊方面的	知識。

He provided me with a lot of knowledge about traveling.

B. 一方面⋯，另一方面⋯

一方面⋯，另一方面⋯ is used to compare two verb phrases or clauses. It is translated as: "on the one hand...on the other hand."

他一方面忙，另一方面又沒有錢，所以不常出外旅遊。

One thing is that he's busy; another is that he doesn't have money, so he doesn't often go out and travel.

我夏天去中國，一方面是為了看朋友，另一方面也想去玩兒玩兒。

I went to China this summer — for one thing to visit friends, and for another to go around and sightsee.

⊞ PRACTICE

完成句子

Complete the sentences below.

1. _____ 在工作方面 _____。

2. _____ 在談對象方面 _____。

3. _____ 在音樂方面 _____。

4. _____ 一方面 _____ 另一方面 _____。

問答

Use either 在⋯方面 or 一方面⋯另一方面⋯ to answer the questions below.

1. 中國人在飲食方面有什麼特點？

2. 畢業以後，你打算做什麼？

3. 這個節目裏你最喜愛的地方是什麼？

4. 为什么一些中国传统节目在逐渐地消失？

5. 中国有些什么娱乐活动？

6. 你暑假有什么计划？

翻译

Translate the following sentences into Chinese. Make sure your translation includes 在···方面 and 一方面···另一方面···.

   With regards to expensive leisure activities, playing golf and bowling have become very popular in recent years. This is because, for one, people like to be trendy, and, for another, both activities provide good opportunities to socialize.

V. 结果 (jiéguǒ): As a result
果然 (guǒrán): As expected

结果 and 果然 look similar; however, the two words do not have the same meaning or usage. The conjunction 结果 must be placed before the subject of the second clause to indicate a result caused by the first clause, and that result is often an unpleasant one. The adverb 果然 is placed before a verb phrase to indicate that what happened is what the speaker expected. The subject can be before or after 果然.

A. 结果 As a result

1st clause	2nd clause
Subject Predicate/Verb phrase,	结果 Subject Verb phrase

他太小气，只给了一点儿零钱作为小费，结果服务员把小费退还给他了。
He was so cheap that he only left a few cents as a tip; as a result, the waiter wouldn't accept the tip.

4. 為什麼一些中國傳統節目在逐漸地消失？

5. 中國有些什麼娛樂活動？

6. 你暑假有什麼計畫？

翻譯

Translate the following sentences into Chinese. Make sure your translation includes 在⋯方面 and 一方面⋯另一方面⋯.

    With regards to expensive leisure activities, playing golf and bowling have become very popular in recent years. This is because, for one, people like to be trendy, and, for another, both activities provide good opportunities to socialize.

V. 結果 (jiéguǒ): As a result
果然 (guǒrán): As expected

結果 and 果然 look similar; however, the two words do not have the same meaning or usage. The conjunction 結果 must be placed before the subject of the second clause to indicate a result caused by the first clause, and that result is often an unpleasant one. The adverb 果然 is placed before a verb phrase to indicate that what happened is what the speaker expected. The subject can be before or after 果然.

A. 結果 As a result

1st clause	2nd clause
Subject Predicate/Verb phrase,	結果 Subject Verb phrase

他太小氣，只給了一點兒零錢作為小費，結果服務員把小費退還給他了。
He was so cheap that he only left a few cents as a tip; as a result, the waiter wouldn't accept the tip.

他没存好收据，   结果不能退换他新买的电视机。

He didn't save his receipt; as a result, he couldn't exchange his newly bought television.

B. 果然 As expected, sure enough

1st clause	2nd clause
Subject Verb phrase	Subject 果然 (Subject) Verb phrase

他没说错，   王先生果然病得很厉害。

He was right; Mr. Wang really is very ill.

我一直要他给我介绍他们家人。中秋节那天，他果然请我去他家吃饭、赏月。

I kept asking him to introduce his family to me. As expected, he invited me to his home to admire the beauty of the moon and eat dinner on the day of the Mid-Autumn Festival.

❀ PRACTICE

完成句子

Complete the sentences below.

1. 这种娱乐活动消费太高，(结果) _____。

2. 他说他常去参加这种娱乐活动，今天我也去试了一下儿，(果然) _____
   _____。

3. _____，结果我说错了。

4. _____，果然我听对了。

5. _____，结果 _____。

6. _____，他果然 _____。

翻译

Translate the following sentences into Chinese. Make sure your translation includes 凡是, 结果, and 果然.

   I hear that in China all foreign movies must go through government inspection. As a result, some movies cannot be shown. So, not surprisingly, you haven't ever heard of this Hollywood movie.

VI. 其中 (qízhōng): Of whom, among which, including

其 means "it, they, the...," referring to an antecedent. 中 is an abbreviation of "在···中," meaning "among." 其中 must be placed at the beginning of the second clause and is often followed by 有 or 是.

他沒存好收據，　　　　　　　　結果不能退換他新買的電視機。

He didn't save his receipt; as a result, he couldn't exchange his newly bought television.

B. 果然 As expected, sure enough

1st clause	2nd clause
Subject Verb phrase	**Subject 果然 (Subject) Verb phrase**

他沒說錯，　　　　　　　　　　王先生果然病得很厲害。

He was right; Mr. Wang really is very ill.

我一直要他給我介紹他們家人。中秋節那天，他果然請我去他家吃飯、賞月。

I kept asking him to introduce his family to me. As expected, he invited me to his home to admire the beauty of the moon and eat dinner on the day of the Mid-Autumn Festival.

❀ PRACTICE

完成句子

Complete the sentences below.

1. 這種娛樂活動消費太高，（結果）_____。

2. 他說他常去參加這種娛樂活動，今天我也去試了一下兒，（果然）_____
   _____。

3. _____，結果我說錯了。

4. _____，果然我聽對了。

5. _____，結果 _____。

6. _____，他果然 _____。

翻譯

Translate the following sentences into Chinese. Make sure your translation includes 凡是, 結果, and 果然.

I hear that in China all foreign movies must go through government inspection. As a result, some movies cannot be shown. So, not surprisingly, you haven't ever heard of this Hollywood movie.

VI. 其中 (qízhōng): Of whom, among which, including

其 means "it, they, the…," referring to an antecedent. 中 is an abbreviation of "在…中," meaning "among." 其中 must be placed at the beginning of the second clause and is often followed by 有 or 是.

1st clause	2nd clause
Subject Verb Object	**其中 (Subject) Verb Object**

我爸爸有很多不同颜色的衬衫，其中他最喜欢那件蓝的。
My father has shirts of many different colors; of all of them, he likes the blue one best.

这家饭馆卖很多种菜，   其中有南方风味的辣菜。
This restaurant has many kinds of food, including some spicy Southern-style dishes.

❁ PRACTICE

模仿造句

Make sentences of your own by following each of the examples given.

1. 在公园里锻炼身体的人不少，其中 _____。
   (Example: 有很多是老人)

2. 我喜欢 _____，其中最好 _____ 是 _____。
   (Example: 听现代流行歌曲，听的，这个人唱的歌)

3. 网页上有很多 _____，其中 _____。
   (Example: 节目，还有些小品)

问答

Use the preposition 其中 to answer the following questions.

1. 休闲的时候，有很多事可以做。哪些是你喜欢做的？

2. 中国有哪些传统节日？哪些跟西方节日相似？哪些跟西方节日完全不同？

翻译

Translate the following sentences into Chinese. Make sure your translation includes 其中 and 却.

   Every Chinese province and city has its own television station, but, of all of them, none is privately owned. This is because all television stations are owned by the government.

1st clause	2nd clause
Subject Verb Object	其中 **(Subject) Verb Object**

我爸爸有很多不同顏色的襯衫，其中他最喜歡那件藍的。

My father has shirts of many different colors; of all of them, he likes the blue one best.

這家飯館賣很多種菜，   其中有南方風味的辣菜。

This restaurant has many kinds of food, including some spicy Southern-style dishes.

✇ PRACTICE

模仿造句

Make sentences of your own by following each of the examples given.

1. 在公園裏鍛煉身體的人不少，其中 _____。

   (Example: 有很多是老人)

2. 我喜歡 _____，其中最好 _____ 是 _____。

   (Example: 聽現代流行歌曲，聽的，這個人唱的歌)

3. 網頁上有很多 _____，其中 _____。

   (Example: 節目，還有些小品)

問答

Use the preposition 其中 to answer the following questions.

1. 休閒的時候，有很多事可以做。哪些是你喜歡做的？

2. 中國有哪些傳統節日？哪些跟西方節日相似？哪些跟西方節日完全不同？

翻譯

Translate the following sentences into Chinese. Make sure your translation includes 其中 and 卻.

    Every Chinese province and city has its own television station, but, of all of them, none is privately owned. This is because all television stations are owned by the government.

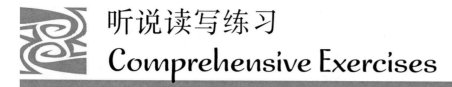

听说读写练习
Comprehensive Exercises

🎧 TASK 1. 听一听、选一选 LISTENING EXERCISES

A. Bingo

In this section, you will hear various Chinese phrases. Demonstrate your understanding of these phrases by numbering their English counterparts in the order in which you hear them.

to take advantage of leisure time

to compare with American society

to be similar to modern songs

to go through government inspection

to say hello

to be gradually disappearing

CCTV 4

in these respects

to have always been popular in the past

not for entertainment (contrary to expectation)

to make one feel annoyed all the time

a type of high-expenditure game

a place where retired people get together

as expected, the phone rang

a quiet gymnasium

the best among all the programs

B. Matching

Listen to the sentences in Chinese and number them in the order in which you hear them.

1. 有些人去健身房并不是为了锻炼身体，而是为了交际。
2. 与美国社会相比，中国退休老人比较注意锻炼身体。
3. 现在中国一方面有传统的娱乐活动，另一方面也有些西方的现代娱乐活动。
4. 中国的电视台一向都是受国家控制的。
5. 与美国相似，现在中国的年轻人也很时兴唱流行歌曲。
6. 一般人对传统文化不感兴趣，结果一些传统习俗逐渐消失。
7. 游戏有很多种，其中，计算机游戏在大学生中最时髦。
8. 听流行歌曲或唱卡拉OK能使人忘掉烦恼。
9. 果然今天晚上电视上没有一个有意思的节目。

聽說讀寫練習
Comprehensive Exercises

🎧 TASK 1. 聽一聽、選一選　LISTENING EXERCISES

A. Bingo

In this section, you will hear various Chinese phrases. Demonstrate your understanding of these phrases by numbering their English counterparts in the order in which you hear them.

to take advantage of leisure time	to have always been popular in the past
to compare with American society	not for entertainment (contrary to expectation)
to be similar to modern songs	to make one feel annoyed all the time
to go through government inspection	a type of high-expenditure game
to say hello	a place where retired people get together
to be gradually disappearing	as expected, the phone rang
CCTV 4	a quiet gymnasium
in these respects	the best among all the programs

B. Matching

Listen to the sentences in Chinese and number them in the order in which you hear them.

1. 有些人去健身房並不是為了鍛鍊身體，而是為了交際。
2. 与美國社會相比，中國退休老人比較注意鍛鍊身體。
3. 現在中國一方面有傳統的娛樂活動，另一方面也有些西方的現代娛樂活動。
4. 中國的電視臺一向都是受國家控制的。
5. 与美國相似，現在中國的年輕人也很時興唱流行歌曲。
6. 一般人對傳統文化不感興趣，結果一些傳統習俗逐漸消失。
7. 遊戲有很多种，其中，計算機遊戲在大學生中最時髦。
8. 听流行歌曲或唱卡拉OK能使人忘掉煩惱。
9. 果然今天晚上電視上沒有一個有意思的節目。

C. *Short Conversations*

Listen to these short conversations. Select the correct answer for each question from the choices provided.

1. 注意/不注意
2. 喜欢/不喜欢
3. 想/不想
4. 爱/不爱
5. 男的/女的

🎧 TASK 2. 听一听、说一说 SHORT PASSAGES

PASSAGE 1

Pre-Listening Activity

Before you begin, answer the following questions, which are designed to help you predict what will happen in the passage.

1. 你们家最喜欢的娱乐休闲活动是什么？
2. 你最爱看哪种电视节目？

Vocabulary

1. 频道	píndào	*n.*	channel
2. 文艺	wényì	*n.*	performing arts
3. 儿童	értóng	*n.*	children
4. 看不过来	kàn bù guòlai	*phr.*	not be able to see everything

Listening Activity

Now listen to the passage and answer the questions that follow. Be sure to make a voice recording on the multimedia CD-ROM explaining each of your choices.

A. Listening for the new words

Did you catch all the new words in the passage?

B. Listening for the main idea

这段话主要谈的是什么？

a) 说话的人喜欢看什么电视节目。

b) 他们家人喜欢看什么电视节目。

C. Short Conversations

Listen to these short conversations. Select the correct answer for each question from the choices provided.

1. 注意/不注意
2. 喜歡/不喜歡
3. 想/不想
4. 愛/不愛
5. 男的/女的

🎧 ❀ TASK 2. 聽一聽、說一說 SHORT PASSAGES

PASSAGE 1

Pre-Listening Activity

Before you begin, answer the following questions, which are designed to help you predict what will happen in the passage.

1. 你們家最喜歡的娛樂休閒活動是什麼？
2. 你最愛看哪種電視節目？

Vocabulary

1. 頻道	píndào	*n.*	channel
2. 文藝	wényì	*n.*	performing arts
3. 兒童	értóng	*n.*	children
4. 看不過來	kàn bù guòlai	*phr.*	not be able to see everything

Listening Activity

Now listen to the passage and answer the questions that follow. Be sure to make a voice recording on the multimedia CD-ROM explaining each of your choices.

A. Listening for the new words

Did you catch all the new words in the passage?

B. Listening for the main idea

這段話主要談的是什麼？

a) 說話的人喜歡看什麼電視節目。

b) 他們家人喜歡看什麼電視節目。

c) 他在比较现在和过去的电视节目。

d) 以上都不对。

C. Listening for details

1. 过去电视节目多不多？你怎么知道呢？

   多／不多

2. 说话的这个人现在家里的电视机比以前多了，是不是？为什么？

   是／不是

3. 他家里的人每个人看电视都有自己的兴趣，对不对？你怎么知道呢？

   对／不对

Post-Listening Activity

Now state your opinion as you record your voice on the multimedia CD-ROM.

你觉得看电视是不是最好的休闲活动？为什么？

PASSAGE 2

Pre-Listening Activity

Before you begin, answer the following questions, which are designed to help you predict what will happen in the passage.

1. 你爸爸妈妈休闲的时候喜欢干什么？

2. 你和你的朋友或室友的休闲方式一样不一样？

Listening Activity

Now listen to the passage and then answer the questions that follow. Be sure to make a voice recording on the multimedia CD-ROM explaining each of your choices.

A. Listening for main idea

说话的这个女的主要在讲什么？

a) 她爸爸妈妈的休闲方式

b) 她室友的休闲方式

c) 她自己的休闲方式

d) 以上都对。

c) 他在比較現在和過去的電視節目。

d) 以上都不對。

C. Listening for details

1. 過去電視節目多不多？你怎麼知道呢？

   多/不多

2. 說話的這個人現在家裏的電視機比以前多了，是不是？為什麼？

   是/不是

3. 他家裏的人每個人看電視都有自己的興趣，對不對？你怎麼知道呢？

   對/不對

Post-Listening Activity

Now state your opinion as you record your voice on the multimedia CD-ROM.

你覺得看電視是不是最好的休閒活動？為什麼？

PASSAGE 2

Pre-Listening Activity

Before you begin, answer the following questions, which are designed to help you predict what will happen in the passage.

1. 你爸爸媽媽休閒的時候喜歡幹什麼？

2. 你和你的朋友或室友的休閒方式一樣不一樣？

Listening Activity

Now listen to the passage and then answer the questions that follow. Be sure to make a voice recording on the multimedia CD-ROM explaining each of your choices.

A. Listening for main idea

說話的這個女的主要在講什麼？

a) 她爸爸媽媽的休閒方式

b) 她室友的休閒方式

c) 她自己的休閒方式

d) 以上都對。

B. Listening for details

1. 说话的这个女的觉得他爸爸妈妈的休闲的方式，好不好？为什么？

    好/不好

2. 说话的这个女的觉得她的室友的休闲方式好不好？为什么？

    好/不好

3. 说话的这个女的所喜欢的休闲活动跟她的室友一样不一样？你怎么知道呢？

    一样/不一样

Post-Listening Activity

Now state your opinion as you record your voice on the multimedia CD-ROM.

你觉得说话的人的看法对不对？为什么？

🎧💿 TASK 3. 看一看、说一说、写一写 SHORT VIDEO

Pre-Listening Activity

Before you begin, answer the following questions, which are designed to help you predict what will happen in the video.

1. 你觉得冬天的时候应该做什么休闲活动？为什么？

2. 你觉得打牌有意思吗？为什么？

Vocabulary

1. 东北	dōngběi	*prop. n.*	Northeast China
2. 这辈子	zhè bèizi	*phr.*	this lifetime

Listening Activity

Now listen to the dialogue and answer the questions that follow. Be sure to make a voice recording on the multimedia CD-ROM explaining each of your choices.

A. Listening for new words

Did you catch all the new words in the dialogue?

B. Listening for details

1. 說話的這個女的覺得他爸爸媽媽的休閒的方式，好不好？為什麼？

   好/不好

2. 說話的這個女的覺得她的室友的休閒方式好不好？為什麼？

   好/不好

3. 說話的這個女的所喜歡的休閒活動跟她的室友一樣不一樣？你怎麼知道呢？

   一樣/不一樣

Post-Listening Activity

Now state your opinion as you record your voice on the multimedia CD-ROM.

你覺得說話的人的看法對不對？為什麼？

🎧 TASK 3. 看一看、說一說、寫一寫 SHORT VIDEO

Pre-Listening Activity

Before you begin, answer the following questions, which are designed to help you predict what will happen in the video.

1. 你覺得冬天的時候應該做什麼休閒活動？為什麼？

2. 你覺得打牌有意思嗎？為什麼？

Vocabulary

1. 東北	dōngběi	*prop. n.*	Northeast China
2. 這輩子	zhè bèizi	*phr.*	this lifetime

Listening Activity

Now listen to the dialogue and answer the questions that follow. Be sure to make a voice recording on the multimedia CD-ROM explaining each of your choices.

A. Listening for new words

Did you catch all the new words in the dialogue?

B. Listening for the main idea

这段对话主要在说什么？

a) 滑雪对身体好不好。

b) 打牌对身体好不好。

c) 假期两人都干了什么。

d) 户外活动好还是户内活动好。

C. Listening for details

1. 这两个人谁去东北了？为什么去东北？

   男的/女的

2. 这两个人谁爱打牌？这个人怎么打牌？

   男的/女的

3. 这两个人是不是常在一起打牌？为什么？

   是/不是

Post-Listening Activity

Now state your opinion as you record your voice on the multimedia CD-ROM, and then write a summary of the dialogue.

请你用自己的话说一说这段对话都讲了些什么。

∩ ✤ TASK 4. 读一读、写一写 READING EXERCISES

This section consists of two parts: Short Stories and Authentic Material.

A. Short Stories

After reading each of the two Chinese 成语故事, respond in Chinese to the questions that follow.

成语故事：乐在其中

这个成语是从孔子的论语里来的。孔子是中国的一个非常有名的思想家。他很喜欢音乐，喜欢弹琴唱歌。有的时候，客人来拜访他，给他唱歌。要是他听得高兴了，他就会让这个人再唱一遍，并且同这个人一起唱歌。所以，他非常注重用音乐来教育人民。

B. Listening for the main idea

這段對話主要在說什麼？

a) 滑雪對身體好不好。

b) 打牌對身體好不好。

c) 假期兩人都幹了什麼。

d) 戶外活動好還是戶內活動好。

C. Listening for details

1. 這兩個人誰去東北了？為什麼去東北？

    男的／女的

2. 這兩個人誰愛打牌？這個人怎麼打牌？

    男的／女的

3. 這兩個人是不是常在一起打牌？為什麼？

    是／不是

Post-Listening Activity

Now state your opinion as you record your voice on the multimedia CD-ROM, and then write a summary of the dialogue.

請你用自己的話說一說這段對話都講了些什麼？

🎧 ▦ TASK 4. 讀一讀、寫一寫 READING EXERCISES

This section consists of two parts: Short Stories and Authentic Material.

A. Short Stories

After reading each of the two Chinese 成語故事, respond in Chinese to the questions that follow.

成語故事：樂在其中

　　這個成語是從孔子的論語裏來的。孔子是中國的一個非常有名的思想家。他很喜歡音樂，喜歡彈琴唱歌。有的時候，客人來拜訪他，給他唱歌。要是他聽得高興了，他就會讓這個人再唱一遍，並且同這個人一起唱歌。所以，他非常注重用音樂來教育人民。

他说过：一个人吃粗粮，喝白水，把自己弯着的胳膊当枕头，就能"乐在其中"了，也就是说，就能高兴了。这个成语里的"乐"是快乐的意思。但是，对孔子来说，音乐的乐会使他联想到快乐的乐，因为音乐是一件能让他快乐的事。

Vocabulary

1. 乐在其中	lè zài qízhōng	*phr.*	therein lies happiness
乐	lè	*n.*	happiness
其	qí	*pron.*	its
2. 孔子	Kǒngzǐ	*prop. n.*	Confucius
3. 论语	Lúnyǔ	*prop. n.*	The Confucian Analects
4. 思想家	sīxiǎngjiā	*n.*	thinker, philosopher
5. 弹琴	tánqín	*v. obj.*	to play a stringed instrument
6. 注重	zhùzhòng	*v.*	to pay attention to
7. 教育	jiàoyù	*v.*	to educate
8. 粗粮	cūliáng	*n.*	unrefined food
9. 胳膊	gēbo	*n.*	the arm
10. 枕头	zhěntou	*n.*	pillow

Questions

1. 用自己的话说一说"乐在其中"是什么意思？

2. 你同意不同意孔子的说法？为什么？

3. 做什么事情或者活动能让你感到"乐在其中"？为什么？

成语故事：乐此不疲

古时候，中国有一个皇帝叫刘秀。他这个人工作总是非常努力，每天都和他的大臣们讨论国家大事，常常到半夜才休息。他的大儿子看到他这样辛苦，就对他说：您虽然像古时候那些伟大的皇帝一样英明，但是您不能像古时候那些人那样保养您的身体。您需要多休息，不要太累了。我希望您能好好地爱惜自己。刘秀听了以后，对他儿子说："这些事情都是我喜欢做的，所以我并不感到疲劳。"

　　他說過：一個人吃粗糧，喝白水，把自己彎著的胳膊當枕頭，就能“樂在其中”了，也就是說，就能高興了。這個成語裏的“樂”是快樂的意思。但是，對孔子來說，音樂的樂會使他聯想到快樂的樂，因為音樂是一件能讓他快樂的事。

Vocabulary

1. 樂在其中	lè zài qízhōng	*phr.*	therein lies happiness
樂	lè	*n.*	happiness
其	qí	*pron.*	its
2. 孔子	Kǒngzǐ	*prop. n.*	Confucius
3. 論語	Lúnyǔ	*prop. n.*	The Confucian Analects
4. 思想家	sīxiǎngjiā	*n.*	thinker, philosopher
5. 彈琴	tánqín	*v. obj.*	to play a stringed instrument
6. 注重	zhùzhòng	*v.*	to pay attention to
7. 教育	jiàoyù	*v.*	to educate
8. 粗糧	cūliáng	*n.*	unrefined food
9. 胳膊	gēbo	*n.*	the arm
10. 枕頭	zhěntou	*n.*	pillow

Questions

1. 用自己的話說一說“樂在其中”是什麼意思？

2. 你同意不同意孔子的說法？為什麼？

3. 做什麼事情或者活動能讓你感到“樂在其中”？為什麼？

成語故事：樂此不疲

　　古時候，中國有一個皇帝叫劉秀。他這個人工作總是非常努力，每天都和他的大臣們討論國家大事，常常到半夜才休息。他的大兒子看到他這樣辛苦，就對他說：您雖然像古時候那些偉大的皇帝一樣英明，但是您不能像古時候那些人那樣保養您的身體。您需要多休息，不要太累了。我希望您能好好地愛惜自己。劉秀聽了以後，對他兒子說：“這些事情都是我喜歡做的，所以我並不感到疲勞。”

Vocabulary

1. 乐此不疲	lè cǐ bù pí	*phr.*	
乐	lè		to find happiness in, to enjoy
此	cǐ		this
疲	pí		tired
2. 皇帝	huángdì	*n.*	emperor
3. 刘秀	Liú Xiù	*prop. n.*	name of a person
4. 大臣	dàchén	*n.*	cabinet ministers
5. 讨论	tǎolùn	*v.*	to discuss
6. 半夜	bànyè	*n.*	midnight
7. 伟大	wěidà	*adj.*	great
8. 英明	yīngmíng	*adj.*	brilliant
9. 保养	bǎoyǎng	*v.*	to take care of (one's health)
10. 爱惜	àixī	*v.*	to cherish

Questions

1. 用自己的话说一说"乐此不疲"是什么意思？

2. 你觉得刘秀的说法对不对？为什么？

3. 你觉得"乐此不疲"这句话有没有道理？为什么？

B. Authentic Material

In this section, you will be exposed to some authentic materials used in China. Read the following newspaper article about the ways people spend their leisure time, and answer the questions.

1. 按照这篇文章说的，中国人的休闲时间多不多？

2. 中国人休闲时，多半做些什么活动？

3. 中国人的这种休闲方式好不好？

Vocabulary

1. 樂此不疲	lè cǐ bù pí	*phr.*	
樂	lè		to find happiness in, to enjoy
此	cǐ		this
疲	pí		tired
2. 皇帝	huángdì	*n.*	emperor
3. 劉秀	Liú Xiù	*prop. n.*	name of a person
4. 大臣	dàchén	*n.*	cabinet ministers
5. 討論	tǎolùn	*v.*	to discuss
6. 半夜	bànyè	*n.*	midnight
7. 偉大	wěidà	*adj.*	great
8. 英明	yīngmíng	*adj.*	brilliant
9. 保養	bǎoyǎng	*v.*	to take care of (one's health)
10. 愛惜	àixī	*v.*	to cherish

Questions

1. 用自己的話說一說 “ 樂此不疲 ” 是什麼意思?

2. 你覺得劉秀的說法對不對? 為什麼?

3. 你覺得 “ 樂此不疲 ” 這句話有沒有道理? 為什麼?

B. Authentic Material

In this section, you will be exposed to some authentic materials used in China. Read the following newspaper article about the ways people spend their leisure time, and answer the questions.

1. 按照這篇文章說的,中國人的休閒時間多不多?

2. 中國人休閒時,多半做些什麼活動?

3. 中國人的這種休閒方式好不好?

中国人的休闲时间真忙

环球时报

最新调查显示，中国老百姓平均每日休闲时间达到了6个小时以上。这意味着所有人可以在每天的1/4时间里想干什么，想怎么休闲就怎么休闲。……很多人的休闲方式可以说"休得越贵族感觉越好，闲得越流行越快乐"。……打牌的打麻将，茶馆、公园、街头、家中，甚至在午休的公司里，打牌和打麻将的人到处都是。……很多中国人的休闲方式太注重吃喝。一些节日和朋友的聚会成了吃喝的代名词，每家的餐桌上都堆满了肉、蛋、鸡、鸭、鱼等食品。亲朋好友间还要频频敬酒、斗酒。……很多人一放假便没日没夜地打牌、上网聊天、看电视等。所以，有的医院一到星期一，吃坏肚子、玩坏身子的病人便格外多，医生们不得不为这些病人起了一些很好听的名字——"假日综合征"患者。……在欧洲，很多国家的生活节奏都很休闲，即便有几天假期，人们通常也都是以日常休闲为主，一般不会出现中国那样的突击消费。很多餐馆、商店在周末和假期都关门休息。人们大多三五成群聚在一起喝喝咖啡……

🎧🦋 TASK 5. 想一想、说一说 PRESENTATION

Please pick one of the following for your presentation.

A. Individual Presentation

Describe an activity that you like a lot. Please make sure to tell the audience why you like the activity, when or how you started it, how long you've been doing it, and how this activity makes you feel. Feel free to make things up, and be creative!

環球時報

最新調查顯示，中國老百姓平均每日休閒時間達到了6個小時以上。這意味著所有人可以在每天的1/4時間裡想乾什麼，想怎麼休閒就怎麼休閒。……很多人的休閒方式可以說"休得越貴族感覺越好，閒得越流行越快樂"。……打牌的打麻將，茶館、公園、街頭、家中，甚至在午休的公司裡，打牌和打麻將的人到處都是。……很多中國人的休閒方式太注重吃喝。一些節日和朋友的聚會成了吃喝的代名詞，每家的餐桌上都堆滿了肉、蛋、雞、鴨、魚等食品。親朋好友間還要頻頻敬酒、斗酒。……很多人一放假便沒日沒夜地打牌、上網聊天、看電視等。所以，有的醫院一到星期一，吃壞肚子、玩壞身子的病人便格外多，醫生們不得不為這些病人起了一些很好聽的名字——"假日綜合征"患者。……在歐洲，很多國家的生活節奏都很休閒，即便有幾天假期，人們通常也都是以日常休閒為主，一般不會出現中國那樣的突擊消費。很多餐館、商店在週末和假期都關門休息。人們大多三五成群聚在一起喝喝咖啡……

🎧🈂 TASK 5. 想一想、説一説 PRESENTATION

Please pick one of the following for your presentation.

A. Individual Presentation

Describe an activity that you like a lot. Please make sure to tell the audience why you like the activity, when or how you started it, how long you've been doing it, and how this activity makes you feel. Feel free to make things up, and be creative!

B. Group Presentation

Setting: Anywhere (be creative)

Cast: Two people

Situation: Two people have just finished an activity. Perhaps they were watching television or seeing a movie. Or they could have been playing a game of Ping-Pong or chess. Whatever it was, now they are done and want to discuss what they've just experienced. The two share their reactions to what has occurred.

🎧 TASK 6. 想一想、写一写 COMPOSITION

Pick one of the following topics.

1. Describe the leisure activities done by people of various ages in your home country. Are there similarities or are they quite different?

2. A Chinese friend who does not know English but is familiar with Chinese resources asks you about English Web resources. Tell your friend about English language Web resources that are the same as, or similar to, the Chinese Web resources that you read about in the text.

B. Group Presentation

Setting: Anywhere (be creative)

Cast: Two people

Situation: Two people have just finished an activity. Perhaps they were watching television or seeing a movie. Or they could have been playing a game of Ping-Pong or chess. Whatever it was, now they are done and want to discuss what they've just experienced. The two share their reactions to what has occurred.

🎧 TASK 6. 想一想、寫一寫 COMPOSITION

Pick one of the following topics.

1. Describe the leisure activities done by people of various ages in your home country. Are there similarities or are they quite different?

2. A Chinese friend who does not know English but is familiar with Chinese resources asks you about English Web resources. Tell your friend about English language Web resources that are the same as, or similar to, the Chinese Web resources that you read about in the text.

44

中医与西医

Traditional Chinese Medicine and Western Medicine

In this lesson you will:
- Describe and discuss traditional Chinese medicine.
- Argue either for or against the use of Chinese medicine.
- Compare traditional Chinese medicine with Western medicine.

中国现有两种医学：西医和中医。一般医院都有中医科。中医已经有两千多年的历史了。中医的医学理论和治疗方法和西医很不一样。中国有句老话："西医治标，中医治本。"也就是说，西医是头疼医头，脚疼医脚[1]。治疗效果固然很好，特别是对急性病，可是药的副作用大。中医的治疗原理是把人的身心看作一个整体，通过调理身体的各种功能来治病。这也就是"治本"，意思是从根本上治疗。此外，中医讲究预防，在病情还没有发展起来的时候，就开始调理，以达到健康的效果。看病方法也和西医大不相同，中医大夫用望（看皮肤

The main entrance of Xi'an Traditional Chinese Medicine Hospital.

196

44

中醫與西醫

Traditional Chinese Medicine and Western Medicine

In this lesson you will:

■ Describe and discuss traditional Chinese medicine.
■ Argue either for or against the use of Chinese medicine.
■ Compare traditional Chinese medicine with Western medicine.

中國現有兩種醫學：西醫和中醫。一般醫院都有中醫科。中醫已經有兩千多年的歷史了。中醫的醫學理論和治療方法和西醫很不一樣。中國有句老話："西醫治標，中醫治本。"也就是說，西醫是頭疼醫頭，腳疼醫腳[1]。治療效果固然很好，特別是對急性病，可是藥的副作用大。中醫的治療原理是把人的身心看作一個整體，通過調理身體的各種功能來治病。這也就是"治本"，意思是從根本上治療。此外，中醫講究預防，在病情還沒有發展起來的時候，就開始調理，以達到健康的效果。看病方法也和西醫大不相同，中醫大夫用望（看皮膚

The main entrance of Xi'an Traditional Chinese Medicine Hospital.

Xueying Wang

197

颜色等）、闻（闻气味等）、问（问病情等）、切（切脉等）的方法来给病人看病。很多西医无法治好的慢性病，中医都能治。中医有一本书，叫"神农本草经"，是世界上最古老的一本医药书，介绍了三百多种有药效的动物、植物和矿物。中医根据不同的病情，把不同的中药按比例搭配，熬成汤让病人喝。当然对很多常见病，中医也有成药。中药的副作用一般要比西药小，价格也比较便宜，难怪现在世界上很多人都开始对中医感兴趣了。

　　由于多年来，中国政府不断地推广中西医结合，很多西医大夫也懂一些中医知识，也常常给病人开中药。还有，医生做手术时用针灸麻醉更是常见。吴文德腰疼一个多月了，去医院看过几次西医，不是验血，就是验尿，再不然就是做B超，但是什么问题也没有查出来。一

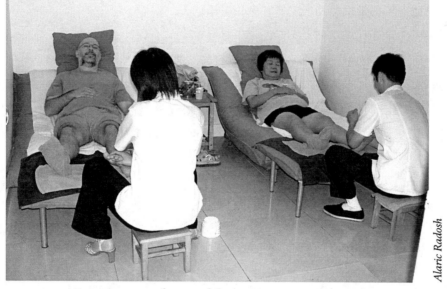

Enjoying a professional foot massage in Nanjing.

天，在学校图书馆陈小云遇到吴文德，她劝吴文德去看看中医。

（在学校图书馆）

陈小云：吴文德，西医好像对腰疼没有什么好办法，你不妨去试试中医吧。你腰疼一个多月了，老吃止痛药也不是个办法。

吴文德：我原先也想去试试中医，后来听李丽莉说中药难吃极了，所以我就没去。不过现在没有其他办法了，只好去试试。

陈小云：我不同意你的看法。良药苦口利于病[2]。如果中药能治好你的病，就算是药苦，你也应该吃下去。快去看中医吧，以免病入膏肓[3]。到时候你后悔都来不及。

吴文德：杯弓蛇影[4]。你别那么紧张，好不好？

顏色等)、聞(聞氣味等)、問(問病情等)、切(切脈等)的方法來給病人看病。很多西醫無法治好的慢性病,中醫都能治。中醫有一本書,叫"神農本草經",是世界上最古老的一本醫藥書,介紹了三百多種有藥效的動物、植物和礦物。中醫根據不同的病情,把不同的中藥按比例搭配,熬成湯讓病人喝。當然對很多常見病,中醫也有成藥。中藥的副作用一般要比西藥小,價格也比較便宜,難怪現在世界上很多人都開始對中醫感興趣了。

由於多年來,中國政府不斷地推廣中西醫結合,很多西醫大夫也懂一些中醫知識,也常常給病人開中藥。還有,醫生做手術時用針灸麻醉更是常見。吳文德腰疼一個多月了,去醫院看過幾次西醫,不是驗血,就是驗尿,再不然就是做B超,但是什麼問題也沒有查出來。一天,在學校圖書館陳小雲遇到吳文德,她勸吳文德去看看中醫。

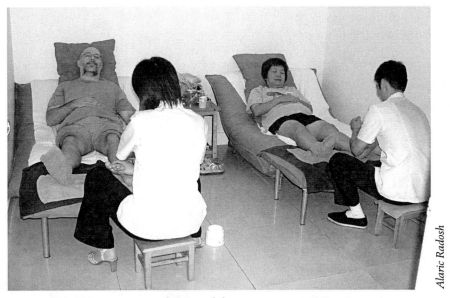

Enjoying a professional foot massage in Nanjing.

(在學校圖書館)

陳小雲:吳文德,西醫好像對腰疼沒有什麼好辦法,你不妨去試試中醫吧。你腰疼一個多月了,老吃止痛藥也不是個辦法。

吳文德:我原先也想去試試中醫,後來聽李麗莉說中藥難吃極了,所以我就沒去。不過現在沒有其他辦法了,只好去試試。

陳小雲:我不同意你的看法。良藥苦口利於病[2]。如果中藥能治好你的病,就算是藥苦,你也應該吃下去。快去看中醫吧,以免病入膏肓[3]。到時候你後悔都來不及。

吳文德:杯弓蛇影[4]。你別那麼緊張,好不好?

（在门诊室里）

高大夫：来，我给你号一下儿脉。……你是不是腰疼腰酸，晚上睡不好觉，总是上厕所，对不对？

吴文德：太对了！你是怎么知道的？

高大夫：你的脉象告诉我的。你的病是肾虚引起的。我给你开一个星期的中药，每天还要做一次针灸，调理调理，一个星期以后再来看看。

（一个星期以后吴文德在学校附近碰到了陈小云）

吴文德：陈小云，难怪你使劲儿向我推荐中医。现在我的腰不疼了，总算没白吃苦。我现在真正相信中医了。

Notes

1. 头疼医头，脚疼医脚。 (Tóu téng yī tóu, jiǎo téng yī jiǎo.)

   Not go to the root of the problem; (lit.) to treat the head for headaches, and to treat the foot for foot aches. This lesson uses this phrase for its literal, not figurative, meaning.

2. 良药苦口利于病。 (Liáng yào kǔ kǒu lì yú bìng.)

   (Lit.) Good medicine may taste bitter, but it is beneficial to curing the disease. This phrase is usually followed by 忠言逆耳利于行 (zhōng yán nì er, lì yú xíng), which means "Sincere advice grates on the ear but is beneficial to one's actions."

3. 病入膏肓 (bìng rù gāo huāng)

   A situation that can no longer be remedied; (lit.) the disease has entered the vitals (implying that it can no longer be reached by any treatment). For more information about this sentence, please see Task 4 in 听说读写练习.

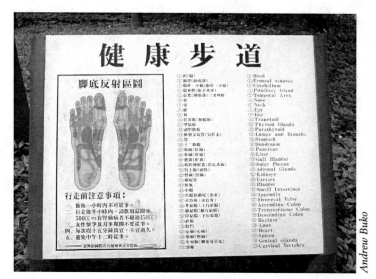

Instructions displayed at the entrance to a therapeutic foot massage path in the Peace Park in Taipei.

（在門診室裏）

高大夫：來，我給你號一下兒脈。……你是不是腰疼腰酸，晚上睡不
　　　　好覺，總是上廁所，對不對？

吳文德：太對了！你是怎麼知道的？

高大夫：你的脈象告訴我的。你的病是腎虛引起的。我給你開一個星
　　　　期的中藥，每天還要做一次針灸，調理調理，一個星期以後
　　　　再來看看。

（一個星期以後吳文德在學校附近碰到了陳小雲）

吳文德：陳小雲，難怪你使勁兒向我推薦中醫。現在我的腰不疼了，
　　　　總算沒白吃苦。我現在真正相信中醫了。

Notes

1. 頭疼醫頭，腳疼醫腳。 (Tóu téng yī tóu, jiǎo téng yī jiǎo.)
   Not go to the root of the problem; (lit.) to treat the head for headaches, and to treat the foot for foot aches. This lesson uses this phrase for its literal, not figurative, meaning.

2. 良藥苦口利於病。 (Liáng yào kǔ kǒu lì yú bìng.)
   (Lit.) Good medicine may taste bitter, but it is beneficial to curing the disease. This phrase is usually followed by 忠言逆耳利於行 (zhōng yán nì er, lì yú xíng), which means "Sincere advice grates on the ear but is beneficial to one's actions."

3. 病入膏肓 (bìng rù gāo huāng)
   A situation that can no longer be remedied; (lit.) the disease has entered the vitals (implying that it can no longer be reached by any treatment). For more information about this sentence, please see Task 4 in 聽說讀寫練習.

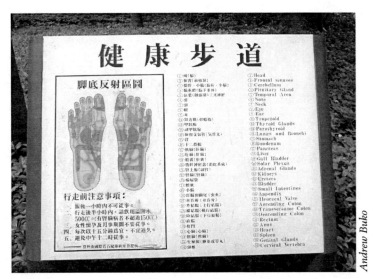

Instructions displayed at the entrance to a therapeutic foot massage path in the Peace Park in Taipei.

4. **杯弓蛇影** (bēi gōng shé yǐng)

To entertain imaginary fears; (lit.) the archer's bow reflected in the cup (appears to be) the shadow of a snake. For more information about this sentence, please see Task 4 in 听说读写练习.

课文问答 *Questions and Answers*

1. 中医用什么方法去了解病人的病情？
2. 中药的成分是什么？比较一下中药和西药的药效。
3. 吴文德喜欢不喜欢看中医？为什么？
4. 中医和西医有些什么不一样的地方？你认为中西医结合是不是一个治病的好方法？为什么？

 生词表
Vocabulary

Character	Pinyin	Part of Speech	English Definition
1. 中医	zhōngyī	*n.*	traditional Chinese medicine

我以后想研究中医。

| 2. 西医 | xīyī | *n.* | Western medicine |

他过去是搞西医的，现在也开始学中医了。

| 3. 医学 | yīxué | *n.* | medical science; (lit.) the study of medicine |

我觉得中国医学史很有意思。

| 4. 理论 | lǐlùn | *n.* | theory |

他只懂一点中医理论，但不能看病或开药。

| 5. 效果 | xiàoguǒ | *n.* | effect, result |

这种药效果很好，你试一试，怎么样？

| 6. 固然 | gùrán | *adv.* | admittedly, although it is true... |

要是能去医院固然好，但是他现在不能去。

| 固 | | *adj.* | tenacious, solid, hard |

| 7. 急性病 | jíxìngbìng | *n.* | acute disease; (lit.) quick-natured disease |

如果是急性病，那就应该去看西医。

4. 杯弓蛇影 (bēi gōng shé yǐng)

To entertain imaginary fears; (lit.) the archer's bow reflected in the cup (appears to be) the shadow of a snake. For more information about this sentence, please see Task 4 in 聽說讀寫練習.

課文問答 *Questions and Answers*

1. 中醫用什麼方法去瞭解病人的病情？
2. 中藥的成分是什麼？比較一下中藥和西藥的藥效。
3. 吳文德喜歡不喜歡看中醫？為什麼？
4. 中醫和西醫有些什麼不一樣的地方？你認為中西醫結合是不是一個治病的好方法？為什麼？

生詞表
Vocabulary

Character	Pinyin	Part of Speech	English Definition
1. 中醫	zhōngyī	*n.*	traditional Chinese medicine

我以後想研究中醫。

2. 西醫	xīyī	*n.*	Western medicine

他過去是搞西醫的，現在也開始學中醫了。

3. 醫學	yīxué	*n.*	medical science; (lit.) the study of medicine

我覺得中國醫學史很有意思。

4. 理論	lǐlùn	*n.*	theory

他只懂一點中醫理論，但不能看病或開藥。

5. 效果	xiàoguǒ	*n.*	effect, result

這種藥效果很好，你試一試，怎麼樣？

6. 固然	gùrán	*adv.*	admittedly, although it is true...

要是能去醫院固然好，但是他現在不能去。

固		*adj.*	tenacious, solid, hard

7. 急性病	jíxìngbìng	*n.*	acute disease; (lit.) quick-natured disease

如果是急性病，那就應該去看西醫。

急性		n.	fast-acting, short-tempered nature, impatient personality; (lit.) quick nature
8. 副	fù	*pref.*	side (effect), vice-(president), assistant (professor)

这是我们公司的副经理。

9. 作用	zuòyòng	n.	function, role, effect

你吃的那种药有没有副作用？

10. 原理	yuánlǐ	n.	fundamental principle; (lit.) the original principle

我只知道这种药的效果，但是不懂得它的原理。

11. 整体	zhěngtǐ	n.	entirety; (lit.) whole body

学习和生活对学生来说是一个整体的两个部分。

12. 通过	tōngguò	v.	to pass through, to pass (a set standard)

这次考试你通过了吗？

13. 病情	bìngqíng	n.	the condition of an illness, the state of a disease

那位医生想跟你再谈一下儿你的病情。

情		n.	situation, circumstance, condition; (lit.) feeling

14. 以	yǐ	*conj.*	(formal) so as to, in order to

请按时服药，以达到有效治疗的目的。

15. 皮肤	pífū	n.	skin

你的皮肤怎么总是这么好？

肤		n.	facial skin, skin

16. 气味	qìwèi	n.	(formal) smell, odor

这种药有一种气味，很难闻。

17. 无法	wúfǎ	*phr.*	no way, no idea

医生说这种病现在西医无法治疗。

18. 慢性病	mànxìngbìng	n.	chronic illness, chronic health condition; (lit.) slow-natured disease

这种慢性病很难治。

慢性		n.	slow-acting nature, slow or phlegmatic temperament

| 急性 | | *n.* | fast-acting, short-tempered nature, impatient personality; (lit.) quick nature |

8. 副　　　　　fù　　　　*pref.*　　　side (effect), vice-(president), assistant (professor)

這是我們公司的副經理。

9. 作用　　　zuòyòng　　*n.*　　　function, role, effect

你吃的那種藥有沒有副作用？

10. 原理　　　yuánlǐ　　　*n.*　　　fundamental principle; (lit.) the original principle

我只知道這種藥的效果，但是不懂得它的原理。

11. 整體　　　zhěngtǐ　　*n.*　　　entirety; (lit.) whole body

學習和生活對學生來說是一個整體的兩個部分。

12. 通過　　　tōngguò　　*v.*　　　to pass through, to pass (a set standard)

這次考試你通過了嗎？

13. 病情　　　bìngqíng　　*n.*　　the condition of an illness, the state of a disease

那位醫生想跟你再談一下兒你的病情。

| 情 | | *n.* | situation, circumstance, condition; (lit.) feeling |

14. 以　　　　yǐ　　　　*conj.*　　(formal) so as to, in order to

請按時服藥，以達到有效治療的目的。

15. 皮膚　　　pífū　　　*n.*　　　skin

你的皮膚怎麼總是這麼好？

| 膚 | | *n.* | facial skin, skin |

16. 氣味　　　qìwèi　　　*n.*　　　(formal) smell, odor

這種藥有一種氣味，很難聞。

17. 無法　　　wúfǎ　　　*phr.*　　no way, no idea

醫生說這種病現在西醫無法治療。

18. 慢性病　　mànxìngbìng　*n.*　　chronic illness, chronic health condition; (lit.) slow-natured disease

這種慢性病很難治。

| 慢性 | | *n.* | slow-acting nature, slow or phlegmatic temperament |

19. 古老   gǔlǎo   *adj.*   ancient

中医是一种古老的医学。

20. 药效   yàoxiào   *n.*   efficacy of a medicine; (lit.) the effect of a medicine

这种草有药效，可以治病。

21. 动物   dòngwù   *n.*   animal, the animal kingdom

你喜欢什么动物？

22. 植物   zhíwù   *n.*   vegetation, plant

这里的很多植物，我都没有见过。

23. 矿物   kuàngwù   *n.*   minerals

这有很多种矿物，世界上其他的地方都没有。

24. 根据   gēnjù   *prep.*   according to

医生说要根据他现在的病情给他开一些新的药。

25. 比例   bǐlì   *n.*   proportion, ratio

这种药你应该按一比二的比例加水：一杯药加两杯水。

26. 搭配   dāpèi   *v.*   to combine, to match up, to intermingle

这两种药你可以搭配着吃。

搭   *v.*   to bring together, to build (by putting pieces together)

27. 熬   áo   *v.*   to stew, to simmer

医生说你的药要熬两个小时以后才能喝。

28. 成药   chéngyào   *n.*   ready-made medicine

成药吃起来很方便。

29. 不断   búduàn   *adv.*   unbroken, uninterrupted, incessant; (lit.) no break

只要你不断地努力，一定能学好中医。

断   *v.*   to cut off, to break

30. 推广   tuīguǎng   *v.*   to spread, to promote, to popularize

他觉得应该在西方推广中医。

                        adj.   broad, wide, vast

31. 结合   jiéhé   *v.*   to unite, to unify, to join in wedlock

我觉得这两种药结合起来效果一定很好。

19. 古老   gǔlǎo   *adj.*   ancient
中醫是一種古老的醫學。

20. 藥效   yàoxiào   *n.*   efficacy of a medicine; (lit.) the effect of a medicine
這種草有藥效，可以治病。

21. 動物   dòngwù   *n.*   animal, the animal kingdom
你喜歡什麼動物？

22. 植物   zhíwù   *n.*   vegetation, plant
這里的很多植物，我都沒有見過。

23. 礦物   kuàngwù   *n.*   minerals
這有很多種礦物，世界上其他的地方都沒有。

24. 根據   gēnjù   *prep.*   according to
醫生說要根據他現在的病情給他開一些新的藥。

25. 比例   bǐlì   *n.*   proportion, ratio
這種藥你應該按一比二的比例加水：一杯藥加兩杯水。

26. 搭配   dāpèi   *v.*   to combine, to match up, to intermingle
這兩種藥你可以搭配著吃。
    搭   *v.*   to bring together, to build (by putting pieces together)

27. 熬   áo   *v.*   to stew, to simmer
醫生說你的藥要熬兩個小時以後才能喝。

28. 成藥   chéngyào   *n.*   ready-made medicine
成藥吃起來很方便。

29. 不斷   búduàn   *adv.*   unbroken, uninterrupted, incessant; (lit.) no break
只要你不斷地努力，一定能學好中醫。
    斷   *v.*   to cut off, to break

30. 推廣   tuīguǎng   *v.*   to spread, to promote, to popularize
他覺得應該在西方推廣中醫。
                                    adj.   broad, wide, vast

31. 結合   jiéhé   *v.*   to unite, to unify, to join in wedlock
我覺得這兩種藥結合起來效果一定很好。

| 结 | | *v.* | to knot, to tie up |
| 合 | | *v.* | to join, to unite, to combine |

32. 手术   shǒushù   *n.*   surgical operation

我最怕做手术。

| 术 | | *n.* | art |

33. 针灸   zhēnjiǔ   *n.*   acupuncture and moxibustion

你去试一试针灸，怎么样？

| 针 | | *n.* | needle |

34. 麻醉   mázuì   *n.*   anaesthesia

在动手术的时候，医生给他用的是针灸麻醉。

| 麻 | | *adj.* | numb |
| 醉 | | *adj.* | intoxicated |

35. 腰   yāo   *n.*   waist, the middle section (of something)

他腰痛得很厉害。

36. 尿   niào   *n.*   urine

看中医的时候医生总是问我尿多不多。

| | | *v.* | to urinate |

那个小孩晚上总是尿床。

37. 不然   bùrán   *conj.*   otherwise, in other case

你吃点中成药，不然去医院看看吧。

38. B超   B Chāo   *n.*   ultrasound

去医院做 B超非常麻烦。

39. 遇到   yù dào   *v. comp.*   to encounter, to come across

我去北京大学的时候，遇到了我以前的一个老师。

40. 劝   quàn   *v.*   to persuade, to advise, to urge

我劝你去看看中医。

41. 不妨   bùfáng   *adv.*   might as well

我认识一个中医。他会针灸，你不妨去试一试。

42. 止痛药   zhǐ tòng yào   *n.*   painkiller

止痛药只能止痛，但不能治病。

| 止痛 | | *v. obj.* | to stop pain |

| 結 | | *v.* | to knot, to tie up |
| 合 | | *v.* | to join, to unite, to combine |

32. 手術　　shǒushù　　*n.*　　surgical operation

我最怕做手術。

| 術 | | *n.* | art |

33. 針灸　　zhēnjiǔ　　*n.*　　acupuncture and moxibustion

你去試一試針灸，怎麼樣？

| 針 | | *n.* | needle |

34. 麻醉　　mázuì　　*n.*　　anaesthesia

在動手術的時候，醫生給他用的是針灸麻醉。

| 麻 | | *adj.* | numb |
| 醉 | | *adj.* | intoxicated |

35. 腰　　yāo　　*n.*　　waist, the middle section (of something)

他腰痛得很属害。

36. 尿　　niào　　*n.*　　urine

看中醫的時候醫生總是問我尿多不多。

| | | *v.* | to urinate |

那個小孩晚上總是尿床。

37. 不然　　bùrán　　*conj.*　　otherwise, in other case

你吃點中成藥，不然去醫院看看吧。

38. B超　　B Chāo　　*n.*　　ultrasound

去醫院做B超非常麻煩。

39. 遇到　　yù dào　　*v. comp.*　　to encounter, to come across

我去北京大學的時候，遇到了我以前的一個老師。

40. 勸　　quàn　　*v.*　　to persuade, to advise, to urge

我勸你去看看中醫。

41. 不妨　　bùfáng　　*adv.*　　might as well

我認識一個中醫。他會針灸，你不妨去試一試。

42. 止痛藥　　zhǐ tòng yào　　*n.*　　painkiller

止痛藥只能止痛，但不能治病。

| 止痛 | | *v. obj.* | to stop pain |

| 止 | | *v.* | to stop |

43. | 原先 | yuánxiān | *adv.* | originally, at first |

我原先想去看西医，但是现在觉得我应该去试一试中医。

44. | 同意 | tóngyì | *v.* | to agree, to approve |

你为什么不同意？

45. | 看法 | kànfǎ | *n.* | way of looking at things |

我跟他的看法不一样。

| 法 | | *b.f.* | way, method, mode |

46. | 以免 | yǐmiǎn | *conj.* | (so as) to avoid, lest |

你应该听医生的话，按时吃药，以免变成慢性病。

47. | 后悔 | hòuhuǐ | *v.* | to regret, to repent |

我现在后悔那个时候没有听医生的话。

48. | 大夫 | dàifu | *v.* | medical doctor |

张大夫人很好，你去找他看吧。

49. | 引起 | yǐnqǐ | *v.* | to trigger, to give rise to |

你的病是感冒引起的，吃点中药很快就会好。

50. | 附近 | fùjìn | *n.* | nearby area, surrounding area |

这儿附近有中医吗？

51. | 相信 | xiāngxìn | *v.* | to believe (in), to trust |

他说他吃了那种中成药以后很快就好了。但是，我不相信。

中医术语 Chinese Medical Terminology

1. | 治标 | zhì biāo | *v. obj.* | (标 = surface) to treat symptoms only (not the underlying cause) |

2. | 治本 | zhì běn | *v. obj.* | to treat the root of the problem |

3. | 调理 | tiáolǐ | *v.* | to regulate and harmonize (the bodily functions) |

| 调 | | *v.* | to mix, to blend |
| 理 | | *v.* | to put in order, to straighten up |

止   *v.*   to stop

43. 原先   yuánxiān   *adv.*   originally, at first
我原先想去看西醫，但是現在覺得我應該去試一試中醫。

44. 同意   tóngyì   *v.*   to agree, to approve
你為什麼不同意？

45. 看法   kànfǎ   *n.*   way of looking at things
我跟他的看法不一樣。

法   *b.f.*   way, method, mode

46. 以免   yǐmiǎn   *conj.*   (so as) to avoid, lest
你應該聽醫生的話，按時吃藥，以免變成慢性病。

47. 後悔   hòuhuǐ   *v.*   to regret, to repent
我現在後悔那個時候沒有聽醫生的話。

48. 大夫   dàifu   *v.*   medical doctor
張大夫人很好，你去找他看吧。

49. 引起   yǐnqǐ   *v.*   to trigger, to give rise to
你的病是感冒引起的，吃點中藥很快就會好。

50. 附近   fùjìn   *n.*   nearby area, surrounding area
這兒附近有中醫嗎？

51. 相信   xiāngxìn   *v.*   to believe (in), to trust
他說他吃了那種中成藥以後很快就好了。但是，我不相信。

中醫術語 Chinese Medical Terminology

1. 治標   zhì biāo   *v. obj.*   (標 = surface) to treat symptoms only
                                                     (not the underlying cause)

2. 治本   zhì běn   *v. obj.*   to treat the root of the problem

3. 調理   tiáolǐ   *v.*   to regulate and harmonize (the bodily
                                                     functions)

調   *v.*   to mix, to blend
理   *v.*   to put in order, to straighten up

4. 切脉/号脉/把脉 qiē mài/hào mài/bǎ mài

                          v. obj.   to feel/take a pulse

5. 脉象   màixiàng   *n.*   pattern of one's pulse

6. 肾虚   shèn xū   *phr.*   deficiency in kidneys

7. 中（草）药   zhōng(cǎo)yào   *n.*   traditional Chinese (herbal) medicine

8. 西药   xīyào   *n.*   Western medicine

9. 中成药   zhōng chéngyào *phr.*   ready-made traditional Chinese medicine

10. 中西医   zhōngxī yī   *phr.*   traditional Chinese and Western medicine

专有名词 Proper Nouns

神农本草经   Shénnóng Běncǎojīng   The Divine Farmer's Classic of Pharmacology

口头用语 Spoken Expressions

1. 不是个办法   búshì ge bànfǎ   not a good method

2. 到时候你···   dào shíhou nǐ...   when the time comes, you would (do something)

3. 白吃   bái chī   to eat in vain, to suffer in vain

书面语 *vs.* 口语 Written Form *vs.* Spoken Form

In Chinese, the "written form" preserves a lot of words and expressions from Classical Chinese and is therefore more concise and formal. As its name implies, the "written form" is used primarily in writing, but it occurs frequently in speech as well.

书面语	口语
1. 肤色	皮肤颜色
2. 药效	药的效果
3. 身心	身体和心理
4. 此外	除了这个以外

4. 切脈／號脈／把脈　qiē mài/hào mài/bǎ mài

　　　　　　　　　　　　　　v. obj.　　　　　　　　to feel/take a pulse

5. 脈象　　　　màixiàng　　　*n.*　　　　　　　pattern of one's pulse

6. 腎虛　　　　shèn xū　　　　*phr.*　　　　　　deficiency in kidneys

7. 中 (草) 藥　zhōng(cǎo)yào　*n.*　　　　　　traditional Chinese (herbal) medicine

8. 西藥　　　　xīyào　　　　　*n.*　　　　　　Western medicine

9. 中成藥　　　zhōng chéngyào　*phr.*　　　　ready-made traditional Chinese medicine

10. 中西醫　　　zhōngxī yī　　　*phr.*　　　　traditional Chinese and Western medicine

專有名詞 Proper Nouns

神農本草經　　　Shénnóng Běncǎojīng　　　　The Divine Farmer's Classic of Pharmacology

口頭用語 Spoken Expressions

1. 不是個辦法　búshì ge bànfǎ　　　　　　not a good method

2. 到時候你…　dào shíhou nǐ...　　　　　　when the time comes, you would (do something)

3. 白吃　　　　bái chī　　　　　　　　　to eat in vain, to suffer in vain

書面語 *vs.* 口語 Written Form vs. Spoken Form

In Chinese, the "written form" preserves a lot of words and expressions from Classical Chinese and is therefore more concise and formal. As its name implies, the "written form" is used primarily in writing, but it occurs frequently in speech as well.

書面語	口語
1. 膚色	皮膚顏色
2. 藥效	藥的效果
3. 身心	身體和心理
4. 此外	除了這個以外

5. 病情   生病的情况

6. 大不相同   非常不一样

7. 无法   没有办法

8. 多年来   很多年以来

9. …时   …的时候

词汇注解 Featured Vocabulary

1. 通过 (tōngguò) vs. 经过 (jīngguò)

| 通过 | *v.* | to go through (a method or channel), by way of |

他常常通过看电影来练习听力。

He often practices listening (to Chinese) by watching movies.

| 经过 | *v.* | to go through (a process), to pass by |

经过一年的努力，他的中文提高了很多。

After working (or studying) very hard for a year, his Chinese has improved a lot.

我在去中国的路上，经过了日本。

On the way to China, I passed by Japan.

| 经过 | *n.* | process, experience |

请你给我们讲一讲那件事情的经过。

Please tell us the ins and outs of that event (i.e., give us the blow-by-blow account).

2. 根据 (gēnjù) vs. 按照 (ànzhào)

| 根据 | *prep.* | based on |

根据他的研究，吃甜的对身体不好。

According to his research, eating sweet stuff is not good for one's health.

| 根据 | *n.* | evidence, basis |

他说的话一点儿根据都没有。

What he said does not have any basis in fact.

| 按照 | *prep.* | according to |

我们应该按照老师说的去做。

We should act according to what the teacher said.

5. 病情   生病的情況

6. 大不相同   非常不一樣

7. 無法   沒有辦法

8. 多年來   很多年以來

9. …時   …的時候

辭彙注解 Featured Vocabulary

1. 通過 (tōngguò) vs. 經過(jīngguò)

| 通過 | *v.* | to go through (a method or channel), by way of |

他常常通過看電影來練習聽力。

He often practices listening (to Chinese) by watching movies.

| 經過 | *v.* | to go through (a process), to pass by |

經過一年的努力，他的中文提高了很多。

After working (or studying) very hard for a year, his Chinese has improved a lot.

我在去中國的路上，經過了日本。

On the way to China, I passed by Japan.

| 經過 | *n.* | process, experience |

請你給我們講一講那件事情的經過。

Please tell us the ins and outs of that event (i.e., give us the blow-by-blow account).

2. 根據 (gēnjù) vs. 按照 (ànzhào)

| 根據 | *prep.* | based on |

根據他的研究，吃甜的對身體不好。

According to his research, eating sweet stuff is not good for one's health.

| 根據 | *n.* | evidence, basis |

他說的話一點兒根據都沒有。

What he said does not have any basis in fact.

| 按照 | *prep.* | according to |

我們應該按照老師說的去做。

We should act according to what the teacher said.

3. 向 (xiàng) vs. 往 (wǎng)

向	*prep.*	toward

(The noun that follows 向 can be a person, a place word, or a directional word such as 前, 后, 左, 右, etc.)

向朋友推荐   to recommend to a friend
向医院的方向开   to drive toward the hospital
向前走   to walk forward

往	*prep.*	toward

(往 is usually followed by a place or directional word.)

往后看   to look back
往火车站跑   to run toward the train station

词汇练习
Vocabulary Exercises

🎧 ✖ TASK 1. 组词 WORD AND PHRASE COMPOSITION

Use the given word or phrase on the left as a guide to help you think of other, similar compound words. Feel free to use a dictionary when needed. Then write down the English definition of each of the compound words you've created.

1. 性 (nature, property): 急性   acute (of diseases)

   _____ 性

   _____ 性

   _____ 性

2. 理 (logic, reason): 原理   fundamental principle

   _____ 理

   _____ 理

   _____ 理

3. 情 (feeling, situation): 病情   the condition of an illness, the state of a disease

   _____ 情

   _____ 情

   _____ 情

3. 向 (xiàng) vs. 往 (wǎng)

向	*prep.*	toward

(The noun that follows 向 can be a person, a place word, or a directional word such as 前, 後, 左, 右, etc.)

向朋友推薦	to recommend to a friend
向醫院的方向開	to drive toward the hospital
向前走	to walk forward

往	*prep.*	toward

(往 is usually followed by a place or directional word.)

往後看	to look back
往火車站跑	to run toward the train station

辭彙練習
Vocabulary Exercises

🎧 ✎ TASK 1. 組詞 WORD AND PHRASE COMPOSITION

Use the given word or phrase on the left as a guide to help you think of other, similar compound words. Feel free to use a dictionary when needed. Then write down the English definition of each of the compound words you've created.

1. 性 (nature, property): 急性　　　　acute (of diseases)

　　_____ 性

　　_____ 性

　　_____ 性

2. 理 (logic, reason): 原理　　　　fundamental principle

　　_____ 理

　　_____ 理

　　_____ 理

3. 情 (feeling, situation): 病情　　　　the condition of an illness, the state of a disease

　　_____ 情

　　_____ 情

　　_____ 情

4. 物 (thing): 药物   medicine

   _____物

   _____物

   _____物

5. 意 (idea, intention): 同意   to agree, to approve

   _____意

   _____意

   _____意

6. 原 (original): 原理   fundamental principle

   原 _____

   原 _____

   原 _____

🎧 TASK 2. 搭配 MATCHING

Match words or phrases from the left column with those in the right column to form phrases.

1. Verb   **Noun (phrase)**

1) 看成   a) 手术

2) 熬成   b) 一个整体

3) 通过   c) 药汤

4) 动   d) 调理

2. Verb   **Noun (phrase)**

1) 推广   a) 病人别喝酒

2) 劝   b) 中医大夫的话

3) 引起   c) 中西医结合

4) 相信   d) 感冒

4. 物 (thing): 藥物   medicine

    _____物

    _____物

    _____物

5. 意 (idea, intention): 同意   to agree, to approve

    _____意

    _____意

    _____意

6. 原 (original): 原理   fundamental principle

    原 _____

    原 _____

    原 _____

🎧 ✸ TASK 2. 搭配 MATCHING

Match words or phrases from the left column with those in the right column to form phrases.

1. Verb   **Noun (phrase)**

1) 看成   a) 手術

2) 熬成   b) 一個整體

3) 通過   c) 藥湯

4) 動   d) 調理

2. Verb   **Noun (phrase)**

1) 推廣   a) 病人別喝酒

2) 勸   b) 中醫大夫的話

3) 引起   c) 中西醫結合

4) 相信   d) 感冒

🎧 TASK 3. 填空 FILL IN THE BLANKS

A. 句子

Read the following sentences and fill in each blank with the appropriate word or phrase from the options given.

1. 按照   经过   根据   通过

a) 他想 _____ 吃中成药来治他的病。

b) 他 _____ 了这次大病以后，再也不敢随便吃东西了。

c) 你应该 _____ 他说的去做。

d) 大夫是 _____ 你的脉象来给你开药。

2. 往   在…上   向   从…上

a) 我 _____ 这本中医书 _____ 看到一个很好的药方。

b) 他 _____ 这本书 _____ 学到了很多中医理论。

c) 我朋友 _____ 我推荐了一位有名的中医大夫。

d) 他 _____ 那家中医院的方向走了过去。

B. 段落

Read the following passages and fill in each blank with the appropriate word or phrase from the options given.

1. 同意   劝   就算   以免

　　我妈妈的病已经有两年了。她的几个美国医生都 _____ 她做手术。但是，做手术很危险。 _____ 手术做得很好，副作用也会很大。我爸爸觉得不应该做这样的手术， _____ 将来后悔。我们家其他的人也都不 _____ 。

2. 原先   只好   向   不妨   效果

　　我不断地 _____ 我的家人推荐中医。 _____ 他们都不相信中医，后来我告诉他们我的几个朋友去看了中医，做了针灸， _____ 都很好。我劝他们 _____ 让妈妈去试一试。他们最后没有别的办法， _____ 同意了。

3. 熬药   整体   调理   根据   引起

　　昨天，我带妈妈去找了一位老中医。他给我妈妈号了脉以后说她的病是心脏 _____ 的。 _____ 他的经验像我妈妈这样的病不用做手术，用中药和针灸

🎧 ✸ TASK 3. 填空 FILL IN THE BLANKS

A. 句子

Read the following sentences and fill in each blank with the appropriate word or phrase from the options given.

1. 按照　　　經過　　　根據　　　通過

a) 他想 _____ 吃中成藥來治他的病。

b) 他 _____ 了這次大病以後，再也不敢隨便吃東西了。

c) 你應該 _____ 他說的去做。

d) 大夫是 _____ 你的脈象來給你開藥。

2. 往　　在…上　　向　　從…上

a) 我 _____ 這本中醫書 _____ 看到一個很好的藥方。

b) 他 _____ 這本書 _____ 學到了很多中醫理論。

c) 我朋友 _____ 我推薦了一位有名的中醫大夫。

d) 他 _____ 那家中醫院的方向走了過去。

B. 段落

Read the following passages and fill in each blank with the appropriate word or phrase from the options given.

1. 同意　　勸　　就算　　以免

　　我媽媽的病已經有兩年了。她的幾個美國醫生都 _____ 她做手術。但是，做手術很危險。_____ 手術做得很好，副作用也會很大。我爸爸覺得不應該做這樣的手術，_____ 將來後悔。我們家其他的人也都不 _____。

2. 原先　　只好　　向　　不妨　　效果

　　我不斷地 _____ 我的家人推薦中醫。_____ 他們都不相信中醫，後來我告訴他們我的幾個朋友去看了中醫，做了針灸，_____ 都很好。我勸他們 _____ 讓媽媽去試一試。他們最後沒有別的辦法，_____ 同意了。

3. 熬藥　　整體　　調理　　根據　　引起

　　昨天，我帶媽媽去找了一位老中醫。他給我媽媽號了脈以後說她的病是心臟 _____ 的。_____ 他的經驗像我媽媽這樣的病不用做手術，用中藥和針灸就可以治。他还说心脏和身体其他的部分是一个 _____ ，所以要通过 _____ 整个身心来治疗。他给我妈妈开了十几种中药，还教她怎么 _____ 。后来，他又给我妈妈做了针灸。很快，我妈妈的病就好了。

语法句型和练习
Grammar Structures and Exercises

I. 固然…，（不过）…(gùrán..., [búguò]...): Granted, even though..., (however...)

In Lesson 31 you learned about the conjunctions 虽然…但是. In this lesson you will learn a similar but more formal structure: 固然…, 不过…固然 concedes that the first fact is true. It is followed by 不过, 但是, 然而, etc., to introduce a contravening fact. The subject of the first clause can be placed before or after 固然. However, in the second clause,不过, 但是, and must be placed before the subject.

1st clause	2nd clause
Subject 固然 Verb phrase,	(不过) Subject Verb phrase

年轻人认为在外边租房子固然贵，　　　不过也比跟爸爸妈妈住在一起好。
Many young people believe that even though renting a home is very expensive, it is better than living with their parents.

固然社会上还存在着一些传统的习俗，但是一般人都已经慢慢地被西化了。
Even though society still holds on to some traditional customs, people in general have slowly become Westernized.

PRACTICE
问答

Use the pattern 固然…，（不过/然而/但是）… to respond to each of the statements.

1. Statement: 中药太苦，所以我不想吃中药。

    Response: 中药固然 _____ ，不过 _____ 。

2. Statement: 西药的副作用大，对身体不好。

    Response: 西药固然 _____ ，然而 _____ 。

3. Statement: 中国人一般不太注意利用休闲时间锻炼身体。

    Response: 中国人固然 _____ ，但是 _____ 。

就可以治。他還說心臟和身體其他的部分是一個 ＿＿＿＿＿＿ ，所以要通過 ＿＿＿＿＿＿
整個身心來治療。他給我媽媽開了十幾種中藥，還教她怎麼 ＿＿＿＿＿＿ 。後來，他
又給我媽媽做了針灸。很快，我媽媽的病就好了。

語法句型和練習
Grammar Structures and Exercises

I. 固然…，（不過）…(gùrán..., [búguò]...): Granted, even though..., (however...)

In Lesson 31 you learned about the conjunctions 雖然…但是. In this lesson you will learn a similar but more formal structure: 固然…, 不過…固然 concedes that the first fact is true. It is followed by 不過, 但是, 然而, etc., to introduce a contravening fact. The subject of the first clause can be placed before or after 固然. However, in the second clause,不過, 但是, and must be placed before the subject.

1st clause	2nd clause
Subject 固然 Verb phrase,	(不過) Subject Verb phrase

年輕人認為在外邊租房子固然貴，　　　不過也比跟爸爸媽媽住在一起好。

Many young people believe that even though renting a home is very expensive, it is better than living with their parents.

固然社會上還存在著一些傳統的習俗，但是一般人都已經慢慢地被西化了。

Even though society still holds on to some traditional customs, people in general have slowly become Westernized.

❧ PRACTICE

問答

Use the pattern 固然…，（不過/然而/但是）… to respond to each of the statements.

1. Statement: 中藥太苦，所以我不想吃中藥。

   Response: 中藥固然 ＿＿＿＿＿＿＿＿＿＿＿＿＿＿ ，不過 ＿＿＿＿＿＿＿＿＿＿＿＿＿＿＿ 。

2. Statement: 西藥的副作用大，對身體不好。

   Response: 西藥固然 ＿＿＿＿＿＿＿＿＿＿＿＿＿＿ ，然而 ＿＿＿＿＿＿＿＿＿＿＿＿＿＿＿ 。

3. Statement: 中國人一般不太注意利用休閒時間鍛煉身體。

   Response: 中國人固然 ＿＿＿＿＿＿＿＿＿＿＿＿＿ ，但是 ＿＿＿＿＿＿＿＿＿＿＿＿＿＿＿ 。

翻译

Translate the following sentences into Chinese. Make sure your translation includes 固然···, 不过/然而/但是···, and 难怪.

Traditional Chinese medicine certainly is very bitter and hard to take, but there are very few side effects and the medicine is relatively cheap. No wonder more and more people are now taking it.

II. 通过···来 (tōngguò...lái): By way of..., in order to...

The verb 通 has different meanings. One of them is "by means of," which is usually followed by a nominal phrase or verb phrase and placed after the subject. 来 in this structure means "in order to" and is placed before the second verb to introduce the aim or result of the 通过 phrase.

Subject	通过 Nominal/Verb phrase 来	Verb Object
有些人	通过学中医来	了解中国文化。

Some people learn about Chinese culture by learning about traditional Chinese medicine.

大学生	喜欢通过网上聊天来	认识新朋友。

College students like to meet new friends by chatting on the Internet.

🔲 PRACTICE

模仿造句

Make sentences of your own by following each of the examples given.

1. 这位医生通过 ＿＿＿＿＿＿＿＿＿＿，来给病人 ＿＿＿＿＿＿＿＿＿＿＿。
   (Example: 中医、西医的结合，治疗)

2. 医生通过 ＿＿＿＿＿＿＿＿＿＿，来控制 ＿＿＿＿＿＿＿＿＿＿＿。
   (Example: 针灸和手术，病人的病情)

3. ＿＿＿＿＿ 通过 ＿＿＿＿＿，来提高 ＿＿＿＿＿＿＿＿＿＿＿。
   (Example: 国家，教育，人们的文化水平)

问答

Use the pattern 通过···来 to answer the following questions.
1. 你怎么提高你的中文水平？

翻譯

Translate the following sentences into Chinese. Make sure your translation includes 固然…, 不過/然而/但是…, and 難怪.

Traditional Chinese medicine certainly is very bitter and hard to take, but there are very few side effects and the medicine is relatively cheap. No wonder more and more people are now taking it.

II. 通過…來 (tōngguò...lái): By way of..., in order to...

The verb 通 has different meanings. One of them is "by means of," which is usually followed by a nominal phrase or verb phrase and placed after the subject. 來 in this structure means "in order to" and is placed before the second verb to introduce the aim or result of the 通過 phrase.

Subject	通過 Nominal/Verb phrase 來	Verb Object
有些人	通過學中醫來	瞭解中國文化。

Some people learn about Chinese culture by learning about traditional Chinese medicine.

大學生	喜歡通過網上聊天來	認識新朋友。

College students like to meet new friends by chatting on the Internet.

❀ PRACTICE

模仿造句

Make sentences of your own by following each of the examples given.

1. 這位醫生通過 ＿＿＿＿＿＿＿＿＿＿＿＿＿＿，來給病人 ＿＿＿＿＿＿＿＿＿＿＿＿＿＿。
   (Example: 中醫、西醫的結合，治療)

2. 醫生通過 ＿＿＿＿＿＿＿＿＿＿＿＿＿＿，來控制 ＿＿＿＿＿＿＿＿＿＿＿＿＿。
   (Example: 針灸和手術，病人的病情)

3. ＿＿＿＿＿＿ 通過 ＿＿＿＿＿＿，來提高 ＿＿＿＿＿＿＿＿＿＿＿＿＿＿＿。
   (Example: 國家，教育，人們的文化水平)

問答

Use the pattern 通過…來 to answer the following questions.

1. 你怎麼提高你的中文水平？

2. 你朋友是怎么找到他的工作的？

翻译

Translate the following sentences into Chinese. Make sure your translation includes 按照 and 通过…来.

According to the tenets of traditional Chinese medical treatment, a person's physical and mental well-being are connected into one entity, and the doctor regulates the function of each of these components in order to cure the disease.

III. …，以…(…, yǐ…): In order to…
…，以免…(…, yǐmiǎn…): So as to avoid…

以 and 以免 look similar; however, the two words do not have the same meaning or usage.

A. …，以… In order to

In terms of meaning, the conjunction 以 is the same as 为了 (Lesson 42). However, 以 must be placed before the verb of the second clause to indicate the aim of the first clause. 为了 is usually placed at the beginning of the first clause. 以 is often used in the written language.

1st clause (Action)	2nd clause (Aim)
Subject Verb phrase,	以 Verb Object

这儿最近开了很多小吃店，   以满足大家的需要。
A lot of snack shops opened up here recently in order to meet people's needs.

医生让他每天跑步，   以达到健康的效果。
The doctor asked him to jog every day in order to reach his health target.

B. …，以免… So as to avoid

以 can be followed by 免 to indicate that the action in the first clause needs to take place in order to avoid the circumstance presented in the second clause; 以免 often serves as a suggestion or warning. It is placed at the beginning of the second clause. Sometimes the more colloquial 省得 is interchangeable with 以免.

1st clause (Action)	2nd clause (Circumstance)
Subject Verb Object,	以免 Verb Object

我们还是先检查一下儿行李吧，以免忘了什么东西。
We should check our luggage so as to avoid forgetting things.

你不要再喝咖啡了，   以免晚上睡不着。
You should stop drinking coffee so as to avoid not being able to sleep at night.

2. 你朋友是怎麼找到他的工作的？

翻譯

Translate the following sentences into Chinese. Make sure your translation includes 按照 and 通過…來.

According to the tenets of traditional Chinese medical treatment, a person's physical and mental well-being are connected into one entity, and the doctor regulates the function of each of these components in order to cure the disease.

III. …，以…(..., yǐ...): In order to...
　　…，以免…(..., yǐmiǎn...): So as to avoid...

以 and 以免 look similar; however, the two words do not have the same meaning or usage.

A. …，以… In order to

In terms of meaning, the conjunction 以 is the same as 為了 (Lesson 42). However, 以 must be placed before the verb of the second clause to indicate the aim of the first clause. 為了 is usually placed at the beginning of the first clause. 以 is often used in the written language.

1st clause (Action)	2nd clause (Aim)
Subject Verb phrase,	以 **Verb Object**

這兒最近開了很多小吃店，　　　　以滿足大家的需要。
A lot of snack shops opened up here recently in order to meet people's needs.

醫生讓他每天跑步，　　　　以達到健康的效果。
The doctor asked him to jog every day in order to reach his health target.

B. …，以免… So as to avoid

以 can be followed by 免 to indicate that the action in the first clause needs to take place in order to avoid the circumstance presented in the second clause; 以免 often serves as a suggestion or warning. It is placed at the beginning of the second clause. Sometimes the more colloquial 省得 is interchangeable with 以免.

1st clause (Action)	2nd clause (Circumstance)
Subject Verb Object,	以免 **Verb Object**

我們還是先檢查一下兒行李吧，以免忘了什麼東西。
We should check our luggage so as to avoid forgetting things.

你不要再喝咖啡了，　　　　以免晚上睡不著。
You should stop drinking coffee so as to avoid not being able to sleep at night.

📖 PRACTICE

问答

Use the preposition 以… along with 以免… to answer the following questions.

1. 一个人得了病，为什么医生让他吃药打针？

_____，以达到 _____。

_____，以免 _____。

2. 医生让你注意调理饮食，每天锻炼身体吗？为什么？

_____，以预防 _____。

_____，以免 _____。

3. 为什么情人节的时候，你给朋友送花送糖？

_____，以表示 _____。

_____，以免 _____。

完成句子

Complete each of the sentences below.

1. _____ 以达到 _____。

2. _____ 以完成 _____。

3. _____ 以改变 _____。

翻译

Translate the following sentences into Chinese. Make sure your translation includes 以 and 以免.

Traditional Chinese medicine pays careful attention to prevention. It attends to regulating the function of every part of the body in order to maintain good health. It also begins regulating (bodily functions) before illness occurs, thereby preventing the illness from reaching the vital organs.

IV. 不是…就是…（再不然）(búshì…jiùshì…[zàibùrán]): If not…then…or else…

In Lesson 43 you learned the structure 不是…而是, which expresses a contrast between two clauses. In this lesson you will learn the structure 不是…就是…（再不然）, which means "either…or…(or else)." This structure links three contrasting nouns, verbs, phrases, or clauses. 再不然 can also be used and is often followed by 就 or 还.

❧ PRACTICE

問答

Use the preposition 以… along with 以免… to answer the following questions.

1. 一個人得了病，為什麼醫生讓他吃藥打針？

    _____，以達到 _____ 。

    _____，以免 _____ 。

2. 醫生讓你注意調理飲食，每天鍛煉身體嗎？為什麼？

    _____，以預防 _____ 。

    _____，以免 _____ 。

3. 為什麼情人節的時候，你給朋友送花送糖？

    _____，以表示 _____ 。

    _____，以免 _____ 。

完成句子

Complete each of the sentences below.

1. _____ 以達到 _____ 。

2. _____ 以完成 _____ 。

3. _____ 以改變 _____ 。

翻譯

Translate the following sentences into Chinese. Make sure your translation includes 以 and 以免.

Traditional Chinese medicine pays careful attention to prevention. It attends to regulating the function of every part of the body in order to maintain good health. It also begins regulating (bodily functions) before illness occurs, thereby preventing the illness from reaching the vital organs.

IV. 不是…就是…（再不然）(búshì…jiùshì…[zàibùrán]): If not...then...or else...

In Lesson 43 you learned the structure 不是…而是, which expresses a contrast between two clauses. In this lesson you will learn the structure 不是…就是…（再不然）, which means "either...or...(or else)." This structure links three contrasting nouns, verbs, phrases, or clauses. 再不然 can also be used and is often followed by 就 or 還.

Statement	1st clause	2nd clause	3rd clause
Subject Verb Object, 不是 **Noun/Verb phrase,**	就是 **Noun/Verb phrase**	再不然就	**/ Verb Object**

去长城，　　　　　　不是乘公共汽车，　　就是坐出租车，　　　　再不然还可以坐火车。

To get to the Great Wall, [you can] take a bus, a taxi, or a train.

你生病了，　　　　　不是吃中药，　　　　就是吃西药，　　　　　再不然就用针灸。

If you get sick, [you need to] take either traditional Chinese medicine or Western medicine or use acupuncture and moxibustion.

❀ PRACTICE

完成句子

Use 不是…就是…，再不然 to complete each of the sentences below.

1. 医生给病人看病的时候，不是 _____ 就是 _____ ，再不然 _____ 。

2. 我每天锻炼身体，不是 _____ 就是 _____ ，再不然 _____ 。

3. 我毕业以后的计划，不是 _____ 就是 _____ ，再不然 _____ 。

4. 一般人庆祝节日的方式，不是 _____ 就是 _____ ，再不然 _____ 。

翻译

Translate the following sentences into Chinese. Make sure your translation includes 自从…以来, 不是…就是…（再不然）and 结果.

Ever since he got sick, he takes medicine, gets shots, or goes to the hospital for acupuncture every day. As a result, his condition has improved a lot.

V. …，不妨…(..., bùfáng...): Why don't (you)..., might as well

This adverbial phrase literally means "there's no harm in …." It implies that one might as well (do something), and serves as a suggestion. 不妨 is usually placed at the beginning of the second clause, after the subject — if there is a subject. Sometimes 如果 or 要是 is used in the first clause.

1st clause	2nd clause
Subject Verb phrase,	**Subject** 不妨 **Verb phrase**

如果你想吃辣菜，　　　　　　我们不妨去那家南方风味的饭馆。

If you want to eat spicy dishes, we might as well try that Southern-style restaurant.

打太极拳对健康有帮助，　　　你不妨劝那位病人学学太极拳。

Practicing tai chi can help people improve their health, so there's no harm in telling that patient to try it.

Statement	1st clause	2nd clause	3rd clause
Subject Verb Object,	不是 **Noun/Verb phrase,**	就是 **Noun/Verb phrase**	再不然就 / **Verb Object**

去長城， 　　　　不是乘公共汽車， 　就是坐出租車， 　　再不然還可以坐火車。

To get to the Great Wall, [you can] take a bus, a taxi, or a train.

你生病了， 　　　　不是吃中藥， 　　　就是吃西藥， 　　　再不然就用針灸。

If you get sick, [you need to] take either traditional Chinese medicine or Western medicine or use acupuncture and moxibustion.

❀ PRACTICE

完成句子

Use 不是…就是…，再不然 to complete each of the sentences below.

1. 醫生給病人看病的時候，不是 _____ 就是 _____ ，再不然 _____ 。

2. 我每天鍛煉身體，不是 _____ 就是 _____ ，再不然 _____ 。

3. 我畢業以後的計畫，不是 _____ 就是 _____ ，再不然 _____ 。

4. 一般人慶祝節日的方式，不是 _____ 就是 _____ ，再不然 _____ 。

翻譯

Translate the following sentences into Chinese. Make sure your translation includes 自從…以來, 不是…就是…（再不然）and 結果.

　　Ever since he got sick, he takes medicine, gets shots, or goes to the hospital for acupuncture every day. As a result, his condition has improved a lot.

V. …, 不妨…(..., bùfáng...): Why don't (you)..., might as well

This adverbial phrase literally means "there's no harm in ...." It implies that one might as well (do something), and serves as a suggestion. 不妨 is usually placed at the beginning of the second clause, after the subject — if there is a subject. Sometimes 如果 or 要是 is used in the first clause.

1st clause	2nd clause
Subject Verb phrase,	**Subject** 不妨 **Verb phrase**

如果你想吃辣菜， 　　　　我們不妨去那家南方風味的飯館。

If you want to eat spicy dishes, we might as well try that Southern-style restaurant.

打太極拳對健康有幫助， 　　你不妨勸那位病人學學太極拳。

Practicing tai chi can help people improve their health, so there's no harm in telling that patient to try it.

Early morning tai chi practice in a park in Hangzhou.

PRACTICE

模仿造句

Make sentences of your own by following each of the examples given.

1. A: 我从来没有看过中医。

   B: 这位中医 _____，你不妨 _____。

   (Example: 治病很有效，去试一试)

2. A: 我每天晚上都睡不好觉。

   B: 你不妨 _____，说不定能帮助你睡觉。

   (Example: 睡觉前喝点儿牛奶)

3. A: 我朋友向我推荐那部电影。

   B: 要是 _____，你不妨 _____。

   (Example: 你有时间，去看看)

4. A: 今晚有没有相声节目？

   B: _____可能 _____，你不妨 _____。

   (Example: 网页上，登着节目表，上网查查)

5. A: 最近我 _____，吃止痛药也没用。

   B: 你不妨 _____。

   (Example: 老头疼，试一试针灸)

Early morning tai chi practice in a park in Hangzhou.

🞉 PRACTICE

模仿造句

Make sentences of your own by following each of the examples given.

1. A: 我從來沒有看過中醫。
   B: 這位中醫 ＿＿＿＿＿＿＿＿＿＿＿＿＿＿＿，你不妨 ＿＿＿＿＿＿＿＿＿＿＿＿＿＿＿。
   (Example: 治病很有效，去試一試)

2. A: 我每天晚上都睡不好覺。
   B: 你不妨 ＿＿＿＿＿＿＿＿＿＿＿＿＿＿＿＿＿＿＿＿，說不定能幫助你睡覺。
   (Example: 睡覺前喝點兒牛奶)

3. A: 我朋友向我推薦那部電影。
   B: 要是 ＿＿＿＿＿＿＿＿＿＿＿＿＿，你不妨 ＿＿＿＿＿＿＿＿＿＿＿＿＿＿＿。
   (Example: 你有時間，去看看)

4. A: 今晚有沒有相聲節目？
   B: ＿＿＿＿＿＿＿＿＿可能 ＿＿＿＿＿＿＿＿＿，你不妨 ＿＿＿＿＿＿＿＿＿。
   (Example: 網頁上，登著節目表，上網查查)

5. A: 最近我 ＿＿＿＿＿＿＿＿＿＿＿＿＿＿＿＿＿＿＿，吃止痛藥也沒用。
   B: 你不妨 ＿＿＿＿＿＿＿＿＿＿＿＿＿＿＿＿＿＿＿＿。
   (Example: 老頭疼，試一試針灸)

翻译

Translate the following sentences into Chinese. Make sure your translation includes 固然…不过 and 不妨.

Traditional Chinese medicine is not that well-known in the U.S. However, I heard some movie stars are seeing doctors of traditional Chinese medicine now, so why don't you give it a try?

VI. 只好…(zhǐhǎo…): Have no choice but…

This adverbial phrase indicates that there is no choice but to do something. 只好 is generally preceded by a clause stating a restricting condition. If the second clause has a subject, 只好 is usually placed after the subject.

1st clause (Reason)	2nd clause (Action)
Subject Verb Object,	**Subject 只好 Verb Object**

外面下大雪，   我只好在家看电视。
It's snowing hard outside, so I might as well stay inside and watch television.

因为带的人民币不够了，   所以我只好用信用卡。
Since I didn't bring enough RMB, I have no choice but to pay with my credit card.

❧ PRACTICE

模仿造句

Make sentences of your own by following each of the examples given.

1. 西医无法治好这个病人的病，所以他只好 _____。
   (Example: 去找中医看)

2. 我因为全身疼得动不了，所以只好 _____。
   (Example: 去试试针灸)

3. 他在中国旅游，可是一句中国话也不会说，所以只好 _____。
   (Example: 去请了一位会讲英文的导游)

问答

Use the word 只好… to answer the following questions.

1. 她为什么不吃肉，光吃素？

翻譯

Translate the following sentences into Chinese. Make sure your translation includes 固然…不過 and 不妨.

　　Traditional Chinese medicine is not that well-known in the U.S. However, I heard some movie stars are seeing doctors of traditional Chinese medicine now, so why don't you give it a try?

VI. 只好…(zhǐhǎo...): Have no choice but...

This adverbial phrase indicates that there is no choice but to do something. 只好 is generally preceded by a clause stating a restricting condition. If the second clause has a subject, 只好 is usually placed after the subject.

1st clause (Reason)	2nd clause (Action)
Subject Verb Object,	**Subject 只好 Verb Object**

外面下大雪，　　　　　　　我只好在家看電視。
It's snowing hard outside, so I might as well stay inside and watch television.

因為帶的人民幣不夠了，　　所以我只好用信用卡。
Since I didn't bring enough RMB, I have no choice but to pay with my credit card.

▨▧ PRACTICE

模仿造句

Make sentences of your own by following each of the examples given.

1. 西醫無法治好這個病人的病，所以他只好 ＿＿＿＿＿＿＿＿＿＿＿＿＿＿＿＿＿＿＿。
   (Example: 去找中醫看)

2. 我因為全身疼得動不了，所以只好 ＿＿＿＿＿＿＿＿＿＿＿＿＿＿＿＿＿＿＿。
   (Example: 去試試針灸)

3. 他在中國旅遊，可是一句中國話也不會說，所以只好 ＿＿＿＿＿＿＿＿＿＿＿＿＿。
   (Example: 去請了一位會講英文的導遊)

問答

Use the word 只好… to answer the following questions.

1. 她為什麼不吃肉，光吃素？

2. 感恩节时你为什么不回家跟家人团聚？

3. 很多人已经六十多岁了，为什么还不退休呢？

翻译

Translate the following sentence into Chinese. Make sure your translation includes 结果 and 只好.

There's no effective Western treatment for chronic backaches, so, as a result, patients have no choice other than to take pain medication every day.

VII. 就算（是）…也… (jiù suàn[shì]...yě...): Even if...(Still have to...)

The conjunction 就算（就是）introduces a hypothetical circumstance, while the following clause describes an inevitable situation despite that hypothetical circumstance. or is used in the second clause.

1st clause (Hypothesis)	2nd clause
就算（是）Subject Verb phrase,	Subject 也/还是 Verb phrase

就算你不喜欢坐出租车，　　　但是为了不耽误时间，你也得坐。
Even if you don't like to take taxis, you'll have to take one in order to avoid wasting time.

就是服务员不跟你要小费，　　你还是应该给他。
Even if the attendant does not ask you for a tip, you should still give him one.

🔲 PRACTICE

连句子

Use 就算 or 就是, whichever is appropriate, to connect each pair of phrases to form a complete sentence.

1. 中药很苦　　　　吃
2. 针灸有效　　　　不想试
3. 不同意　　　　　不应该错过这个好机会

2. 感恩節時你為什麼不回家跟家人團聚？

3. 很多人已經六十多歲了，為什麼還不退休呢？

翻譯

Translate the following sentence into Chinese. Make sure your translation includes 結果 and 只好.

There's no effective Western treatment for chronic backaches, so, as a result, patients have no choice other than to take pain medication every day.

VII. 就算 (是)⋯也⋯ (jiù suàn[shì]...yě...): Even if...(Still have to...)

The conjunction 就算 (就是) introduces a hypothetical circumstance, while the following clause describes an inevitable situation despite that hypothetical circumstance. or is used in the second clause.

1st clause (Hypothesis)	2nd clause
就算 (是) Subject Verb phrase,	Subject 也/還是 Verb phrase

就算你不喜歡坐出租車，　　　但是為了不耽誤時間，你也得坐。
Even if you don't like to take taxis, you'll have to take one in order to avoid wasting time.

就是服務員不跟你要小費，　　你還是應該給他。
Even if the attendant does not ask you for a tip, you should still give him one.

⧉ PRACTICE

連句子

Use 就算 or 就是, whichever is appropriate, to connect each pair of phrases to form a complete sentence.

1. 中藥很苦　　　　吃
2. 針灸有效　　　　不想試
3. 不同意　　　　　不應該錯過這個好機會

❀ PRACTICE

模仿造句

Make a sentence of your own by following each of the examples given.

1. A: 你看过中医没有？看中医比看西医便宜。

   B: 没看过。就算 _____。

   (Example: 看中医便宜，我还是不想去)

2. A: 你有没有时间跟我打麻将？

   B: 有。就是 _____。

   (Example: 我没有时间我也要跟你打麻将)

3. A: _____，你还学不学了？

   B: 学。就是 _____。

   (Example: 跳舞，学不好我也要学)

翻译

Translate the following sentence into Chinese. Make sure your translation includes 就算 and 无论如何.

Even though the basic tenets of traditional Chinese medicine and Western medicine differ, essentially they share the same goals — no matter what, the patients' illnesses must be cured.

❧ PRACTICE

模仿造句

Make a sentence of your own by following each of the examples given.

1. A: 你看過中醫沒有？看中醫比看西醫便宜。

   B: 沒看過。就算 _____。

   (Example: 看中醫便宜，我還是不想去)

2. A: 你有沒有時間跟我打麻將？

   B: 有。就是 _____。

   (Example: 我沒有時間我也要跟你打麻將)

3. A: _____，你還學不學了？

   B: 學。就是 _____。

   (Example: 跳舞，學不好我也要學)

翻譯

Translate the following sentence into Chinese. Make sure your translation includes 就算 and 無論如何.

Even though the basic tenets of traditional Chinese medicine and Western medicine differ, essentially they share the same goals — no matter what, the patients' illnesses must be cured.

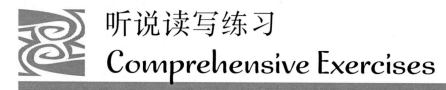

听说读写练习
Comprehensive Exercises

🎧 TASK 1. 听一听、选一选 LISTENING EXERCISES

A. Bingo

In this section, you will hear various Chinese phrases. Demonstrate your understanding of these phrases by numbering their English counterparts in the order in which you hear them.

basic principles of Chinese traditional medicine

ancient medical theories

to encourage him to use acupuncture for anesthesia

the side effects are minimal

to require surgery

after treating and regulating (the ailment)

chronic diseases and acute diseases

no harm in giving acupuncture a try

to take painkillers continually

to avoid causing a backache

the effects of ready-made medicine

the results are very good

to be extremely regretful

to write out prescriptions according to the condition of the illness

to have agreed originally

to combine traditional Chinese medicine and Western medicine

B. Matching

Listen to the sentences in Chinese and number them in the order in which you hear them.

1. 他原先想看西医，后来我劝他不妨去试试针灸。

2. 他现在不是吃中药，就是打针或者去医院作针灸。

3. 这种中药是把很多种植物矿物按一定的比例搭配熬成的。

4. 他不相信任何西药，我只好给他熬中药喝。

5. 我觉得通过中医西医结合来治疗，效果最好，副作用也小。

6. 这种成药就算是治疗慢性病的效果不错，但是对急性病不一定好。

7. 你别吃那么多止痛药，应该去看看你的腰痛是什么引起的，以免将来后悔。

8. 西医的很多药药效固然很快，但是副作用常常也不小。

9. 他根据我的病情，向我推荐了几种成药。

聽說讀寫練習
Comprehensive Exercises

🎧 🖉 TASK 1. 聽一聽、選一選 LISTENING EXERCISES

A. Bingo

In this section, you will hear various Chinese phrases. Demonstrate your understanding of these phrases by numbering their English counterparts in the order in which you hear them.

basic principles of Chinese traditional medicine

ancient medical theories

to encourage him to use acupuncture for anesthesia

the side effects are minimal

to require surgery

after treating and regulating (the ailment)

chronic diseases and acute diseases

no harm in giving acupuncture a try

to take painkillers continually

to avoid causing a backache

the effects of ready-made medicine

the results are very good

to be extremely regretful

to write out prescriptions according to the condition of the illness

to have agreed originally

to combine traditional Chinese medicine and Western medicine

B. Matching

Listen to the sentences in Chinese and number them in the order in which you hear them.

1. 他原先想看西醫，後來我勸他不妨去試試針灸。
2. 他現在不是吃中藥，就是打針或者去醫院作針灸。
3. 這種中藥是把很多種植物礦物按一定的比例搭配熬成的。
4. 他不相信任何西藥，我只好給他熬中藥喝。
5. 我覺得通過中醫西醫結合來治療，效果最好，副作用也小。
6. 這種成藥就算是治療慢性病的效果不錯，但是對急性病不一定好。
7. 你別吃那麼多止痛藥，應該去看看你的腰痛是什麼引起的，以免將來後悔。
8. 西醫的很多藥藥效固然很快，但是副作用常常也不小。
9. 他根據我的病情，向我推薦了幾種成藥。

C. Short Conversations

Listen to these short conversations. Select the correct answer for each question from the choices provided.

1. 西医/中医
2. 应该/不应该
3. 女的/男的
4. 同意/不同意
5. 相信/不相信
6. 是/不是

🎧 TASK 2. 听一听、说一说 SHORT PASSAGES

PASSAGE 1

Pre-Listening Activity

Before you begin, answer the following questions, which are designed to help you predict what will happen in the passage.

1. 你喜欢看中医还是西医？
2. 你认识的人中有没有只相信中医的？

Vocabulary

1. 中草药	Zhōngcǎoyào	*n.*	Chinese herbal medicine
2. 舌苔	shétāi	*n.*	coating or fur on the tongue
3. 病史	bìngshǐ	*n.*	medical history

Listening Activity

Now listen to the passage and answer the questions that follow. Be sure to make a voice recording on the multimedia CD-ROM explaining each of your choices.

A. Listening for new words

Did you catch all the new words in the passage?

B. Listening for the main idea

这段话主要谈的是什么？

a) 西医和中医的不同之处。
b) 赵亮和王明对中西医的看法。

C. Short Conversations

Listen to these short conversations. Select the correct answer for each question from the choices provided.

1. 西醫/中醫

2. 應該/不應該

3. 女的/男的

4. 同意/不同意

5. 相信/不相信

6. 是/不是

🎧 TASK 2. 聽一聽、說一說 SHORT PASSAGES

PASSAGE 1

Pre-Listening Activity

Before you begin, answer the following questions, which are designed to help you predict what will happen in the passage.

1. 你喜歡看中醫還是西醫？

2. 你認識的人中有沒有只相信中醫的？

Vocabulary

1. 中草藥	Zhōngcǎoyào	n.	Chinese herbal medicine
2. 舌苔	shétāi	n.	coating or fur on the tongue
3. 病史	bìngshǐ	n.	medical history

Listening Activity

Now listen to the passage and answer the questions that follow. Be sure to make a voice recording on the multimedia CD-ROM explaining each of your choices.

A. Listening for new words

Did you catch all the new words in the passage?

B. Listening for the main idea

這段話主要談的是什麼？

a) 西醫和中醫的不同之處。

b) 趙亮和王明對中西醫的看法。

c) 西医、中医的好处。

d) 西医、中医的坏处。

C. Listening for details

1. 赵亮受他爷爷和爸爸的影响很大，对不对？你怎么知道呢？

   对/不对

2. 王明根本就不理解中医的医疗方法，对不对？你怎么知道呢？

   对/不对

3. 说话的人是不是觉得赵亮和王明的看法都很对？你怎么知道呢？

   是/不是

Post-Listening Activity

Now state your opinion as you record your voice on the multimedia CD-ROM.

你同意赵亮的看法还是王明的看法？为什么？

PASSAGE 2

Pre-Listening Activity

Before you begin, answer the following questions, which are designed to help you predict what will happen in the passage.

1. 你了解不了解西医的理论？

2. 你或者你家人看过中医吗？

Listening Activity

Now listen to the passage and answer the questions that follow. Be sure to make a voice recording on the multimedia CD-ROM explaining each of your choices.

A. Listening for new words

Did you catch all the new words in the passage?

B. Listening for the main idea

这段话主要谈的是什么？

a) 中医和西医的好处和坏处。

b) 中国人对西医和中医的看法。

c) 西醫、中醫的好處。

d) 西醫、中醫的壞處。

C. Listening for details

1. 趙亮受他爺爺和爸爸的影響很大，對不對？你怎麼知道呢？

   對/不對

2. 王明根本就不理解中醫的醫療方法，對不對？你怎麼知道呢？

   對/不對

3. 說話的人是不是覺得趙亮和王明的看法都很對？你怎麼知道呢？

   是/不是

Post-Listening Activity

Now state your opinion as you record your voice on the multimedia CD-ROM.

你同意趙亮的看法還是王明的看法？為什麼？

PASSAGE 2

Pre-Listening Activity

Before you begin, answer the following questions, which are designed to help you predict what will happen in the passage.

1. 你瞭解不瞭解西醫的理論？

2. 你或者你家人看過中醫嗎？

Listening Activity

Now listen to the passage and answer the questions that follow. Be sure to make a voice recording on the multimedia CD-ROM explaining each of your choices.

A. Listening for new words

Did you catch all the new words in the passage?

B. Listening for the main idea

這段話主要談的是什麼？

a) 中醫和西醫的好處和壞處。

b) 中國人對西醫和中醫的看法。

c) 西医为什么比中医好。

d) 中医为什么比西医好。

C. Listening for details

1. 说话的人认为西医比中医好，对不对？你怎么知道呢？

   对/不对

2. 生病生了很长时间了，老是治不好，你应该看中医还是西医？为什么？

   中医/西医

3. 不管是中药还是西药都没有副作用，对不对？你怎么知道呢？

   对/不对

Post-Listening Activity

Now state your opinion as you record your voice on the multimedia CD-ROM.

你会不会去看中医？为什么？

🎧 TASK 3. 看一看、说一说、写一写 SHORT VIDEO

Pre-Listening Activity

Before you begin, answer the following questions, which are designed to help you predict what will happen in the video.

1. 你有病的时候愿意不愿意吃药？为什么？

2. 如果西药治不好你的病，你愿意不愿意试试中药？

Vocabulary

1. 脸色	liǎnsè	*phr.*	complexion; facial expression
2. 食物中毒	shíwùzhòngdú	*phr.*	food poisoning
3. 见效	jiànxiào	*v.*	to take effect, show results (of medicines,etc.)
4. 涩	sè	*adj.*	puckery
5. 既然…就	jìrán…jiù	*conj.*	since, now that
6. 证明	zhèngmíng	*v.*	to prove, to testify

Listening Activity

Now listen to the dialogue and then answer the questions that follow. Be sure to make a voice recording explaining each of your choices on the multimedia CD-ROM.

c) 西醫為什麼比中醫好。

d) 中醫為什麼比西醫好。

C. Listening for details

1. 說話的人認為西醫比中醫好，對不對？你怎麼知道呢？

   對/不對

2. 生病生了很長時間了，老是治不好，你應該看中醫還是西醫？為什麼？

   中醫/西醫

3. 不管是中藥還是西藥都沒有副作用，對不對？你怎麼知道呢？

   對/不對

Post-Listening Activity

Now state your opinion as you record your voice on the multimedia CD-ROM.

　　你會不會去看中醫？為什麼？

🎧 TASK 3. 看一看、說一說、寫一寫 SHORT VIDEO

Pre-Listening Activity

Before you begin, answer the following questions, which are designed to help you predict what will happen in the video.

1. 你有病的時候願意不願意吃藥？為什麼？

2. 如果西藥治不好你的病，你願意不願意試試中藥？

Vocabulary

1. 臉色	liǎnsè	*phr.*	complexion; facial expression
2. 食物中毒	shíwùzhòngdú	*phr.*	food poisoning
3. 見效	jiànxiào	*v.*	to take effect, show results (of medicines,etc.)
4. 澀	sè	*adj.*	puckery
5. 既然…就	jìrán…jiù	*conj.*	since, now that
6. 證明	zhèngmíng	*v.*	to prove, to testify

Listening Activity

Now listen to the dialogue and then answer the questions that follow. Be sure to make a voice recording explaining each of your choices on the multimedia CD-ROM.

A. Listening for new words

Did you catch all the new words in the dialogue?

B. Listening for the main idea

这段话主要谈的是什么？

a) 说话的人在讨论他们自己是喜欢吃中药还是喜欢吃西药。

b) 说话的两个人在谈中药和西药的相同之处。

c) 说话的两个人对西药和中药的看法有很多相同之处。

d) 说话的两个人对西医和中医理论的看法有很多不同之处。

C. Listening for details

1. 那个女的生了病以后只吃中药不吃西药，是不是？为什么？

   是/不是

2. 说话的那个男的认为得慢性病以后应该吃西药还是吃中药？为什么？

   西药/中药

3. 两个人争了半天，最后说话的那个女的相信中医了没有？你怎么知道呢？

   相信/不相信

Post-Listening Activity

Now state your opinion as you record your voice on the multimedia CD-ROM, and write a summary of the dialogue.

请你用自己的话说一说这段对话都讲了些什么？

⌒🎧 TASK 4. 读一读、写一写 READING EXERCISES

This section consists of two parts: Short Stories and Authentic Material.

A. Short Stories

After reading each of the two Chinese 成语故事, respond in Chinese to the questions that follow.

成语故事：病入膏肓

　　古时候有一个国王生了病，全国的名医都被请来给国王看病，但是谁也治不好国王的病。后来听说秦国有一个非常有名的医生，国王就马上派人去请。那个医生还没有到，国王就做了一个梦。他梦见两个坏孩子。一个坏孩子说："有一个很好的医生要来看病，恐怕要伤害我们，我们躲到什么地方去呢？"另一个坏孩子

A. Listening for new words

Did you catch all the new words in the dialogue?

B. Listening for the main idea

這段話主要談的是什麼？

a) 說話的人在討論他們自己是喜歡吃中藥還是喜歡吃西藥。

b) 說話的兩個人在談中藥和西藥的相同之處。

c) 說話的兩個人對西藥和中藥的看法有很多相同之處。

d) 說話的兩個人對西醫和中醫理論的看法有很多不同之處。

C. Listening for details

1. 那個女的生了病以後只吃中藥不吃西藥，是不是？為什麼？

   是／不是

2. 說話的那個男的認為 得慢性病以後應該吃西藥還是吃中藥？為什麼？

   西藥／中藥

3. 兩個人爭了半天，最後說話的那個女的相信中醫了沒有？你怎麼知道呢？

   相信／不相信

Post-Listening Activity

Now state your opinion as you record your voice on the multimedia CD-ROM, and write a summary of the dialogue.

請你用自己的話說一說這段對話都講了些什麼？

🎧 TASK 4. 讀一讀、寫一寫 READING EXERCISES

This section consists of two parts: Short Stories and Authentic Material.

A. Short Stories

After reading each of the two Chinese 成語故事, respond in Chinese to the questions that follow.

成語故事：病入膏肓

古時候有一個國王生了病，全國的名醫都被請來給國王看病，但是誰也治不好國王的病。後來聽說秦國有一個非常有名的醫生，國王就馬上派人去請。那個醫生還沒有到，國王就做了一個夢。他夢見兩個壞孩子。一個壞孩子說："有一個很好的醫生要來看病，恐怕要傷害我們，我們躲到什麼地方去呢？"另一個壞孩子说：”你看这个地方是心，那个地方是腹，心和腹中间的那个地方叫膏肓。我们躲在那儿，再好的医生也伤害不到我们，你放心吧。”

第二天早上医生到了以后，给这个国王看了病，说："您的病已经入膏肓了。因为针灸，汤药都达不到那个地方，所以没有办法治了。"国王听了说："这真是一位高明的医生。"于是就送了他很多礼物，让他回去了。过了不久，国王真的病死了。

Vocabulary

1.	病入膏肓	bìng rù gāo huāng		
	膏	gāo		fat on top of the heart
	肓	huāng		the area between the heart and the diaphragm
	膏肓	gāo huāng		represents an area medicine can not reach, or where diseases are thought to be beyond cure
2.	国王	guówáng	*n.*	king
3.	秦国	Qínguó	*prop. n.*	the state of Qin
4.	梦	mèng	*n.*	dream
			v.	to dream
5.	伤害	shānghài	*v.*	to harm
6.	躲	duǒ	*v.*	to hide
7.	腹	fù	*n.*	abdomen, stomach
8.	高明	gāomíng	*adj.*	brilliant

Questions

1. 请用自己的话讲一讲"病入膏肓"是什么意思。
2. 你觉得国王请的医生棒不棒，为什么？
3. 你能用"病入膏肓"造句子吗？

成语故事：杯弓蛇影

古时候，有个人叫杜宣。有一天，一个朋友请他去他们家喝酒。他拿起酒杯来的时候，看见酒里边有一条小蛇。他很害怕，不想喝，但是，他又不敢不喝。最后說："你看這個地方是心，那個地方是腹，心和腹中間的那個地方叫膏肓。我們躲在那兒，再好的醫生也傷害不到我們，你放心吧。"

　　第二天早上醫生到了以後，給這個國王看了病，說："您的病已經入膏肓了。因為針灸，湯藥都達不到那個地方，所以沒有辦法治了。"國王聽了說："這真是一位高明的醫生。"於是就送了他很多禮物，讓他回去了。過了不久，國王真的病死了。

Vocabulary

1. 病入膏肓	bìng rù gāo huāng		
膏	gāo		fat on top of the heart
肓	huāng		the area between the heart and the diaphragm
膏肓	gāo huāng		represents an area medicine can not reach, or where diseases are thought to be beyond cure
2. 國王	guówáng	*n.*	king
3. 秦國	Qínguó	*prop. n.*	the state of Qin
4. 夢	mèng	*n.*	dream
		v.	to dream
5. 傷害	shānghài	*v.*	to harm
6. 躲	duǒ	*v.*	to hide
7. 腹	fù	*n.*	abdomen, stomach
8. 高明	gāomíng	*adj.*	brilliant

Questions

1. 請用自己的話講一講"病入膏肓"是什麼意思。
2. 你覺得國王請的醫生棒不棒，為什麼？
3. 你能用"病入膏肓"造句子嗎？

成語故事：杯弓蛇影

　　古時候，有個人叫杜宣。有一天，一個朋友請他去他們家喝酒。他拿起酒杯來的時候，看見酒裏邊有一條小蛇。他很害怕，不想喝，但是，他又不敢不喝。最後他勉强把酒喝下去了。但是，回家以后，就开始觉得肚子疼，并且疼得非常厉害，连饭也不能吃。医生来给他看了病，做了针灸，吃了汤药，各种治疗方法都用了，但是怎么也治不好他的病。

后来，他的这位朋友来看他。他告诉他朋友他的病的原因。他的朋友想了半天，还是不明白他的酒杯里边怎么会有一条小蛇。所以他的这位朋友又把他请到家里，像上次一样又给他倒了一杯酒。这时，他们才发现，酒杯里的小蛇原来是墙上挂着的一把弓箭的影子。

杜宣回家以后，很快病就好了。

Vocabulary

1. 杯弓蛇影	bēi gōng shé yǐng		
弓		*n.*	bow
蛇		*n.*	snake
影		*b.f.*	shadow
2. 杜宣	Dù Xuān	*prop. n.*	person's name
3. 勉强	miǎnqiǎng	*adv.*	reluctantly
4. 弓箭	gōngjiàn	*n.*	bow and arrow
5. 影子	yǐngzi	*n.*	shadow

Questions

1. 请用自己的话讲一讲"杯弓蛇影"是什么意思。

2. 你觉得杜宣为什么病了？

3. 你从"杯弓蛇影"的故事中学到了什么？

B. Authentic Material

In this section, you will be exposed to some authentic materials used in China. Read the following Web page about acupuncture, and answer the questions. (http://www.acusky.com/)

Questions

1. 一个人对针灸完全不了解，可以上什么网页查看？

2. "针灸"又被叫做什么？

3. 一个人得了病，想用针灸治疗，他可以查看哪个网页？

他勉強把酒喝下去了。但是，回家以後，就開始覺得肚子疼，並且疼得非常厲害，連飯也不能吃。醫生來給他看了病，做了針灸，吃了湯藥，各種治療方法都用了，但是怎麼也治不好他的病。

後來，他的這位朋友來看他。他告訴他朋友他的病的原因。他的朋友想了半天，還是不明白他的酒杯裏邊怎麼會有一條小蛇。所以他的這位朋友又把他請到家裏，像上次一樣又給他倒了一杯酒。這時，他們才發現，酒杯裏的小蛇原來是牆上掛著的一把弓箭的影子。

杜宣回家以後，很快病就好了。

Vocabulary

1. 杯弓蛇影	bēi gōng shé yǐng		
弓		*n.*	bow
蛇		*n.*	snake
影		*b.f.*	shadow
2. 杜宣	Dù Xuān	*prop. n.*	person's name
3. 勉強	miǎnqiǎng	*adv.*	reluctantly
4. 弓箭	gōngjiàn	*n.*	bow and arrow
5. 影子	yǐngzi	*n.*	shadow

Questions

1. 請用自己的話講一講"杯弓蛇影"是什麼意思。
2. 你覺得杜宣為什麼病了？
3. 你從"杯弓蛇影"的故事中學到了什麼？

B. Authentic Material

In this section, you will be exposed to some authentic materials used in China. Read the following Web page about acupuncture, and answer the questions. (http://www.acusky.com/)

Questions

1. 一個人對針灸完全不瞭解，可以上什麼網頁查看？
2. "針灸"又被叫做什麼？
3. 一個人得了病，想用針灸治療，他可以查看哪個網頁？

欢迎你

进入本站论坛

针灸疗法是祖国医学遗产的一部分，也是我国特有的一种民族医疗方法。千百年来，对保卫健康、繁衍民族，有过卓越的贡献，直到现在，仍然担当着这个任务，为广大群众所信仰。据古代文献《山海经》和《内经》，有用"石镵"刺破痈肿的记载，以及《孟子》："七年之病，求三年之艾"的说法，再根据近年在我国各地所挖出的历史文物来考证，"针灸疗法"的起源，可能就在石器时

● 最近更新 专病专治—蜂针疗法 ●   更新
时间 2005-09-23

👁 **初识针灸**

内容介绍

对于" 东方神针 "你知道多少？这个栏目的知识并不难懂，你会从各个方面对针灸疗法和祖国的传统医学有一个大概的了解……

📖 **基础理论**

内容介绍

祖国医学博大精深，你如果想系统的学习一下针灸方面的理论知识，就进来看看，包含《经络学》、《腧穴学》、《刺灸法》的内容……

👥 **专病专治**

内容介绍

联合国世界卫生组织提出了**43**种推荐针灸治疗的适应病症，这里对针灸科最常见的几类疾病的症状、诊断、治疗方法等作了介绍，可以作临床治疗的参考之用……

🖾 **论坛留言**

内容介绍

如果您有什么关于针灸学知识的问题，如果有什么疾病的治疗需要针灸疗法的帮助，如果您对本网站有什么意见建议…欢迎进入

● 欢迎参加本站调查 ●

请问您属于以下哪一类访问者？

○ 医学专业人士
○ 医学业余爱好者
○ 寻医问药者
○ 随便逛逛
○ 其他

提交　查看结果

针灸学是一门古老而神奇的科学，早在公元6世纪，针灸学术便开始传播到国外，目前，在亚洲、西欧、东欧、拉美等已有120多个国家和地区应用针灸术为本国人民治病，不少国家还先后成立了针灸学术团体、针灸教育机构和研究机构。著名的巴黎大学医学院就开设有针灸课。据报道，针灸治疗有效的病种达307种，其中效果显著的就有100多种。1980年，联合国世

🎧 TASK 5. 想一想、说一说 PRESENTATION

Please pick one of the following for your presentation.

A. Individual Presentation

You are having a conversation with a cousin in the U.S. who is studying to become a doctor. Recommend that (s)he take a year or two to learn something about Chinese medicine and explain the advantages of combining the two types of medicine.

●最近更新 专病专治—蜂针疗法 ●　　　　更新
时间 2005-09-23

👁 初識針灸
内容介紹

對於 " 東方神針 " 你知道多少？這個欄目的知識
並不難懂，你會從各個方面對針灸療法和祖國的
傳統 醫學有一個大概的了解 ……

🖼 基礎理論
内容介紹

祖國醫學博大精深，你如果想系統的學習一下針
灸方面的理論知識，就進來看看，包含《經絡學》、
《腧穴學》、《刺灸法》的内容 ……

👥 專病專治
内容介紹

聯合國世界衛生組織提出了**43**种推薦針灸治療的
適應病症，這裡對針灸科最常見的幾類疾病的症
狀、診斷、治療方法等作了介紹，可以作臨床治
療的參考之用 ……

👥 論壇留言
内容介紹

如果您有什麼關於針灸學知識的問題，如果有什
麼疾病的治療需要針灸療法的幫助，如果您對本
網站有什麼意見建議…歡迎進入

🎧 TASK 5. 想一想、説一説 PRESENTATION

Please pick one of the following for your presentation.

A. Individual Presentation

You are having a conversation with a cousin in the U.S. who is studying to become a doctor. Recommend that (s)he take a year or two to learn something about Chinese medicine and explain the advantages of combining the two types of medicine.

B. Group Presentation

Setting: At a drugstore

Cast: Two friends

Situation: Someone has been feeling sick and has brought a friend to the drugstore with him/her to buy medicine. The sick person is opposed to the use of Chinese medicine, so (s)he is horrified to find that there is only Chinese medicine at the drugstore. Why don't they have Western medicine? A debate erupts about the advantages and disadvantages of traditional Chinese medicine. Construct a dialogue of at least twelve sentences between the two friends. Why is Chinese traditional medicine better or worse than Western medicine? Be sure to include vocabulary and grammar learned in this lesson.

TASK 6. 想一想、写一写 COMPOSITION

Search the Web and find information on any country other than China that uses Chinese medicine. Write a brief summary of your findings.

B. Group Presentation

Setting: At a drugstore

Cast: Two friends

Situation: Someone has been feeling sick and has brought a friend to the drugstore with him/her to buy medicine. The sick person is opposed to the use of Chinese medicine, so (s)he is horrified to find that there is only Chinese medicine at the drugstore. Why don't they have Western medicine? A debate erupts about the advantages and disadvantages of traditional Chinese medicine. Construct a dialogue of at least twelve sentences between the two friends. Why is Chinese traditional medicine better or worse than Western medicine? Be sure to include vocabulary and grammar learned in this lesson.

∩ ✤ TASK 6. 想一想、寫一寫 COMPOSITION

Search the Web and find information on any country other than China that uses Chinese medicine. Write a brief summary of your findings.

45
教育
The Chinese Education System

In this lesson you will:

■ Talk about the Chinese education system.

■ Argue either for or against certain aspects of the Chinese education system.

■ Compare the Chinese education system with that of your own country.

中国的学校有私立和公立两种：私立学校一般是学生通过了考试交了钱即可被录取。公立学校分为普通学校和重点学校两种。普通学校录取的是住在附近的学生。重点学校录取的是通过考试选出来的学生。中国的教育体系来自于科举制度，以考试为主。中国学校都是通过考试来决定每年学生升级还是留级。连初中和高中的录取以及上什么学校一般也都是以考试分数来决定。学生的考试成绩有时还会影响到学生交多少学费。例如，在一些重点学校，考试成绩好的尖子学生不仅可以不交学费，而且还可以拿奖学金。考分高的学生交的学费要低于刚达到录取线的学生，有时，差几分的学生，如果能走后门，又愿意多交钱，也可以上重点学校。所以，学生竞争激烈，无论是几年

Xueying Wang

Parents anxiously wait outside a middle school as their children take high school entrance exams.

45
教育
The Chinese Education System

In this lesson you will:

■ Talk about the Chinese education system.
■ Argue either for or against certain aspects of the Chinese education system.
■ Compare the Chinese education system with that of your own country.

中國的學校有私立和公立兩種：私立學校一般是學生通過了考試交了錢即可被錄取。公立學校分為普通學校和重點學校兩種。普通學校錄取的是住在附近的學生。重點學校錄取的是通過考試選出來的學生。中國的教育體係來自於科舉制度，以考試為主。中國學校都是通過考試來決定每年學生升級還是留級。連初中和高中的錄取以及上什麼學校一般也都是以考試分數來決定。學生的考試成績有時還會影響到學生交多少學費。例如，在一些重點學校，考試成績好的尖子學生不僅可以不交學費，而且還可以拿獎學金。考分高的學生交的學費要低於剛達到錄取線的學生，有時，差幾分的學生，如果能走後門，又願意多交錢，也可以上重點學校。所以，學生競爭激烈，無論是幾年

Parents anxiously wait outside a middle school as their children take high school entrance exams.

259

级，都必须专心致志[1]，努力学习，家长、老师、以及社会也都以学生的成绩来衡量一个学生的好坏。为了学习进步，为了不让父母失望，学生常常学到深夜，压力极大。

考大学被称之为高考，在中国是一件大事。高考是全国统一考试，简称统考，即全中国在同一天，同一个时间，考同一门课。高考结束以后，每个学校的录取分数线都不一样，都是由各省规定的。重点大学的录取分数线要高于普通大学。除了大学以外，还有广播电视大学、函授大学等等。名落孙山[2]的学生可以再上一年补习班，第二年重考。一天，李丽莉和吴文德、陈小云对中国教育制度进行讨论。他们谈到了中国和美国教育制度的不同之处。下面请听他们的对话：

吴文德：我听说中国现在有了私立学校，但是好学生都不上私立学校。难道公立学校比私立学校还好吗？

陈小云：是啊。公立的重点学校非常好，师资是一流的，学生也都是经过考试挑选出来的。我们前几十年没有私立学校。很多望子成龙的家长为了让孩子受到更好的教育，愿意多出学费，后来终于有了私立学校。但是他们学生的来源以及师资水平都远不如公立的重点学校。

李丽莉：我今天跟一个学生聊天，他告诉我中国的高中生在申请大学时，只可以报三个志愿。如果考生没被第一志愿录取，当申请材料被转到另外两个学校时，那儿的招生人数基本上满了。他们上大学的可能性就非常小。

吴文德：那太危险了。除非第一志愿被录取，否则就有可能错过上大学的机会。

A banner encouraging students to score well on the exams.

級，都必須專心致志[1]，努力學習，家長、老師、以及社會也都以學生的成績來衡量一個學生的好壞。為了學習進步、為了不讓父母失望，學生常常學到深夜，壓力極大。

考大學被稱之為高考，在中國是一件大事。高考是全國統一考試，簡稱統考，即全中國在同一天，同一個時間，考同一門課。高考結束以後，每個學校的錄取分數線都不一樣，都是由各省規定的。重點大學的錄取分數線要高於普通大學。除了大學以外，還有廣播電視大學，函授大學等等。名落孫山[2]的學生可以再上一年補習班，第二年重考。一天，李麗莉和吳文德、陳小雲對中國教育制度進行討論。他們談到了中國和美國教育制度的不同之處。下面請聽他們的對話：

吳文德：我聽說中國現在有了私立學校，但是好學生都不上私立學校。難道公立學校比私立學校還好嗎？

陳小雲：是啊。公立的重點學校非常好，師資是一流的，學生也都是經過考試挑選出來的。我們前幾十年沒有私立學校。很多望子成龍的家長為了讓孩子受到更好的教育，願意多出學費，後來終於有了私立學校。但是他們學生的來源以及師資水平都遠不如公立的重點學校。

李麗莉：我今天跟一個學生聊天，他告訴我中國的高中生在申請大學時，只可以報三個志願。如果考生沒被第一志願錄取，當申請材料被轉到另外兩個學校時，那兒的招生人數基本上滿了。他們上大學的可能性就非常小。

吳文德：那太危險了。除非第一志願被錄取，否則就有可能錯過上大學的機會。

A banner encouraging students to score well on the exams.

This middle school proudly displays its premier status at the front gate.

陈小云：对啊。所以，高考对学生压力很大。

李丽莉：我还听说，在申请大学的同时，学生得填写自己的专业。录取以后，专业就定了，一般不允许换专业。

吴文德：我上大学的时候，一会儿想当律师，一会儿想学医，一会儿想搞国际关系。直到大学二年级才把专业定了下来。没上大学就定专业，那不是赶鸭子上架吗？

李丽莉：像你这样的人在中国读学士是没门儿的。

吴文德：你可别小看了我。说不定我将来还要来中国读硕士或博士呢？

陈小云：行了，别逗能了。现代的社会是行行出状元[3]。读学位并不是唯一的出路。

Notes

1. 专心致志   (zhuān xīn zhì zhì)

To focus one's energy on what one is doing; (lit.) to focus one's heart and mind on one thing. For more information about this phrase, please see Task 4 in 听说读写练习.

2. 名落孙山   (míng luò Sūn Shān)

Used as a euphemism to describe someone who did not pass an exam; (lit.) one's rank/grade (in an examination) falls behind that of Sun Shan (who barely passed his exam). For more information about this phrase, please see Task 4 in 听说读写练习.

This middle school proudly displays its premier status at the front gate.

陳小雲：對啊。所以，高考對學生壓力很大。

李麗莉：我還聽說，在申請大學的同時，學生得填寫自己的專業。錄取以後，專業就定了，一般不允許換專業。

吳文德：我上大學的時候，一會兒想當律師，一會兒想學醫，一會兒想搞國際關係。直到大學二年級才把專業定了下來。沒上大學就定專業，那不是趕鴨子上架嗎？

李麗莉：像你這樣的人在中國讀學士是沒門兒的。

吳文德：你可別小看了我。說不定我將來還要來中國讀碩士或博士呢？

陳小雲：行了，別逞能了。現代的社會是行行出狀元[3]。讀學位並不是唯一的出路。

Notes

1. 專心致志　(zhuān xīn zhì zhì)

To focus one's energy on what one is doing; (lit.) to focus one's heart and mind on one thing. For more information about this phrase, please see Task 4 in 聽說讀寫練習.

2. 名落孫山　(míng luò Sūn Shān)

Used as a euphemism to describe someone who did not pass an exam; (lit.) one's rank/grade (in an examination) falls behind that of Sun Shan (who barely passed his exam). For more information about this phrase, please see Task 4 in 聽說讀寫練習.

3. **行行出状元**   (hángháng chū zhuàngyuán)
Every profession can have outstanding performers.

行行	hángháng	*n.*	every field, profession, occupation
出	chū	*v.*	to emerge
状元	zhuàngyuán	*n.*	the person who earns the highest grade in the imperial examination system

课文问答 *Questions and Answers*

1. 中国教育制度的特点是什么？结果怎么样？
2. 请你比较一下儿中国的公立学校和私立学校。
3. 在中国，大学生怎么定专业？跟你们国家有什么不同之处？
4. 中国的教育制度和你们国家的教育制度有什么相同之处，有什么不同之处？你更喜欢哪个国家的教育制度？为什么？

Studying for exams.

 生词表
Vocabulary

Character	Pinyin	Part of Speech	English Definition
1. 教育	jiàoyù	*n.*	education

普及教育在中国是一个很重要的问题。

| | | *v.* | to educate, to teach |

那个妈妈不知道怎么教育自己的孩子。

3. 行行出狀元　(hángháng chū zhuàngyuán)

Every profession can have outstanding performers.

行行	hángháng	*n.*	every field, profession, occupation
出	chū	*v.*	to emerge
狀元	zhuàngyuán	*n.*	the person who earns the highest grade in the imperial examination system

課文問答 *Questions and Answers*

1. 中國教育制度的特點是什麼？結果怎麼樣？

2. 請你比較一下兒中國的公立學校和私立學校。

3. 在中國，大學生怎麼定專業？跟你們國家有什麼不同之處？

4. 中國的教育制度和你們國家的教育制度有什麼相同之處，有什麼不同之處？你更喜歡哪個國家的教育制度？為什麼？

Studying for exams.

Chris Vee

 生詞表
Vocabulary

Character	Pinyin	Part of Speech	English Definition
1. 教育	jiàoyù	*n.*	education

普及教育在中國是一個很重要的問題。

| | | *v.* | to educate, to teach |

那個媽媽不知道怎麼教育自己的孩子。

2. 公立　　　　gōnglì　　　*adj.*　　　　public; (lit.) publicly owned/established

中国公立学校的教育水平都很高吗？

3. 即　　　　　jí　　　　　*adv.*　　　　namely, that is, thence; (lit.) the classical Chinese word for 就 or 就是

你吃了药以后，即可去休息。

4. 普通　　　　pǔtōng　　　*adj.*　　　　ordinary, common, average

这个地方的房子很普通。

5. 重点　　　　zhòngdiǎn　　*n.*　　　　the most important (point, center, etc.)

你为什么一定要上重点高中？

6. 体系　　　　tǐxì　　　　　*n.*　　　　system, structure

大学只是教育体系的一个部分。

7. 来自于　　　láizì yú　　　*phr.*　　　to originate from

我们的学生来自于世界各地。

来自　　　　　　　　　　　*v. comp.*　　to originate from
于　　　　　　　　　　　　*prep.*　　　from

8. 科举　　　　kējǔ　　　　*n.*　　　　imperial civil service examination system

你给我讲一讲科举是什么意思，好吗？

9. 制度　　　　zhìdù　　　　*n.*　　　　rules, regulations, institution, system

你觉得中国的教育制度有些什么问题？

10. 以…为　　　yǐ…wéi　　　*phr.*　　　to take...as, to regard...as, to treat...as

学生应该以学习为主，不应该以工作为主。

以　　　　　　　　　　　　*prep.*　　　relying, taking, using, by means of
为　　　　　　　　　　　　*v.*　　　　to be

11. 升级　　　　shēng jí　　*v. obj.*　　to rise to a higher level, to rise to another grade

我学习虽然不好，但是升级应该没有问题？

12. 留级　　　　liú jí　　　　*v. obj.*　　to be kept back a grade, to fail to proceed to a higher level

你们学校每年有没有学生留级？

13. 学费　　　　xuéfèi　　　　*n.*　　　　school fees, tuition

我想自己挣钱交学费。

14. 不仅　　　　bùjǐn　　　　*adv.*　　　not only

他不仅想上大学，而且想上最好的重点大学。

2. 公立   gōnglì   *adj.*   public; (lit.) publicly owned/established

中國公立學校的教育水平都很高嗎？

3. 即   jí   *adv.*   namely, that is, thence; (lit.) the classical Chinese word for 就 or 就是

你吃了藥以後，即可去休息。

4. 普通   pǔtōng   *adj.*   ordinary, common, average

這個地方的房子很普通。

5. 重點   zhòngdiǎn   *n.*   the most important (point, center, etc.)

你為什麼一定要上重點高中？

6. 體系   tǐxì   *n.*   system, structure

大學只是教育體系的一個部分。

7. 來自於   láizì yú   *phr.*   to originate from

我們的學生來自於世界各地。

來自   *v. comp.*   to originate from
於   *prep.*   from

8. 科舉   kējǔ   *n.*   imperial civil service examination system

你給我講一講科舉是什麼意思，好嗎？

9. 制度   zhìdù   *n.*   rules, regulations, institution, system

你覺得中國的教育制度有些什麼問題？

10. 以⋯為   yǐ...wéi   *phr.*   to take...as, to regard...as, to treat...as

學生應該以學習為主，不應該以工作為主。

以   *prep.*   relying, taking, using, by means of
為   *v.*   to be

11. 升級   shēng jí   *v. obj.*   to rise to a higher level, to rise to another grade

我學習雖然不好，但是升級應該沒有問題？

12. 留級   liú jí   *v. obj.*   to be kept back a grade, to fail to proceed to a higher level

你們學校每年有沒有學生留級？

13. 學費   xuéfèi   *n.*   school fees, tuition

我想自己掙錢交學費。

14. 不僅   bùjǐn   *adv.*   not only

他不僅想上大學，而且想上最好的重點大學。

| 仅 | | *b.f.* | (lit.) the classical Chinese word for 只 |

15. （分数）线   (fēnshù) xiàn   *n.*   the cutoff point for admission to schools
这个学校的录取分数线比别的学校的都要高。

| 线 | | *n.* | thread, line |

16. 竞争   jìngzhēng   *v.*   to compete
你为什么总要跟别人竞争呢？

| | | *n.* | competition |
没有竞争就没有意思。

17. 激烈   jīliè   *adj.*   intense, fierce
考大学竞争是不是总是这么激烈？

18. 专心   zhuānxīn   *v. obj.*   to focus one's mind/heart, to concentrate
我觉得最重要的是自己专心学习，不是去跟别人竞争。

19. 努力   nǔlì   *adj.*   to exert one's strength, to exert oneself
只要你努力，就一定能考上大学。

| | | *adv.* | hard |
希望你以后努力学习。

| | | *n.* | effort |
你的努力没有浪费。

20. 以及   yǐjí   *conj.*   including, going as far as
所有的学生以及老师都觉得这次考试太难了。

21. 衡量   héngliáng   *v.*   to measure, to gauge
你觉得一个学生的成绩应该拿什么来衡量？

22. 进步   jìnbù   *v.*   to make progress
在朋友们的帮助下，他的学习进步了。

| | | *n.* | progress |
今年这个孩子的成绩有了很大的进步。

23. 父母   fùmǔ   *n.*   parents
你父母最近还好吗？

24. 失望   shīwàng   *v. obj.*   to feel disappointed; (lit.) to lose hope
结婚以后，他非常失望。

| 僅 | | b.f. | (lit.) the classical Chinese word for 只 |

15. （分數）線　　(fēnshù) xiàn　　n.　　the cutoff point for admission to schools

這個學校的錄取分數線比別的學校的都要高。

| 線 | | n. | thread, line |

16. 競爭　　jìngzhēng　　v.　　to compete

你為什麼總要跟別人競爭呢？

| | | n. | competition |

沒有競爭就沒有意思。

17. 激烈　　jīliè　　adj.　　intense, fierce

考大學競爭是不是總是這麼激烈？

18. 專心　　zhuānxīn　　v. obj.　　to focus one's mind/heart, to concentrate

我覺得最重要的是自己專心學習，不是去跟別人競爭。

19. 努力　　nǔlì　　adj.　　to exert one's strength, to exert oneself

只要你努力，就一定能考上大學。

| | | adv. | hard |

希望你以後努力學習。

| | | n. | effort |

你的努力沒有浪費。

20. 以及　　yǐjí　　conj.　　including, going as far as

所有的學生以及老師都覺得這次考試太難了。

21. 衡量　　héngliáng　　v.　　to measure, to gauge

你覺得一個學生的成績應該拿什麼來衡量？

22. 進步　　jìnbù　　v.　　to make progress

在朋友們的幫助下，他的學習進步了。

| | | n. | progress |

今年這個孩子的成績有了很大的進步。

23. 父母　　fùmǔ　　n.　　parents

你父母最近還好嗎？

24. 失望　　shīwàng　　v. obj.　　to feel disappointed; (lit.) to lose hope

結婚以後，他非常失望。

25. 压力　　　　　yālì　　　　　　*n.*　　　　　　　pressure

我父母给我的压力太大了。

26. 统一　　　　　tǒngyī　　　　　*adv.*　　　　　　in a unified way, all together

明天我们几个学校是不是统一考试？

27. 规定　　　　　guīdìng　　　　*v.*　　　　　　　to set as a rule

他父母规定他每天晚上一定要学习五个小时。

　　　　　　　　　　　　　　　　n.　　　　　　　rule, regulation

那是学校的规定。

28. 进行　　　　　jìnxíng　　　　*v.*　　　　　　　to carry on

专家对中国的考试制度进行了研究。

29. 讨论　　　　　tǎolùn　　　　　*v.*　　　　　　　to discuss

这个问题我们应该讨论讨论再做决定。

　　　　　　　　　　　　　　　　n.　　　　　　　discussion

这次的讨论对我很有帮助。

30. 难道　　　　　nándào　　　　*adv.*　　　　　　(used in a rhetorical question) could it be possible that...?

难道你还想再上一次大学吗？

31. 师资　　　　　shīzī　　　　　*n.*　　　　　　　faculty of an educational institution

这个学校的师资怎么样？

32. 一流　　　　　yīliú　　　　　*adj.*　　　　　　first-rate, first-class

这儿的学生都是一流的。

33. 挑选　　　　　tiāoxuǎn　　　*v.*　　　　　　　to pick and select

这些书有的有用，有的没用，你应该挑选挑选。

34. 终于　　　　　zhōngyú　　　*adv.*　　　　　　finally, at last

他今年终于考上大学了。

35. 来源　　　　　láiyuán　　　　*n.*　　　　　　　origin, source

他父母想了解一下儿这个学校的师资来源。

36. 不如　　　　　bùrú　　　　　*conj.*　　　　　　not as good as

你去北京逛商店不如去上海。

25. 壓力   yālì   *n.*   pressure
我父母給我的壓力太大了。

26. 統一   tǒngyī   *adv.*   in a unified way, all together
明天我們幾個學校是不是統一考試？

27. 規定   guīdìng   *v.*   to set as a rule
他父母規定他每天晚上一定要學習五個小時。
    n.   rule, regulation
那是學校的規定。

28. 進行   jìnxíng   *v.*   to carry on
專家對中國的考試制度進行了研究。

29. 討論   tǎolùn   *v.*   to discuss
這個問題我們應該討論討論再做決定。
    n.   discussion
這次的討論對我很有幫助。

30. 難道   nándào   *adv.*   (used in a rhetorical question) could it be possible that...?
難道你還想再上一次大學嗎？

31. 師資   shīzī   *n.*   faculty of an educational institution
這個學校的師資怎麼樣？

32. 一流   yīliú   *adj.*   first-rate, first-class
這兒的學生都是一流的。

33. 挑選   tiāoxuǎn   *v.*   to pick and select
這些書有的有用，有的沒用，你應該挑選挑選。

34. 終於   zhōngyú   *adv.*   finally, at last
他今年終於考上大學了。

35. 來源   láiyuán   *n.*   origin, source
他父母想瞭解一下兒這個學校的師資來源。

36. 不如   bùrú   *conj.*   not as good as
你去北京逛商店不如去上海。

37. 志愿   zhìyuàn   *n.*   preference (when choosing a vocation, an academic discipline, a profession, a career); (lit.) aspiration

今年你报了哪几个志愿？

38. 材料   cáiliào   *n.*   building material, material, data, information

你申请大学的材料都准备好了吗？

39. 招生   zhāo shēng   *v. obj.*   to recruit students

我们学校明年要从全国各地招生。

40. 人数   rénshù   *n.*   number of people

这个大学今年的新生人数比去年的多。

41. 基本上   jīběn shàng   *adv.*   basically, generally speaking

第四十五课的练习我基本上已经做完了。

42. 性   xìng   *b.f.*   -ness, nature

我觉得我考上北京大学的可能性不大。

43. 危险   wēixiǎn   *adj.*   dangerous, risky

你开车开得那么快，太危险了。

                                        n.   danger, risk

那边有危险，别过去了。

44. 除非···否则   chúfēi...fǒuzé   *conj.*   unless...otherwise...

除非你努力，否则你考不上北京大学。

45. 错过   cuòguò   *v.*   to miss (an opportunity)

你别错过了去日本工作的机会。

46. 同时   tóngshí   *n.*   (at) the same time

在上大学的同时，我还有两个工作。

47. 专业   zhuānyè   *n.*   profession, area of specialization

你以后想搞什么专业？

48. 年级   niánjí   *n.*   grade, year (in school)

你是几年级的学生？

49. 学位   xuéwèi   *n.*   academic degree

拿了学位以后我就想去中国工作。

37. 志願　　zhìyuàn　　*n.*　　preference (when choosing a vocation, an academic discipline, a profession, a career); (lit.) aspiration

今年你報了哪幾個志願？

38. 材料　　cáiliào　　*n.*　　building material, material, data, information

你申請大學的材料都準備好了嗎？

39. 招生　　zhāo shēng　　*v. obj.*　　to recruit students

我們學校明年要從全國各地招生。

40. 人數　　rénshù　　*n.*　　number of people

這個大學今年的新生人數比去年的多。

41. 基本上　　jībǐn shàng　　*adv.*　　basically, generally speaking

第四十五課的練習我基本上已經做完了。

42. 性　　xìng　　*b.f.*　　-ness, nature

我覺得我考上北京大學的可能性不大。

43. 危險　　wēixiǎn　　*adj.*　　dangerous, risky

你開車開得那麼快，太危險了。

　　　　　　　　　　　　　　n.　　danger, risk

那邊有危險，別過去了。

44. 除非⋯否則　　chúfēi...fǒuzé　　*conj.*　　unless...otherwise...

除非你努力，否則你考不上北京大學。

45. 錯過　　cuòguò　　*v.*　　to miss (an opportunity)

你別錯過了去日本工作的機會。

46. 同時　　tóngshí　　*n.*　　(at) the same time

在上大學的同時，我還有兩個工作。

47. 專業　　zhuānyè　　*n.*　　profession, area of specialization

你以後想搞什麼專業？

48. 年級　　niánjí　　*n.*　　grade, year (in school)

你是幾年級的學生？

49. 學位　　xuéwèi　　*n.*　　academic degree

拿了學位以後我就想去中國工作。

50. 唯一   wéiyī   *adv.*   the one and only

我唯一想去的地方就是北京。

                               adj.

他是我唯一的朋友。

51. 出路   chūlù   *n.*   outlet, exit; (lit.) a way out

念学位不是你的唯一出路。你为什么一定要念学位呢？

学校教育等级 Terms for Chinese Schools

1. 小学   xiǎoxué   *n.*   elementary school

2. 初中   chūzhōng   *n.*   middle school

3. 中专   zhōngzhuān   *n.*   vocational middle school

4. 高中   gāozhōng   *n.*   high school

5. 高专   gāozhuān   *n.*   vocational high school

6. 大学   dàxué   *n.*   college/university

7. 函授大学   hánshòu dàxué   *n.*   correspondence school
   函授   *v.*   to teach by correspondence
   函职   *n.*   (formal) correspondence, letter
   授   *v.*   (formal) to give, to teach

8. 研究院   yánjiū yuàn   *n.*   graduate school

学校年级名称 Grade Levels of Chinese Schools

Year Number	Elementary	Middle	High	College
First Year	一年级	初一	高一	大一
Second Year	二年级	初二	高二	大二
Third Year	三年级	初三	高三	大三
Fourth Year	四年级			大四
Fifth Year	五年级			
Sixth Year	六年级			

50. 唯一   wéiyī   *adv.*   the one and only

我唯一想去的地方就是北京。

                                  adj.

他是我唯一的朋友。

51. 出路   chūlù   *n.*   outlet, exit; (lit.) a way out

念學位不是你的唯一出路。你為什麼一定要念學位呢？

學校教育等級 Terms for Chinese Schools

1. 小學	xiǎoxué	*n.*	elementary school
2. 初中	chūzhōng	*n.*	middle school
3. 中專	zhōngzhuān	*n.*	vocational middle school
4. 高中	gāozhōng	*n.*	high school
5. 高專	gāozhuān	*n.*	vocational high school
6. 大學	dàxué	*n.*	college/university
7. 函授大學	hánshòu dàxué	*n.*	correspondence school
函授		*v.*	to teach by correspondence
函		*n.*	(formal) correspondence, letter
授		*v.*	(formal) to give, to teach
8. 研究院	yánjiū yuàn	*n.*	graduate school

學校年級名稱 Grade Levels of Chinese Schools

Year Number	Elementary	Middle	High	College
First Year	一年級	初一	高一	大一
Second Year	二年級	初二	高二	大二
Third Year	三年級	初三	高三	大三
Fourth Year	四年級			大四
Fifth Year	五年級			
Sixth Year	六年級			

学位名称 Degrees Awarded

1. 学士	xuéshì	*n.*	bachelor's degree
2. 硕士	shuòshì	*n.*	master's degree
3. 博士	bóshì	*n.*	doctoral degree

口头用语 Spoken Expressions

1. 尖子	jiānzi	top, top student
2. 走后门	zǒu hòumén	(lit. and met.) to go through the back door
3. 赶鸭子上架	gǎn yāzi shàng jià	(lit.) to force the duck onto the shelf; (met.) to force someone to do something beyond his/her ability
4. 小看	xiǎokàn	belittle
5. 逞能	chěng néng	to brag, to show off one's abilities

书面语 *vs.* 口语 Written Form vs. Spoken Form

In Chinese, the "written form" preserves a lot of words and expressions from Classical Chinese and is therefore more concise and formal than the "spoken form." As its name implies, the "written form" is used primarily in writing, but it occurs frequently in speech as well.

书面语	口语
1. 即可	就可以
2. 分为	分成
3. 来自（于）	从···来的
4. 简称	简单的名称
5. 不仅	不但
6. 低于	比···低
7. 录取线	录取分数线
8. 有时	有的时候
9. 极大	非常大
10. 以及	和
11. 统考	统一考试

學位名稱 Degrees Awarded

1. 學士	xuéshì	*n.*	bachelor's degree
2. 碩士	shuòshì	*n.*	master's degree
3. 博士	bóshì	*n.*	doctoral degree

口頭用語 Spoken Expressions

1. 尖子	jiānzi	top, top student
2. 走後門	zǒu hòumén	(lit. and met.) to go through the back door
3. 趕鴨子上架	gǎn yāzi shàng jià	(lit.) to force the duck onto the shelf; (met.) to force someone to do something beyond his/her ability
4. 小看	xiǎokàn	belittle
5. 逞能	chěng néng	to brag, to show off one's abilities

書面語 *vs.* 口語 Written Form vs. Spoken Form

In Chinese, the "written form" preserves a lot of words and expressions from Classical Chinese and is therefore more concise and formal than the "spoken form." As its name implies, the "written form" is used primarily in writing, but it occurs frequently in speech as well.

書面語	口語
1. 即可	就可以
2. 分為	分成
3. 來自 (於)	從⋯來的
4. 簡稱	簡單的名稱
5. 不僅	不但
6. 低於	比⋯低
7. 錄取線	錄取分數線
8. 有時	有的時候
9. 極大	非常大
10. 以及	和
11. 統考	統一考試

12. 各校   每个学校
13. 当…时   在…的时候

词汇注解 Featured Vocabulary

1. 通过 (tōngguò) vs. 通过…来 (tōngguò…lái)

通过	*v.*	to pass
通过考试		to pass an exam
通过…来…	*v. phr.*	to go through (a method or a channel) in order to...
通过看电视来学中文		to learn Chinese by watching TV

2. 好坏/高低/冷热 (hǎo huài/gāodī/lěng rè)

In Chinese, some antonymous adjectives can be used together to form a noun.

好坏	quality
高低	height
冷热	temperature
长短	length
大小	size

3. 不如 (bùrú)

不如	*v.*	to be inferior to (usually used in a comparison sentence to indicate a preferred choice)

南方菜不如北方菜好吃。

Southern food does not taste as good as Northern food.

4. 基本 (jībǎn) vs. 基本上 (jībǎn shàng)

基本	*adj.*	basic, fundamental
基本知识		basic knowledge
基本问题		fundamental questions
基本上	*adv.*	on the whole, basically

很多人基本上没有吃过中药。

On the whole, many people have not taken traditional Chinese medicine.

5. 性 (xìng)

性	*b.f.*	-ness, -ity (性 can be added to the end of a verb, a noun, or an adjective to form a noun phrase.)

After a verb:	记性	memory
After a noun:	文化性	cultural characteristic
After an adjective:	重要性	importance

12. 各校   每個學校
13. 當⋯時   在⋯的時候

辭彙注解 Featured Vocabulary

1. 通過 (tōngguò) vs. 通過⋯來 (tōngguò⋯lái)

通過	*v.*	to pass
通過考試		to pass an exam

通過⋯來⋯	*v. phr.*	to go through (a method or a channel) in order to...
通過看電視來學中文		to learn Chinese by watching TV

2. 好壞/高低/冷熱 (hǎo huài/gāodī/lěng rè)

In Chinese, some antonymous adjectives can be used together to form a noun.

好壞	quality
高低	height
冷熱	temperature
長短	length
大小	size

3. 不如 (bùrú)

不如	*v.*	to be inferior to (usually used in a comparison sentence to indicate a preferred choice)

南方菜不如北方菜好吃。

Southern food does not taste as good as Northern food.

4. 基本 (jīběn) vs. 基本上 (jīběn shàng)

基本	*adj.*	basic, fundamental
基本知識		basic knowledge
基本問題		fundamental questions

基本上	*adv.*	on the whole, basically

很多人基本上沒有吃過中藥。

On the whole, many people have not taken traditional Chinese medicine.

5. 性 (xìng)

性	*b.f.*	-ness, -ity (性 can be added to the end of a verb, a noun, or an adjective to form a noun phrase.)

After a verb:	記性	memory
After a noun:	文化性	cultural characteristic
After an adjective:	重要性	importance

6. 可能性 (kěnéng xìng) vs. 有可能 (yǒu kěnéng) vs. 可能 (kěnéng)

可能性	*n.*	possibility

我今年去中国的可能性不大。
The chances of my going to China this year are very small.

有可能	*n.*	a possibility, probability

我今年有可能去中国。
There is a possibility that I will go to China this year.

可能	*adj.*	likely, possible

这很可能。
This is very likely.

可能	*aux.*	to be possible, to be likely

他今年可能去上海。
He is likely to go to Shanghai this year.

7. 错过 (cuòguò) vs. 错 (cuò)

错过	*v. comp.*	to miss (an opportunity)

他错过了留学的机会。
He missed the opportunity to study abroad.

错	*adj.*	wrong, incorrect

我错了，你没错。
I am wrong; you are not.

8. 将来/以后 (jiānglái/yǐhòu) vs. 出路 (chūlù)

将来/以后	*t.w.*	in the future

将来 is more formal than 以后 and also indicates a longer period of time.

我们都不知道将来会什么样。
None of us knows what the future will be like.

出路	*n.*	a way out (of a place or situation); future prospects

你现在要是不好好学习，毕业以后就没有出路。
If you don't study hard now, you will have no future after you graduate.

6. 可能性 (kěnéng xìng) vs. 有可能 (yǒu kěnéng) vs. 可能 (kěnéng)

可能性	*n.*	possibility

我今年去中國的可能性不大。
The chances of my going to China this year are very small.

有可能	*n.*	a possibility, probability

我今年有可能去中國。
There is a possibility that I will go to China this year.

可能	*adj.*	likely, possible

這很可能。
This is very likely.

可能	*aux.*	to be possible, to be likely

他今年可能去上海。
He is likely to go to Shanghai this year.

7. 錯過 (cuòguò) vs. 錯 (cuò)

錯過	*v. comp.*	to miss (an opportunity)

他錯過了留學的機會。
He missed the opportunity to study abroad.

錯	*adj.*	wrong, incorrect

我錯了，你沒錯。
I am wrong; you are not.

8. 將來/以後 (jiānglái/yǐhòu) vs. 出路 (chūlù)

將來/以後	*t.w.*	in the future

將來 is more formal than 以後 and also indicates a longer period of time.

我们都不知道將來会什麼樣。
None of us knows what the future will be like.

出路	*n.*	a way out (of a place or situation); future prospects

你現在要是不好好學習，畢業以後就沒有出路。
If you don't study hard now, you will have no future after you graduate.

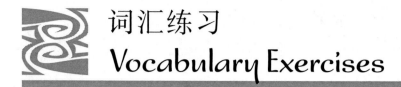

词汇练习
Vocabulary Exercises

🎧 🦋 TASK 1. 组词 WORD AND PHRASE COMPOSITION

Use the given word or phrase on the left as a guide to help you think of other, similar compound words. Feel free to use a dictionary when needed. Then write down the English definition of each of the compound words you've created.

1. 立 (to set up, stand): 公立   public
    _____ 立
    _____ 立
    _____ 立

2. 级 (grade, class): 升级   upgrade
    _____ 级
    _____ 级
    _____ 级

3. 点 (point): 重点   the most important (point, center, etc.)
    _____ 点
    _____ 点
    _____ 点

4. 数 (number): 分数   score
    _____ 数
    _____ 数
    _____ 数

5. 专 (specially): 专门   specialized
    专 _____
    专 _____
    专 _____

辭彙練習
Vocabulary Exercises

🎧 🗿 TASK 1. 組詞 WORD AND PHRASE COMPOSITION

Use the given word or phrase on the left as a guide to help you think of other, similar compound words. Feel free to use a dictionary when needed. Then write down the English definition of each of the compound words you've created.

1. 立 (to set up, stand): 公立   public

    _____ 立

    _____ 立

    _____ 立

2. 級 (grade, class): 升級   upgrade

    _____ 級

    _____ 級

    _____ 級

3. 點 (point): 重點   the most important (point, center, etc.)

    _____ 點

    _____ 點

    _____ 點

4. 數 (number): 分數   score

    _____ 數

    _____ 數

    _____ 數

5. 專 (specially): 專門   specialized

    專 _____

    專 _____

    專 _____

6. 心 (mind): 专心   to concentrate on

_____ 心

_____ 心

_____ 心

🎧 TASK 2. 搭配 MATCHING

A. 修饰语词组

Match the following words and phrases with the appropriate modifiers.

Phrases	Modifiers
1) 竞争	a) 很高
2) 分数	b) 很多
3) 这种可能性	c) 非常激烈
4) 他们的规定	d) 很大

B. 动宾词组

Match verbs in the left column with nouns in the right column to form phrases.

Verbs	Nouns
1) 受	a) 几个志愿
2) 报	b) 大学教育
3) 定	c) 奖学金
4) 拿	d) 专业

🎧 TASK 3. 填空 FILL IN THE BLANKS

A. 句子

Read the following sentences and fill in each blank with the appropriate word or phrase from the options given.

1. 错过   基本上   基本   走错

a) 我今年 _____ 了一个去国外留学的好机会。

b) 我去他们宿舍找他的时候，_____ 路了。

c) 现在他们学的都是很 _____ 的单词，所以应该会读会写。

d) 我 _____ 已经决定明年不再参加高考了。

6. 心 (mind): 專心　　　　　　　　　　　to concentrate on

_____ 心

_____ 心

_____ 心

🎧 TASK 2. 搭配 MATCHING

A. 修飾語詞組

Match the following words and phrases with the appropriate modifiers.

Phrases	Modifiers
1) 競爭	a) 很高
2) 分數	b) 很多
3) 這種可能性	c) 非常激烈
4) 他們的規定	d) 很大

B. 動賓詞組

Match verbs in the left column with nouns in the right column to form phrases.

Verbs	Nouns
1) 受	a) 幾個志願
2) 報	b) 大學教育
3) 定	c) 獎學金
4) 拿	d) 專業

🎧 TASK 3. 填空 FILL IN THE BLANKS

A. 句子

Read the following sentences and fill in each blank with the appropriate word or phrase from the options given.

1. 錯過　　　基本上　　　基本　　　　走錯

a) 我今年 _____ 了一個去國外留學的好機會。

b) 我去他們宿舍找他的時候，_____ 路了。

c) 現在他們學的都是很 _____ 的單詞，所以應該會讀會寫。

d) 我 _____ 已經決定明年不再參加高考了。

2. 有可能　　可能　　可能性

a) 他今年考上大学的 ＿＿＿＿＿＿ 非常小。

b) 他 ＿＿＿＿＿＿ 要上电视大学或者函授大学。

c) 他爸爸妈妈 ＿＿＿＿＿＿ 会感到很失望。

3. 出路　　以后　　将来

a) 他 ＿＿＿＿＿＿ 要去美国读博士。

b) 高考 ＿＿＿＿＿＿ ，你应该好好休息休息。

c) 现在上大学不是学生唯一的 ＿＿＿＿＿＿ 了。

B. 段落

Read the following passages and fill in each blank with the appropriate word or phrase from the options given.

1. 通过　　将来　　低于　　压力　　可能性　　不如

我的分数 ＿＿＿＿＿＿ 重点学校的录取线，所以我没考上。我爸爸妈妈给我付了钱让我上私立学校。当然我们学校的师资 ＿＿＿＿＿＿ 重点学校，也不是一流的。学生也不是＿＿＿＿＿考试选出来的。＿＿＿＿＿考大学，我们考上的＿＿＿＿＿也不大。但是我在这儿学习比较轻松，＿＿＿＿＿不那么大，所以我很喜欢我的学校。

2. 基本上　　志愿　　难道　　唯一　　为主

我妈妈最近常常问我以后考不上大学怎么办。我总觉得上大学也不是 ＿＿＿＿＿＿＿ 的出路。＿＿＿＿＿＿ 每个人都一定要上大学吗？我爸爸说我应该以学校的学习 ＿＿＿＿＿＿ ，但是同时还应该学一点别的。现在我 ＿＿＿＿＿＿ 每个星期六都跟我爸爸去爬山。我的 ＿＿＿＿＿＿ 是当一个爬山运动员。

2. 有可能　　可能　　可能性

a) 他今年考上大學的 ＿＿＿＿＿＿ 非常小。

b) 他 ＿＿＿＿＿＿要上電視大學或者函授大學。

c) 他爸爸媽媽 ＿＿＿＿＿＿會感到很失望。

3. 出路　　以後　　將來

a) 他 ＿＿＿＿＿＿要去美國讀博士。

b) 高考 ＿＿＿＿＿＿，你應該好好休息休息。

c) 現在上大學不是學生唯一的 ＿＿＿＿＿＿ 了。

B. 段落

Read the following passages and fill in each blank with the appropriate word or phrase from the options given.

1. 通過　　　將來　　　低於　　　壓力　　　可能性　　　不如

　　我的分數 ＿＿＿＿＿ 重點學校的錄取線，所以我沒考上。我爸爸媽媽給我付了錢讓我上私立學校。當然我們學校的師資 ＿＿＿＿＿ 重點學校，也不是一流的。學生也不是 ＿＿＿＿＿ 考試選出來的。＿＿＿＿＿ 考大學，我們考上的 ＿＿＿＿＿ 也不大。但是我在這兒學習比較輕鬆，＿＿＿＿＿ 不那麼大，所以我很喜歡我的學校。

2. 基本上　　志願　　難道　　唯一　　為主

　　我媽媽最近常常問我以後考不上大學怎麼辦。我總覺得上大學也不是 ＿＿＿＿＿＿的出路。＿＿＿＿＿ 每個人都一定要上大學嗎？我爸爸說我應該以學校的學習 ＿＿＿＿＿，但是同時還應該學一點別的。現在我 ＿＿＿＿＿ 每個星期六都跟我爸爸去爬山。我的 ＿＿＿＿＿ 是當一個爬山運動員。

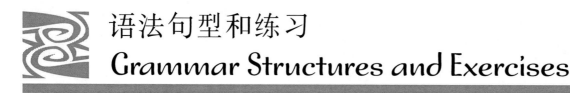

语法句型和练习
Grammar Structures and Exercises

I. The preposition 以 (yǐ): Indicating "take/consider/use"

In Lesson 44 you learned the conjunction 以, which means "in order to." In this lesson you will learn other usages of the preposition 以.

A. 以⋯为（主）(yǐ...wéi [zhǔ]): Take...as...

In the structure 以⋯为⋯, 以 means "consider" or "take" and is usually followed by a noun or verb phrase. 为 means "as" or "to be" and can be followed by a noun or adjectival phrase. "以⋯为 Noun phrase" is used to focus attention on some aspect of the sentence subject. "以⋯为（最）Adjective" can be used to point out the most outstanding item of the aforementioned plural subject. The structure "以⋯为⋯" can function as a predicate or attributive.

	Predicate
Subject	以 Noun 为 Noun phrase
中国北方人的食物	以面食为主。

Northern people's food is primarily based on wheat products.

	Predicate
Subject	以 Noun 为 Adjective phrase
大学生的休闲活动	以计算机游戏最为流行。

Among college students' recreational activities, computer games are the most popular.

	Attributive
Subject Verb	以 Noun 为 Noun phrase 的 Object
他们有没有	以素菜为主的菜单？

Do they have any menus that primarily contain vegetarian dishes?

B. 以⋯（来）Verb (yǐ...[lái]): Use/take

In the structure "以⋯（来）Verb," 以 means "use" or "take" and points out the basis or manner of an action. 以 must be placed after the subject and can be followed by a noun or verb phrase. 来 is optional and must be placed before the main verb.

Subject	以 Noun phrase （来）Verb Object
我们	以给他送花的方式来表示对他的感谢。

We express thanks to him by sending flowers.

Subject	以 Verb phrase （来）Verb Object
他	以吃止痛药来治自己的头疼。

He used painkillers to alleviate his headache.

語法句型和練習
Grammar Structures and Exercises

I. The preposition 以 (yǐ): Indicating "take/consider/use"

In Lesson 44 you learned the conjunction 以, which means "in order to." In this lesson you will learn other usages of the preposition 以.

A. 以⋯為(主) (yǐ...wéi [zhǔ]): Take...as...

In the structure 以⋯為⋯, 以 means "consider" or "take" and is usually followed by a noun or verb phrase. 為 means "as" or "to be" and can be followed by a noun or adjectival phrase. "以⋯為 Noun phrase" is used to focus attention on some aspect of the sentence subject. "以⋯為(最) Adjective" can be used to point out the most outstanding item of the aforementioned plural subject. The structure "以⋯為⋯" can function as a predicate or attributive.

	Predicate
Subject	以 **Noun** 為 **Noun phrase**
中國北方人的食物	以麵食為主。

Northern people's food is primarily based on wheat products.

	Predicate
Subject	以 **Noun** 為 **Adjective phrase**
大學生的休閒活動	以電腦遊戲最為流行。

Among college students' recreational activities, computer games are the most popular.

	Attributive
Subject Verb	以 **Noun** 為 **Noun phrase** 的 **Object**
他們有沒有	以素菜為主的菜單?

Do they have any menus that primarily contain vegetarian dishes?

B. 以⋯(來) Verb (yǐ...[lái]): Use/take

In the structure "以⋯(來)Verb," 以 means "use" or "take" and points out the basis or manner of an action. 以 must be placed after the subject and can be followed by a noun or verb phrase. 來 is optional and must be placed before the main verb.

Subject	以 **Noun phrase** (來) **Verb Object**
我們	以給他送花的方式來表示對他的感謝。

We express thanks to him by sending flowers.

Subject	以 **Verb phrase** (來) **Verb Object**
他	以吃止痛藥來治自己的頭疼。

He used painkillers to alleviate his headache.

❈ PRACTICE

模仿造句

Make sentences of your own by following each of the examples given.

1. 我的 _____ 以 _____ 为主。

   (Example: 研究报告，中国的社会问题)

2. 我看过的_____ 中以 _____ 最为 _____。

   (Example: 节目，相声，好笑)

3. 他上什么大学都是以 _____ 来决定。

   (Example: 他爸爸妈妈的愿望)

4. 一般人常常以一个人的 _____ 来衡量这个人的 _____。

   (Example: 工作成绩，能力)

完成句子

Please complete each of the sentences below.

1. _____ 以 _____ 为主。

2. _____ 以 _____ 为基础。

3. _____ 以 _____ 为代表。

4. _____ 以 _____ 为最有名。

5. _____ 以 _____ 最为重要。

6. _____ 以 _____ 为最多。

7. _____ 以 _____ 来决定 _____。

8. _____ 以 _____ 来表示 _____。

9. _____ 以 _____ 来计算 _____。

10. _____ 以 _____ 来衡量 _____。

翻译

Translate the following sentences into Chinese. Make sure your translation includes 以…为主, 以…来衡量, and 无论…还是.

The Chinese education system is always based on exams. No matter how smart a student really is, schools still use test results as a measurement of the student's abilities.

❈ PRACTICE

模仿造句

Make sentences of your own by following each of the examples given.

1. 我的 _____ 以 _____ 為主。

   (Example: 研究報告，中國的社會問題)

2. 我看過的_____ 中以 _____ 最為 _____。

   (Example: 節目，相聲，好笑)

3. 他上什麼大學都是以 _____ 來決定。

   (Example: 他爸爸媽媽的願望)

4. 一般人常常以一個人的 _____ 來衡量這個人的 _____。

   (Example: 工作成績，能力)

完成句子

Please complete each of the sentences below.

1. _____ 以 _____ 為主。

2. _____ 以 _____ 為基礎。

3. _____ 以 _____ 為代表。

4. _____ 以 _____ 為最有名。

5. _____ 以 _____ 最為重要。

6. _____ 以 _____ 為最多。

7. _____ 以 _____ 來決定 _____。

8. _____ 以 _____ 來表示 _____。

9. _____ 以 _____ 來計算 _____。

10. _____ 以 _____ 來衡量 _____。

翻譯

Translate the following sentences into Chinese. Make sure your translation includes 以…為主, 以…來衡量, and 無論…還是.

The Chinese education system is always based on exams. No matter how smart a student really is, schools still use test results as a measurement of the student's abilities.

II. The preposition 于 (yú): Indicating "from" or "than"

The preposition 于 has many meanings. In this lesson you will learn two of them. These two structures are both used in written language.

A. Indicating "from"

In this structure, 于 is suffixed to a verb or a verb plus a complement. In the phrase 来自于, 于 is optional.

Subject	Verb (+ comp.) 于	Object
这些节日都	来自（于）	不同的宗教信仰。

These holidays originate from various religious beliefs.

Verb 于	Object	Subject Verb Object
出于	对中国文化的好奇，	他才问了老师那么多问题。

It's because of curiosity about Chinese culture that he asked his teacher so many questions.

B. Indicating "than"

In this structure, 于 is suffixed to an adjective to mean "than," and it indicates a comparison, e.g. 低于, 高于, etc.

1st noun phrase	Adjective 于	2nd noun phrase
在家打牌的人	远远多于	户外运动的人。

People who play cards at home far outnumber those who exercise outdoors.

❋ PRACTICE

用下列词语填空并造自己的句子

来自于   出于   少于   高于   低于   难于

1. 这次高考内容 _____ 上一次考试的内容。

2. 中国的教育体系 _____ 古代的科举制度。

3. 普通大学的录取分数线 _____ 重点大学的分数线。

4. 爸爸妈妈愿意多出学费，让孩子受到更好的教育。这个观念 _____ 他们望子成龙的愿望。

5. 重点大学的师资水平 _____ 普通大学的师资水平。

6. 对中医感兴趣的人还是 _____ 找西医看病的人。

II. The preposition 於 (yú): Indicating "from" or "than"

The preposition 於 has many meanings. In this lesson you will learn two of them. These two structures are both used in written language.

A. Indicating "from"

In this structure, 於 is suffixed to a verb or a verb plus a complement. In the phrase 來自於, 於 is optional.

Subject	Verb (+ comp.) 於	Object
這些節日都	來自（於）	不同的宗教信仰。

These holidays originate from various religious beliefs.

Verb 於	Object	Subject Verb Object
出於	對中國文化的好奇，	他才問了老師那麼多問題。

It's because of curiosity about Chinese culture that he asked his teacher so many questions.

B. Indicating "than"

In this structure, 於 is suffixed to an adjective to mean "than," and it indicates a comparison, e.g. 低於, 高於, etc.

1st noun phrase	Adjective 於	2nd noun phrase
在家打牌的人	遠遠多於	戶外運動的人。

People who play cards at home far outnumber those who exercise outdoors.

◩ PRACTICE

用下列詞語填空并造自己的句子

來自於　　　出於　　　少於　　　高於　　　低於　　　難於

1. 這次高考內容 _____ 上一次考試的內容。

2. 中國的教育體係 _____ 古代的科舉制度。

3. 普通大學的錄取分數線 _____ 重點大學的分數線。

4. 爸爸媽媽願意多出學費，讓孩子受到更好的教育。這個觀念 _____ 他們望子成龍的願望。

5. 重點大學的師資水平 _____ 普通大學的師資水平。

6. 對中醫感興趣的人還是 _____ 找西醫看病的人。

造句

1. _____ 来自于 _____ 。
2. _____ 出于 _____ 。
3. _____ 少于 _____ 。
4. _____ 高于 _____ 。
5. _____ 低于 _____ 。
6. _____ 难于 _____ 。

翻译

Translate the following sentences into Chinese. Make sure your translation includes 之所以…是因为, 高于, and 毕业于.

The reason the tuition of this middle school is so much higher that that of others is because it has a first-rate faculty. These teachers all graduated from China's premier universities.

III. 难道…（吗）(nándào...[ma]): Is it possible that...

难道…（吗）is a rhetorical question expressing disbelief. 难道 is often placed before the entire predicate, and the optional 吗 is placed at end of the question. 难道 is often followed by a negative form such as 难道不（没）. 难道…（吗）, like all rhetorical questions, does not require an answer.

Statement	Subject 难道 Verb (Object)...吗?
我不喜欢吃肉，	你难道不知道吗？

I don't like to eat meat. Is it possible that you didn't know that?

Statement	难道 Subject Verb (Object)...吗?
现在我们都放弃了，	难道你还要我们参加表演吗？

We have all given up now. You mean you still want us to participate in the performance?

❖ PRACTICE

改写句子

Use 难道…（吗）to rewrite the following sentences.

1. 我大学还没毕业呢！你怎么不知道？

2. 你在中国学校教书，你应该了解中国的教育体系。

3. 你是重点大学的尖子学生，以后你一定会有出路。

造句

1. _____ 來自於 _____ 。
2. _____ 出於 _____ 。
3. _____ 少於 _____ 。
4. _____ 高於 _____ 。
5. _____ 低於 _____ 。
6. _____ 難於 _____ 。

翻譯

Translate the following sentences into Chinese. Make sure your translation includes 之所以⋯是因為, 高於, and 畢業於.

The reason the tuition of this middle school is so much higher that that of others is because it has a first-rate faculty. These teachers all graduated from China's premier universities.

III. 難道⋯（嗎）(nándào...[ma]): Is it possible that...

難道⋯（嗎）is a rhetorical question expressing disbelief. 難道 is often placed before the entire predicate, and the optional 嗎 is placed at end of the question. 難道 is often followed by a negative form such as 難道不（沒）. 難道⋯（嗎）, like all rhetorical questions, does not require an answer.

Statement	Subject 難道 Verb (Object)...嗎?
我不喜歡吃肉，	你難道不知道嗎？

I don't like to eat meat. Is it possible that you didn't know that?

Statement	難道 Subject Verb (Object)...嗎?
現在我們都放棄了，	難道你還要我們參加表演嗎？

We have all given up now. You mean you still want us to participate in the performance?

PRACTICE

改寫句子

Use 難道⋯（嗎）to rewrite the following sentences.

1. 我大學還沒畢業呢！你怎麼不知道？

2. 你在中國學校教書，你應該瞭解中國的教育體係。

3. 你是重點大學的尖子學生，以後你一定會有出路。

⊠ PRACTICE

模仿造句

Make sentences of your own by following each of the examples given.

1. 这么简单的问题，_____。
   (Example: 你难道不会回答吗？)

2. 他已经是大学四年级的学生了，_____。
   (Example: 难道还没有定专业吗？)

3. 你们从小就认识，_____。
   (Example: 难道你不了解他吗？)

翻译

Translate the following sentences into Chinese. Make sure your translation includes 难道…吗.

Can it be true that getting a college degree is the only path in life? Actually, it doesn't matter if you failed the college entrance exam. In today's society, one can excel in every field; there are many opportunities for success.

IV. …，终于… (..., zhōngyú...): At long last, in the end

In Lesson 24 you learned 总算, which indicates that a result is hard-earned but sure. In this lesson you will learn another adverbial phrase, 终于, which also expresses a long-awaited and finally fulfilled result. 终于 usually modifies verbs of more than one syllable. It must be placed after the subject of the clause if there is a subject.

1st clause	2nd clause (Result)
(Subject) Verb phrase	**Subject 终于 Verb phrase**

经过紧张的练习，   我们队终于在运动会上得了游泳比赛第一名。
Our team finally won the swim meet after undergoing a period of intense training.

我朋友费了很多时间教我，   我终于学会从网上下载信息。
I finally learned how to download information from the Internet after my friend spent a lot of time teaching me.

❧ PRACTICE

模仿造句

Make sentences of your own by following each of the examples given.

1. 這麼簡單的問題，_____。
   (Example: 你難道不會回答嗎？)

2. 他已經是大學四年級的學生了，_____。
   (Example: 難道還沒有定專業嗎？)

3. 你們從小就認識，_____。
   (Example: 難道你不瞭解他嗎？)

翻譯

Translate the following sentences into Chinese. Make sure your translation includes 難道…嗎.

　　Can it be true that getting a college degree is the only path in life? Actually, it doesn't matter if you failed the college entrance exam. In today's society, one can excel in every field; there are many opportunities for success.

IV. …，終於… (..., zhōngyú...): At long last, in the end

In Lesson 24 you learned 总算, which indicates that a result is hard-earned but sure. In this lesson you will learn another adverbial phrase, 總算, which also expresses a long-awaited and finally fulfilled result. 終於 usually modifies verbs of more than one syllable. It must be placed after the subject of the clause if there is a subject.

1st clause	2nd clause (Result)
(Subject) Verb phrase	Subject 終於 Verb phrase

經過緊張的練習，　　　　　　　我們隊終於在運動會上得了游泳比賽第一名。
Our team finally won the swim meet after undergoing a period of intense training.

我朋友費了很多時間教我，　　我終於學會從網上下載資訊。
I finally learned how to download information from the Internet after my friend spent a lot of time teaching me.

❀ PRACTICE

模仿造句

Make sentences of your own by following each of the examples given.

1. 他想了很长时间，终于决定 _____。
   (Example: 放弃这次考研机会)

2. 他努力专心地 _____ 终于 _____。
   (Example: 学习，考上了他最喜欢的大学)

3. 经过多年的 _____ ，他终于 _____。
   (Example: 研究，写出了一本中文语法书)

4. 我朋友 _____ 很多次，今年终于_____。
   (Example: 申请了，拿到了奖学金)

5. 由于长时间不断的_____ ，他的 _____ 终于 _____。
   (Example: 锻炼，身体，健康起来了)

问答

Use 终于 to answer the following questions.

1. 你是怎么定自己的专业的？

2. 你朋友为什么决定不考大学了？

翻译

Translate the following sentences into Chinese. Make sure your translation includes 为了 and 终于.

In order to fulfill his parents' wishes for him to attain the highest success, my friend continuously studied hard. Finally, he got accepted into medical school.

🎕 PRACTICE

模仿造句

Make sentences of your own by following each of the examples given.

1. 他想了很長時間，終於決定 _____。
   (Example: 放棄這次考研機會)

2. 他努力專心地 _____ 終於 _____。
   (Example: 學習，考上了他最喜歡的大學)

3. 經過多年的 _____，他終於 _____。
   (Example: 研究，寫出了一本中文語法書)

4. 我朋友 _____ 很多次，今年終於_____。
   (Example: 申請了，拿到了獎學金)

5. 由於長時間不斷的_____，他的 _____ 終於 _____。
   (Example: 鍛煉，身體，健康起來了)

問答

Use 終於 to answer the following questions.

1. 你是怎麼定自己的專業的？

2. 你朋友為什麼決定不考大學了？

翻譯

Translate the following sentences into Chinese. Make sure your translation includes 為了 and 終於.

In order to fulfill his parents' wishes for him to attain the highest success, my friend continuously studied hard. Finally, he got accepted into medical school.

V. The conjunction 除非…(chúfēi…): Unless

The conjunction 除非 means "unless" and leads into the necessary prerequisite of a certain event; it can be used in conjunction with 才 (then) or 否则 (otherwise) in the second clause.

A. 除非…否则 (chúfēi…fǒuzé): Unless…otherwise…

In the 除非…否则 structure, 除非 states the necessary prerequisite for avoiding the dire consequence stated in the second clause. 否则 makes the sentence more forceful by emphasizing that dire consequence. 除非 can be placed before or after the subject in the first clause, while 否则 must be placed after the subject in the second clause. 否则 is interchangeable with the more colloquial phrase 要不然 and sometimes can be used without 除非.

1st clause (Condition)	2nd clause (Consequence)
Subject 除非 (Subject) Verb Object,	**否则 Subject Predicate**

这个病人除非动手术，   否则他的病情会越来越坏。
Unless this patient undergoes surgery, his illness will get more and more serious.

除非你吃中药，   要不然你的咳嗽不会好。
Your cough will not get better unless you take your medicine.

B. 除非…(才) (chúfēi…[cái]): Only if…then…

The structure 除非…才 indicates that there is only one way to produce a certain result. 除非 can be placed before or after the subject, and 才 must be placed after the subject, if there is a subject.

1st clause (Condition)	2nd clause (Result)
Subject 除非 Verb Object,	**才 Verb phrase**

你除非先考上重点高中，   才有可能上重点大学。
Only if you get into a premier high school will you have the chance of getting into a top-ranked university.

除非 Subject Verb Object,	**Subject 才 Verb phrase**

除非单位提供住房，   他们才不用借钱买房子。
They will be able to avoid borrowing money to buy a house only if the division provides them with housing.

V. The conjunction 除非…(chúfēi...): Unless

The conjunction 除非 means "unless" and leads into the necessary prerequisite of a certain event; it can be used in conjunction with 才 (then) or 否則 (otherwise) in the second clause.

A. 除非…否則 (chúfēi…fǒuzé): Unless...otherwise...

In the 除非…否則 structure, 除非 states the necessary prerequisite for avoiding the dire consequence stated in the second clause. 否則 makes the sentence more forceful by emphasizing that dire consequence. 除非 can be placed before or after the subject in the first clause, while 否則 must be placed after the subject in the second clause. 否則 is interchangeable with the more colloquial phrase 要不然 and sometimes can be used without 除非.

1st clause (Condition)	2nd clause (Consequence)
Subject 除非 (Subject) Verb Object,	**否則 Subject Predicate**
這個病人除非動手術，	否則他的病情會越來越壞。

Unless this patient undergoes surgery, his illness will get more and more serious.

除非你吃中藥，	要不然你的咳嗽不會好。

Your cough will not get better unless you take your medicine.

B. 除非…(才) (chúfēi…[cái]): Only if...then...

The structure 除非…才 indicates that there is only one way to produce a certain result. 除非 can be placed before or after the subject, and 才 must be placed after the subject, if there is a subject.

1st clause (Condition)	2nd clause (Result)
Subject 除非 Verb Object,	**才 Verb phrase**
你除非先考上重點高中，	才有可能上重點大學。

Only if you get into a premier high school will you have the chance of getting into a top-ranked university.

除非 Subject Verb Object,	**Subject 才 Verb phrase**
除非單位提供住房，	他們才不用借錢買房子。

They will be able to avoid borrowing money to buy a house only if the division provides them with housing.

❀ PRACTICE

连词

Use 除非…否则 and 除非…才 to connect each group of phrases.

(Condition)	(Result)	(Consequence)
1. 考上重点大学	会有好出路	毕业后找不到好工作
2. 拿到奖学金	付得起学费	付不起学费
3. 走后门	上重点大学	没有机会上大学
4. 有问题	给你打电话	不会给你打电话

完成句子

Complete each of the sentences below using 除非…否则 and 除非…才.
(Condition)

1. _____ 病情得到控制 _____。

2. _____ 多去户外运动 _____。

3. _____ 你按照我说的方法去做 _____。

4. _____ 你帮我忙 _____。

5. _____ 你解释清楚 _____。

6. _____ 你会讨价还价 _____。

翻译

Translate the following sentences into Chinese. Make sure your translation includes 就算…还是 and 除非.

A: Even if the competition among students is not that great, students themselves are still under a lot of pressure to study.

B: Because more and more people want to attend college, unless there is no longer an exam system (for college entrance) in the education system, the competition among students will get more heated and there will be more pressure to study!

🔲 PRACTICE

連詞

Use 除非⋯否則 and 除非⋯才 to connect each group of phrases.

(Condition)	(Result)	(Consequence)
1. 考上重點大學	會有好出路	畢業後找不到好工作
2. 拿到獎學金	付得起學費	付不起學費
3. 走後門	上重點大學	沒有機會上大學
4. 有問題	給你打電話	不會給你打電話

完成句子

Complete each of the sentences below using 除非⋯否則 and 除非⋯才.
(Condition)

1. _____ 病情得到控制 _____。

2. _____ 多去戶外運動 _____。

3. _____ 你按照我說的方法去做 _____。

4. _____ 你幫我忙 _____。

5. _____ 你解釋清楚 _____。

6. _____ 你會討價還價 _____。

翻譯

Translate the following sentences into Chinese. Make sure your translation includes 就算⋯還是 and 除非.

A: Even if the competition among students is not that great, students themselves are still under a lot of pressure to study.

B: Because more and more people want to attend college, unless there is no longer an exam system (for college entrance) in the education system, the competition among students will get more heated and there will be more pressure to study!

VI. 在…的同时，还/也… (zài...de tóngshí, hái/yě…): Indicating simultaneous events

This structure indicates that two events happen at the same time. The duration of the two events should be equal or nearly equal. If the first clause has a subject, 在…的同时 must be placed after the subject. In the second clause, 还 or 也 also follows the subject, if there is a subject. This structure is mostly used in the written language. "一边…一边" (Lesson 37) is more colloquial. 同时 is also used as an adverb and usually appears in the second clause.

1st clause	2nd clause
Subject 在 Verb phrase 的同时，	还/也 Verb phrase

赵亮在大学读博士的同时，   也在高中教数学。

At the same time that Zhao Liang was getting his Ph.D. at the university, he was also teaching math to high school students.

人们在改变饮食习惯的同时，还开始注意利用休闲时间多做户外活动。

Along with changing their eating habits, people are also starting to pay attention to doing outdoor activities in their free time.

🔳 PRACTICE

完成句子

Complete each of the sentences below using 在…的同时.

1. _____ 申请学校 _____。

2. _____ 报考公立大学 _____。

翻译

Translate the following sentence into Chinese. Make sure your translation includes 在…的同时.

In order to pass this year's college-entrance examination, this student, while going to regular high school, also enrolled in supplementary night classes.

VII. 直到…才 (zhídào...cái): Not until…did…

This adverb 才 indicates that a certain event did not occur until a certain time. 直到 indicates a long continuous time up until a certain event, and that event can be indicated by a noun, verb phrase, or a clause. The adverb 直 is optional and is used to emphasize that time continues without interruption. 直到 can be placed before or after the subject, while 才 or 还 must be placed after the subject — if there is a subject — in the second clause.

VI. 在⋯的同時，還/也⋯ (zài...de tóngshí, hái/yě...): Indicating simultaneous events

This structure indicates that two events happen at the same time. The duration of the two events should be equal or nearly equal. If the first clause has a subject, 在⋯的同時 must be placed after the subject. In the second clause, 還 or 也 also follows the subject, if there is a subject. This structure is mostly used in the written language. "一邊⋯一邊" (Lesson 37) is more colloquial. 同時 is also used as an adverb and usually appears in the second clause.

1st clause	2nd clause
Subject 在 Verb phrase 的同時,	**還/也 Verb phrase**

趙亮在大學讀博士的同時，　　也在高中教數學。

At the same time that Zhao Liang was getting his Ph.D. at the university, he was also teaching math to high school students.

人們在改變飲食習慣的同時，還開始注意利用休閒時間多做戶外活動。

Along with changing their eating habits, people are also starting to pay attention to doing outdoor activities in their free time.

🔲 PRACTICE

完成句子

Complete each of the sentences below using 在⋯的同時.

1. ＿＿＿＿＿＿＿＿＿＿＿＿ 申請學校 ＿＿＿＿＿＿＿＿＿＿＿＿＿。
2. ＿＿＿＿＿＿＿＿＿＿＿＿ 報考公立大學 ＿＿＿＿＿＿＿＿＿＿＿。

翻譯

Translate the following sentence into Chinese. Make sure your translation includes 在⋯的同時.

    In order to pass this year's college-entrance examination, this student, while going to regular high school, also enrolled in supplementary night classes.

VII. 直到⋯才 (zhídào...cái): Not until...did...

This adverb 才 indicates that a certain event did not occur until a certain time. 直到 indicates a long continuous time up until a certain event, and that event can be indicated by a noun, verb phrase, or a clause. The adverb 直 is optional and is used to emphasize that time continues without interruption. 直到 can be placed before or after the subject, while 才 or 還 must be placed after the subject — if there is a subject — in the second clause.

1st clause (Time)	2nd clause (Event)
Subject 直到 Time,	**(Subject) 才 Verb phrase**

他直到上了火车   才发现忘了带行李。

It wasn't until he got on the train that he realized he had forgotten his luggage.

直到一位中医治好了我的病，我才开始相信中国医学的理论和方法。

I didn't believe the theories and treatments of traditional Chinese medicine until a traditional Chinese doctor cured my illness.

直到今天   我才认识到中医的好处。

It is only today that I realize the benefits of traditional Chinese medicine.

✺ PRACTICE

完成句子

Complete each of the sentences below.

1. 他直到上了大学，才＿＿＿＿＿＿＿＿＿＿＿＿＿＿＿＿＿＿＿＿＿。

2. 直到大学毕业，＿＿＿＿＿＿＿＿＿＿＿＿＿＿＿＿＿＿＿＿＿＿＿＿。

3. 直到被大学录取，＿＿＿＿＿＿＿＿＿＿＿＿＿＿＿＿＿＿＿＿＿＿。

4. 这个学生直到留级，＿＿＿＿＿＿＿＿＿＿＿＿＿＿＿＿＿＿＿＿＿＿。

5. 直到今天，＿＿＿＿＿＿＿＿＿＿＿＿＿＿＿＿＿＿＿＿＿＿＿＿＿＿。

6. 他直到十八岁，＿＿＿＿＿＿＿＿＿＿＿＿＿＿＿＿＿＿＿＿＿＿＿＿。

7. 他直到＿＿＿＿＿＿＿＿＿＿＿＿＿＿＿＿＿＿＿＿＿＿＿＿，才放弃。

8. 直到＿＿＿＿＿＿＿＿＿＿＿＿＿＿＿＿＿＿＿＿＿＿，他才同意。

9. 直到＿＿＿＿＿＿＿＿＿＿＿＿＿＿＿＿＿＿＿，我才改变这个习惯。

10. ＿＿＿＿＿＿＿＿＿＿＿＿＿＿＿ 直到 ＿＿＿＿＿＿＿＿＿＿＿＿＿，才表示感谢。

翻译

Translate the following sentences into Chinese. Make sure your translation includes 直到…才.

American universities are different from Chinese universities. Many American students do not declare their majors until the second or third year of college. However, Chinese students all must declare their majors when applying to college.

1st clause (Time)	2nd clause (Event)
Subject 直到 Time,	**(Subject) 才 Verb phrase**

他直到上了火車　　　　　才發現忘了帶行李。

It wasn't until he got on the train that he realized he had forgotten his luggage.

直到一位中醫治好了我的病，我才開始相信中國醫學的理論和方法。

I didn't believe the theories and treatments of traditional Chinese medicine until a traditional Chinese doctor cured my illness.

直到今天　　　　　　　　我才認識到中醫的好處。

It is only today that I realize the benefits of traditional Chinese medicine.

▨▨ PRACTICE

完成句子

Complete each of the sentences below.

1. 他直到上了大學，才＿＿＿＿＿＿＿＿＿＿＿＿＿＿＿＿＿＿＿＿。

2. 直到大學畢業，＿＿＿＿＿＿＿＿＿＿＿＿＿＿＿＿＿＿＿＿＿。

3. 直到被大學錄取，＿＿＿＿＿＿＿＿＿＿＿＿＿＿＿＿＿＿＿。

4. 這個學生直到留級，＿＿＿＿＿＿＿＿＿＿＿＿＿＿＿＿＿＿。

5. 直到今天，＿＿＿＿＿＿＿＿＿＿＿＿＿＿＿＿＿＿＿＿＿＿。

6. 他直到十八歲，＿＿＿＿＿＿＿＿＿＿＿＿＿＿＿＿＿＿＿＿。

7. 他直到＿＿＿＿＿＿＿＿＿＿＿＿＿＿＿＿＿＿＿，才放棄。

8. 直到＿＿＿＿＿＿＿＿＿＿＿＿＿＿＿＿＿＿，他才同意。

9. 直到＿＿＿＿＿＿＿＿＿＿＿＿＿＿＿＿，我才改變這個習慣。

10. ＿＿＿＿＿＿＿＿＿＿直到＿＿＿＿＿＿＿＿＿＿，才表示感謝。

翻譯

Translate the following sentences into Chinese. Make sure your translation includes 直到…才.

　　American universities are different from Chinese universities. Many American students do not declare their majors until the second or third year of college. However, Chinese students all must declare their majors when applying to college.

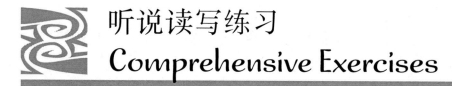

听说读写练习
Comprehensive Exercises

🎧 🦀 TASK 1. 听一听、选一选 LISTENING EXERCISES

A. Bingo

In this section, you will hear various Chinese phrases. Demonstrate your understanding of these phrases by numbering their English counterparts in the order in which you hear them.

the competition is very intense   the materials for applying to universities

top-ranked teachers   to have no regulations

the only way out   the possibility of staying in the same grade

education system   might as well take the exam again

premier high schools and regular high schools   admissions system of vocational middle schools

the pressure is very high   the possibility of this kind of danger is very high

to use testing scores to evaluate   basically, to have no need to pay tuition

to obtain a master's degree or Ph.D.   to obtain two scholarships at the same time

B. Matching

Listen to the sentences in Chinese and number them in the order in which you hear them.

1. 我觉得你不应该只以分数来衡量他的学习好坏。

2. 除非你上重点高中，否则你以后考大学会很困难。

3. 我终于发现上大学并不是唯一的出路。

4. 在决定学什么专业的时候，你应该以自己的兴趣为主。

5. 这个学校的录取分数线高于其他的大学。

6. 我觉得这个学校的师资远不如你们学校。

7. 你怎么直到这个时候才想到别的出路。

8. 你难道觉得竞争还不够激烈，压力还不够大吗？

9. 这些中专以及高专不仅比较容易考上，而且有很多有意思的专业。

聽說讀寫練習
Comprehensive Exercises

🎧 TASK 1. 聽一聽、選一選　LISTENING EXERCISES

A. Bingo

In this section, you will hear various Chinese phrases. Demonstrate your understanding of these phrases by numbering their English counterparts in the order in which you hear them.

the competition is very intense	the materials for applying to universities
top-ranked teachers	to have no regulations
the only way out	the possibility of staying in the same grade
education system	might as well take the exam again
premier high schools and regular high schools	admissions system of vocational middle schools
the pressure is very high	the possibility of this kind of danger is very high
to use testing scores to evaluate	basically, to have no need to pay tuition
to obtain a master's degree or Ph.D.	to obtain two scholarships at the same time

B. Matching

Listen to the sentences in Chinese and number them in the order in which you hear them.

1. 我覺得你不應該只以分數來衡量他的學習好壞。
2. 除非你上重點高中，否則你以後考大學會很困難。
3. 我終於發現上大學並不是唯一的出路。
4. 在決定學什麼專業的時候，你應該以自己的興趣為主。
5. 這個學校的錄取分數線高於其他的大學。
6. 我覺得這個學校的師資遠不如你們學校。
7. 你怎麼直到這個時候才想到別的出路。
8. 你難道覺得競爭還不夠激烈，壓力還不夠大嗎？
9. 這些中專以及高專不僅比較容易考上，而且有很多有意思的專業。

C. Short Conversations

Listen to these short conversations. Select the correct answer for each question from the choices provided.

1. 有/没有

2. 是/不是

3. 大/不太大

4. 多/少

5. 重点公立学校/私立学校

🎧❃ TASK 2. 听一听、说一说 SHORT PASSAGES

PASSAGE 1

Pre-Listening Activity

Before you begin, answer the following questions, which are deigned to help you predict what will happen in the passage.

1. 你小时候爱不爱学习？为什么？

2. 你现在觉得学习重要不重要？

Vocabulary

1. 放学	fàngxué	v. obj.	to get out of classes
2. 论文	lùnwén	n.	thesis
3. 贪	tān	v.	to be greedy for
4. 书包	shūbāo	n.	book bag
5. 分公司	fēn gōngsī	n.	branch office (company)

Listening Activity

Now listen to the passage and answer the questions that follow. Be sure to make a voice recording on the multimedia CD-ROM explaining each of your choices.

A. Listening for new words

Did you catch all the new words in the passage?

C. Short Conversations

Listen to these short conversations. Select the correct answer for each question from the choices provided.

1. 有／沒有

2. 是／不是

3. 大／不太大

4. 多／少

5. 重點公立學校／私立學校

🎧 ✒ TASK 2. 聽一聽、說一說 SHORT PASSAGES

PASSAGE 1

Pre-Listening Activity

Before you begin, answer the following questions, which are deigned to help you predict what will happen in the passage.

1. 你小時候愛不愛學習？為什麼？

2. 你現在覺得學習重要不重要？

Vocabulary

1. 放學	fàngxué	*v. obj.*	to get out of classes
2. 論文	lùnwén	*n.*	thesis
3. 貪	tān	*v.*	to be greedy for
4. 書包	shūbāo	*n.*	book bag
5. 分公司	fēn gōngsī	*n.*	branch office (company)

Listening Activity

Now listen to the passage and answer the questions that follow. Be sure to make a voice recording on the multimedia CD-ROM explaining each of your choices.

A. Listening for new words

Did you catch all the new words in the passage?

B. Listening for the main idea

这段话主要谈的是什么？

a) 只有读书才有出路。

b) 读书不是唯一的出路。

c) 读了博士就能找到好工作。

d) 以上都不对。

C. Listening for details

1. 我小的时候读书认真不认真？你怎么知道？

   认真/不认真

2. 我弟弟的学历比我高还是低？为什么？

   高/低

3. 毕业后我和弟弟谁的出路好？你怎么知道？

   我/弟弟

Post-Listening Activity

Now state your opinion as you record your voice on the multimedia CD-ROM.

说话的人觉得学习重要不重要？你同意不同意他的看法？

PASSAGE 2

Pre-Listening Activity

Before you begin, answer the following questions, which are designed to help you predict what will happen in the passage.

1. 你从小学到中学，从中学到大学都参加了什么样的统一考试？

2. 你觉得考试重要不重要？为什么？

Vocabulary

1. 名词	míngcí	*n.*	noun
2. 缩写	suōxiě	*n.*	abbreviation
3. 教育部	jiàoyù bù	*prop. n.*	Education Department
4. 出题	chū tí	*v. obj.*	to make up test questions

B. Listening for the main idea

這段話主要談的是什麼？

a) 只有讀書才有出路。

b) 讀書不是唯一的出路。

c) 讀了博士就能找到好工作。

d) 以上都不對。

C. Listening for details

1. 我小的時候讀書認真不認真？你怎麼知道？

   認真/不認真

2. 我弟弟的學歷比我高還是低？為什麼？

   高/低

3. 畢業後我和弟弟誰的出路好？你怎麼知道？

   我/弟弟

Post-Listening Activity

Now state your opinion as you record your voice on the multimedia CD-ROM.

說話的人覺得學習重要不重要？你同意不同意他的看法？

PASSAGE 2

Pre-Listening Activity

Before you begin, answer the following questions, which are designed to help you predict what will happen in the passage.

1. 你從小學到中學，從中學到大學都參加了什麼樣的統一考試？

2. 你覺得考試重要不重要？為什麼？

Vocabulary

1. 名詞	míngcí	*n.*	noun
2. 縮寫	suōxiě	*n.*	abbreviation
3. 教育部	jiàoyù bù	*prop. n.*	Education Department
4. 出題	chū tí	*v. obj.*	to make up test questions

Listening Activity

Now listen to the passage and then answer the questions that follow. Be sure to make a voice recording on the multimedia CD-ROM explaining each of your choices.

A. Listening for new words

Did you catch all the new words in the passage?

B. Listening for the main idea

这段话主要谈的是什么？

a) 中国的考试制度和一些考试的名称。

b) 怎么准备中考，高考和考研。

c) 中国学生都怕考试。

d) 以上都不对。

C. Listening for details

1. 学生要上高中必须参加高考，对不对？你怎么知道？

   对/不对

2. 中国所有的统一考试都由学校出题，对不对？你怎么知道？

   对/不对

3. 在中国考试的分数非常重要。对不对？为什么？

   对/不对

Post-Listening Activity

Now state your opinion as you record your voice on the multimedia CD-ROM.

你了解中国的考试制度吗？你对中国的考试制度有什么看法？

🎧 💿 TASK 3. 看一看、说一说、写一写 SHORT VIDEO

Pre-Listening Activity

Before you begin, answer the following questions, which are designed to help you predict what will happen in the video.

1. 你父母亲对你上大学有什么希望？

2. 你上大学的学费是谁付的？为什么？

Listening Activity

Now listen to the passage and then answer the questions that follow. Be sure to make a voice recording on the multimedia CD-ROM explaining each of your choices.

A. Listening for new words

Did you catch all the new words in the passage?

B. Listening for the main idea

這段話主要談的是什麼？

a) 中國的考試制度和一些考試的名稱。

b) 怎麼準備中考，高考和考研。

c) 中國學生都怕考試。

d) 以上都不對。

C. Listening for details

1. 學生要上高中必須參加高考，對不對？你怎麼知道？

   對/不對

2. 中國所有的統一考試都由學校出題，對不對？你怎麼知道？

   對/不對

3. 在中國考試的分數非常重要。對不對？為什麼？

   對/不對

Post-Listening Activity

Now state your opinion as you record your voice on the multimedia CD-ROM.

你瞭解中國的考試制度嗎？你對中國的考試制度有什麼看法？

🎧 ✿ TASK 3. 看一看、說一說、寫一寫 SHORT VIDEO

Pre-Listening Activity

Before you begin, answer the following questions, which are designed to help you predict what will happen in the video.

1. 你父母親對你上大學有什麼希望？

2. 你上大學的學費是誰付的？為什麼？

Vocabulary

1. 失望	shīwàng	*v. obj.*	to be disappointed
2. 复读	fù dú	*v.*	to repeat a grade
3. 对···来说	duì...láishuō	*phr.*	concerning, with regards to, speaking from the point of view of...
4. 后路	hòulù	*n.*	line of retreat, room for maneuver/escape

Listening Activity

Now listen to the dialogue and answer the questions that follow. Be sure to make a voice recording on the multimedia CD-ROM explaining each of your choices.

A. Listening for new words

Did you catch all the new words in the dialogue?

B. Listening for the main idea

这段话主要谈的是什么？

a) 怎么才能取得好的高考成绩。

b) 如何找一个好工作。

c) 高考的成绩和父母的期望。

d) 以上都不对。

C. Listening for details

1. 说话的这两个人谁没考上大学？爸爸妈妈觉得怎么样？

   男的/女的

2. 没考上大学的人准备怎么办？爸爸妈妈觉得怎么样？

   复读/找工作

3. 没考上大学的人最担心什么？你怎么知道？

   找不到工作/爸爸妈妈难过

Post-Listening Activity

Now state your opinion as you record your voice on the multimedia CD-ROM, and then write a summary of the dialogue.

请你用自己的话说一说这段对话都讲了些什么？

Vocabulary

1. 失望	shīwàng	*v. obj.*	to be disappointed
2. 複讀	fù dú	*v.*	to repeat a grade
3. 對⋯來說	duì...láishuō	*phr.*	concerning, with regards to, speaking from the point of view of...
4. 後路	hòulù	*n.*	line of retreat, room for maneuver/escape

Listening Activity

Now listen to the dialogue and answer the questions that follow. Be sure to make a voice recording on the multimedia CD-ROM explaining each of your choices.

A. Listening for new words

Did you catch all the new words in the dialogue?

B. Listening for the main idea

這段話主要談的是什麼？

a) 怎麼才能取得好的高考成績。

b) 如何找一個好工作。

c) 高考的成績和父母的期望。

d) 以上都不對。

C. Listening for details

1. 說話的這兩個人誰沒考上大學？爸爸媽媽覺得怎麼樣？

   男的/女的

2. 沒考上大學的人準備怎麼辦？爸爸媽媽覺得怎麼樣？

   複讀/找工作

3. 沒考上大學的人最擔心什麼？你怎麼知道？

   找不到工作/爸爸媽媽難過

Post-Listening Activity

Now state your opinion as you record your voice on the multimedia CD-ROM, and then write a summary of the dialogue.

請你用自己的話說一說這段對話都講了些什麼？

🎧 📖 TASK 4. 读一读、写一写 READING EXERCISES

This section consists of two parts: Short Stories and Authentic Material.

A. Short Stories

After reading each of the two Chinese stories, respond in Chinese to the questions that follow.

成语故事：名落孙山

在中国古时候要做官都要经过考试。考试考得越好，官就做得越大。有一次，一个叫孙山的人又聪明又有才，他要到一个很远的地方去参加考试。他的邻居有一个儿子，也要去参加考试。他的邻居就叫孙山带着他的儿子一起去，这样可以帮助照顾照顾他的儿子。

考完试以后，他们俩很快就看到了他们考试的成绩。孙山虽然被录取了，但是他在被录取的人中是最后一名，邻居的儿子没有考上，所以他决定留下来复习，准备参加下一次的考试。孙山回到家以后，他的邻居问他："我的儿子考得怎么样？考上了没有？"孙山这个人很会说话。他不愿意说："您儿子没有考上。"所以他笑着对他的邻居说："考试录取的名单上我的名字在最后，您儿子还在我的后边。"

Vocabulary

1. 名落孙山	(míng luò Sūn Shān)		
孙山	Sūn Shān	*prop. n.*	(from a classical Chinese story) name of a person
2. 官	guān	*n.*	government official
3. 邻居	línjū	*n.*	neighbor
4. 照顾	zhàogù	*v.*	to take care of

Questions

1. 用你自己的话讲一讲"名落孙山"是什么意思？

2. 看完这个故事，你觉得那个孙山聪明不聪明？为什么？

3. 你听说过什么名落孙山的故事吗？请你说一说。

成语故事：专心致志

古时候有一个下棋下得非常好的人。他的名字叫秋。全国没有人能下赢他。有一天，有两个年轻人从很远的地方来跟他学下棋。一个学生很努力，老师说什么，

🎧 🖼 TASK 4. 讀一讀、寫一寫 READING EXERCISES

This section consists of two parts: Short Stories and Authentic Material.

A. Short Stories

After reading each of the two Chinese stories, respond in Chinese to the questions that follow.

成語故事：名落孫山

在中國古時候要做官都要經過考試。考試考得越好，官就做得越大。有一次，一個叫孫山的人又聰明又有才，他要到一個很遠的地方去參加考試。他的鄰居有一個兒子，也要去參加考試。他的鄰居就叫孫山帶著他的兒子一起去，這樣可以幫助照顧照顧他的兒子。

考完試以後，他們倆很快就看到了他們考試的成績。孫山雖然被錄取了，但是他在被錄取的人中是最後一名，鄰居的兒子沒有考上，所以他決定留下來復習，準備參加下一次的考試。孫山回到家以後，他的鄰居問他：“我的兒子考得怎麼樣？考上了沒有？”孫山這個人很會說話。他不願意說：“您兒子沒有考上。”所以他笑著對他的鄰居說：“考試錄取的名單上我的名字在最後，您兒子還在我的後邊。”

Vocabulary

1. 名落孫山	(míng luò Sūn Shān)		
孫山	Sūn Shān	*prop. n.*	(from a classical Chinese story) name of a person
2. 官	guān	*n.*	government official
3. 鄰居	línjū	*n.*	neighbor
4. 照顧	zhàogù	*v.*	to take care of

Questions

1. 用你自己的話講一講“名落孫山”是什麼意思？
2. 看完這個故事，你覺得那個孫山聰明不聰明？為什麼？
3. 你听说过什么名落孫山的故事嗎？請你說一說。

成語故事：專心致志

古時候有一個下棋下得非常好的人。他的名字叫秋。全國沒有人能下贏他。有一天，有兩個年輕人從很遠的地方來跟他學下棋。一個學生很努力，老師說什麼，他都仔细地听，认真地写下来，所以那个学生进步很快。另外的那个学生虽然好像也在听老师讲课，但是他的心早就飞到窗户外边去了。一天，他看见一只天鹅从天上飞了过来，他马上就想到怎么把那只天鹅射下来。他在上课的时候不是想这个就是想那个，就是不肯花时间想怎么能下好棋。所以他学下棋的时间虽然跟那个好学生一样长，但是他却没学到真正的下棋本领。秋老师每天都叫他跟那个好学生下棋，他总是输，从来没赢过。不管老师怎么说他，他学习还是不专心。最后，老师只好让他回家去了。

Vocabulary

1. 专心致志   (zhuān xīn zhì zhì)
   专   zhuān   *v.*   to focus
   致   zhì   *v.*   to concentrate
   志   zhì   *n.*   aspiration
2. 年轻人   niánqīng rén   *n.*   young people
3. 好像   hǎoxiàng   *v.*   to seem
4. 天鹅   tiān'é   *n.*   swan
5. 射   shè   *v.*   to shoot (an arrow)
6. 本领   běnlǐng   *n.*   ability, capacity

Questions

1. 用你自己的话讲一讲"专心致志"是什么意思？
2. 看完这个故事，你觉得为什么两个学生一起学下棋，一个学得很好，一个就学不好？
3. 用你自己的话讲一个"专心致志"的故事。

B. Authentic Material

In this section, you will be exposed to some authentic materials used in China. Read the following Internet articles, and answer the questions.

Questions

1. 高考成绩重要不重要？有什么好处？
2. 高考名落孙山的学生多不多？大约有多少？
3. 高考时间有没有改变？

他都仔細地聽，認真地寫下來，所以那個學生進步很快。另外的那個學生雖然好像也在聽老師講課，但是他的心早就飛到窗戶外邊去了。一天，他看見一隻天鵝從天上飛了過來，他馬上就想到怎麼把那只天鵝射下來。他在上課的時候不是想這個就是想那個，就是不肯花時間想怎麼能下好棋。所以他學下棋的時間雖然跟那個好學生一樣長，但是他卻沒學到真正的下棋本領。秋老師每天都叫他跟那個好學生下棋，他總是輸，從來沒贏過。不管老師怎麼說他，他學習還是不專心。最後，老師只好讓他回家去了。

Vocabulary

1. 專心致志	(zhuān xīn zhì zhì)			
專	zhuān	*v.*		to focus
致	zhì	*v.*		to concentrate
志	zhì	*n.*		aspiration
2. 年輕人	niánqīng rén	*n.*		young people
3. 好像	hǎoxiàng	*v.*		to seem
4. 天鵝	tiān'é	*n.*		swan
5. 射	shè	*v.*		to shoot (an arrow)
6. 本領	běnlǐng	*n.*		ability, capacity

Questions

1. 用你自己的話講一講 "專心致志" 是什麼意思？
2. 看完這個故事，你覺得為什麼兩個學生一起學下棋，一個學得很好，一個就學不好？
3. 用你自己的話講一個 "專心致志" 的故事？

B. Authentic Material

In this section, you will be exposed to some authentic materials used in China. Read the following Internet articles, and answer the questions.

Questions

1. 高考成績重要不重要？有什麼好處？
2. 高考名落孫山的學生多不多？大約有多少？
3. 高考時間有沒有改變？

Google News BETA

网页　图片　**新闻**　论坛　网页目录　**更多 »**

高考　　　　　　　　　　　　　[搜索新闻]　[搜索所有网页]　使用偏好

新闻

| 焦点 |
| 国际/港台 |
| 内地 |
| 财经 |
| 科技 |
| 体育 |
| 娱乐 |
| 社会 |

✉ 新闻快讯

关于
Google 新闻
或提供建议

约有15,900项符合高考的查询结果, 以下是第1-10项。(搜索用时0.31秒)

按内容相关性进行排序　按日期排序

特别時期高考從六月開始
博客中国 - 11小时前
高考前几天, 在电话中家长告诉记者, 非典时期停了一个月课, 孩子说毕竟是个损失。如果在学校系统地复习一个月, 那就不一样了。再加上今年高考提前了一个月, 所以无形中就等于少了两个月。所以孩子就拼命学, 高考前几天还要学到…

高考成绩有助拓宽你的出国留学路
网易 - 8小时前
高考录取工作目前已经进入尾声, 相当一部分应届高中毕业生最终选择了出国留学。在日前举办的一场大型公益留学咨询会上, 笔者发现咨询者中不乏放弃高考的学生, 究其原因, 学生和家长回答得"理直气壮"——反正迟早要出国, 参不…

高考落选考生预计近10万
南方日报 - 14小时前
本报讯 (记者/梅志清通讯员/廖翊华) 昨日, 省报生办透露, 今年高考落选考生预计近10万人, 已被录取的考生千万要珍惜难得的读大学机会。现在专科录取正在紧张进行, 预计将在8月10日、11日两天进行专科补报志愿…

南宁一考生高考考出好成绩获50万港币奖学金
新华网广西频道 - 8小时前
…你看, 他就是这么有信心和主见, 几乎不用我们操什么心。就说这次高考填报志愿, 他也没有过多征求我们的意见, 他说: "我都这么大了, 我会为自己选到一所适合自己发展的学校。"他看准香港中文大学就直接报了, 得到学校50…

🎧🌸 TASK 5. 想一想、说一说 PRESENTATION

Please pick one of the following for your presentation.

A. Individual Presentation

1. You are friends with an overseas Chinese graduate student living in the U.S. with his wife and infant child. He is considering staying in the U.S. so his child will not have to go through the Chinese education system. He asks you for your thoughts on the advantages and disadvantages of this decision. Referring to information in the text, respond to his request.

网页　图片　**新闻**　论坛　网页目录　**更多 »**

Google News BETA

高考   搜索新闻   搜索所有网页   使用偏好

新闻

约有**15,900**项符合高考的查询结果, 以下是第**1-10**项。(搜索用时**0.31**秒)

焦点
国际/港台
内地
财经
科技
体育
娱乐
社会

按内容相关性进行排序   按日期排序

特別時期高考從六月開始
博客中國 - 11小时前

高考前幾天，在電話中家長告訴記者，非典時期停了一個月課，孩子說畢竟是個損失。如果在學校系統地復習一個月，那就不一樣了。再加上今年高考提前了一個月，所以無形中就等於少了兩個月。所以孩子就拼命學，高考前幾天還要學到 …

✉ 新聞快讯

关于
Google 新闻
或提供建议

高考成績有助拓寬你的出國留學路
網易 - 8小時前

高考錄取工作目前已經進入尾聲，相當一部分應屆高中畢業生最終選擇了出國留學。在日前舉辦的一場大型公益留學諮詢會上，筆者發現咨詢者中不乏放棄高考的學生，究其原因，學生和家長回答得 " 理直氣壯 " ——反正遲早要出國，參不 …

高考落選考生預計近10萬
南方日報 - 14小時前

本報訊（記者/梅志清通訊員/廖翊華）昨日，省報生辦透露，今年高考落選考生預計近10萬人，已被錄取的考生千萬要珍惜難得的讀大學機會。現在專科錄取正在緊張進行，預計將在8月10日、11日兩天進行專科補報志願 …

南寧一考生高考考出好成績獲50萬港幣獎學金
新華網廣西頻道 - 8小時前

…你看，他就是這麼有信心和主見，幾乎不用我們操什麼心。就說這次高考填報志願，他也沒有過多徵求我們的意見，他說：" 我都這麼大了，我會為自己選到一所適合自己發展的學校。" 他看準香港中文大學就直接報了，得到學校50…

🎧 TASK 5. 想一想、説一説 PRESENTATION

Please pick one of the following for your presentation.

A. Individual Presentation

1. You are friends with an overseas Chinese graduate student living in the U.S. with his wife and infant child. He is considering staying in the U.S. so his child will not have to go through the Chinese education system. He asks you for your thoughts on the advantages and disadvantages of this decision. Referring to information in the text, respond to his request.

2. A Chinese high-school senior comes to you with a problem. She can't afford to pay college tuition, and she isn't sure that she wants to attend college anyway. Based on the information in the text, tell her about other options besides college for continuing her education, as well as anything you know about financial aid opportunities that help pay college tuition.

B. Group Presentation

Setting: In a home
Cast: Parents and their child, who is graduating from a high school
Situation: The parents desperately want their child to attend college. However, their child does not want to go. Carry out a debate about whether or not the child should go to college. Who will win the argument?

∩ ⬤ TASK 6. 想一想、写一写 COMPOSITION

Write an essay that could be included as part of your application for a summer program (real or fictitious) in China. Be sure to discuss how the program could help you achieve your goals and why you should be selected for this program. If you need help finding a summer program, go to http://www.yahoo.com.cn/.

2. A Chinese high-school senior comes to you with a problem. She can't afford to pay college tuition, and she isn't sure that she wants to attend college anyway. Based on the information in the text, tell her about other options besides college for continuing her education, as well as anything you know about financial aid opportunities that help pay college tuition.

B. Group Presentation

Setting: In a home
Cast: Parents and their child, who is graduating from a high school
Situation: The parents desperately want their child to attend college. However, their child does not want to go. Carry out a debate about whether or not the child should go to college. Who will win the argument?

○ TASK 6. 想一想、寫一寫 COMPOSITION

Write an essay that could be included as part of your application for a summer program (real or fictitious) in China. Be sure to discuss how the program could help you achieve your goals and why you should be selected for this program. If you need help finding a summer program, go to http://www.yahoo.com.cn/.

Appendix:

List of Grammar Points

Chinese-English Vocabulary Glossary, Arranged Alphabetically by Pinyin

This vocabulary glossary includes all regular vocabulary, spoken expressions, and supplementary vocabulary for *Chinese Odyssey, Volumes 5 & 6*. An "s" after a lesson number means that the word comes from a supplementary vocabulary list. For proper nouns, see the Glossary of Proper Nouns.

Simplified	Traditional	Pinyin	Part of Speech	Definition	Lesson
安静	安靜	ānjìng	adj.	quiet, tranquil	43
按照	按照	ànzhào	prep.	following the pattern of, according to	41
熬	熬	áo	v.	to stew, to simmer	44
B超	B超	B chāo	n.	ultrasound	44
白吃	白吃	bái chī	s.e.	to eat in vain, to suffer in vain	44
百姓	百姓	bǎixìng	n.	ordinary people; (lit.) the hundred surnames	48
半成品	半成品	bànchéngpǐn	n.	(lit.) half-finished product	41
包括	包括	bāokuò	v.	to include, to contain	49
包子	包子	bāozi	n.	steamed bun (with filling)	41
保	保	bǎo	b.f.	to protect, to safeguard, to defend, to guarantee	47
保持	保持	bǎochí	v.	to maintain, to keep	49
保护	保護	bǎohù	v., n.	to protect, to preserve; protection	50
保龄球	保齡球	bǎolíng qiú	n.	bowling; (lit.) bowling ball	43
保险	保險	bǎoxiǎn	adj., n.	safe, secure; insurance; (lit.) protection against danger	47
保障	保障	bǎozhàng	n.	guarantee, security, protection	47

329

Simplified	Traditional	Pinyin	Part of Speech	Definition	Lesson
保证金	保證金	bǎozhèngjīn	n.	financial aid; (lit.) security money	48
报酬	報酬	bàochou	n.	reward, remuneration	49
报告	報告	bàogào	n.	report	50
爆炸	爆炸	bàozhà	n., v.	explosion; to explode	47
北方	北方	běifāng	n.	north, northern direction	41
背	背	bèi	n.	back (of the body)	49
背景	背景	bèijǐng	n.	background	49
本地	本地	běndì	n.	this locality, this place	50
比方	比方	bǐfang	n.	example, illustration	41
比方说	比方說	bǐfang shuō	phr.	for example, for instance	41
比例	比例	bǐlì	n.	proportion, ratio	44
闭	閉	bì	b.f.	to close up, to shut tight	50
毕业	畢業	bì yè	v.obj.	to graduate	43
避	避	bì	b.f.	to evade, to keep away	47
避免	避免	bìmiǎn	v.	to avoid	47
变化	變化	biànhuà	n.	change, transformation	46
表示	表示	biǎoshì	n., v.	indication; to express, to show, to demonstrate, to indicate	41
饼(子)	餅(子)	bǐng (zi)	n.	pancake	41
并不是…而是	並不是…而是	bìng búshì…érshì	conj.	contrary to what one would expect, it is not true that…, it is however true that…	43
病情	病情	bìngqíng	n.	the condition of an illness, the state of a disease	44
博士	博士	bóshì	n.	doctoral degree	45
不断	不斷	búduàn	adv.	unbroken, uninterrupted, incessant; (lit.) no break	44

Simplified	Traditional	Pinyin	Part of Speech	Definition	Lesson
不妨	不妨	bùfáng	v.	to have no harm in, might as well	44
不管	不管	bùguǎn	conj.	regardless of	41
不合	不合	bùhé	v.	to not get along with each other, to be in disharmony	46
不仅	不僅	bùjǐn	adv.	not only	45
不堪	不堪	bùkān	v.	(formal) cannot bear, cannot put up with	50
不堪设想	不堪設想	bùkān shèxiǎng	phr.	(usually in the negative) inconceivable, unthinkable, unbearable to think about	50
不然	不然	bùrán	conj.	otherwise, in other case	44
不如	不如	bùrú	conj.	not as good as	45
不是个办法	不是個辦法	bùshì ge bànfǎ	s.e.	not a good method	44
不足	不足	bùzú	adj.	insufficient, not enough	47
部长	部長	bùzhǎng	n.	minister	49
材料	材料	cáiliào	n.	building material, material, data, information	45
裁员	裁員	cáiyuán	v.	to reduce staff, to downsize	48
采取	採取	cǎiqǔ	v.	to adopt (a way of doing things)	49
采用	採用	cǎiyòng	v.	to (choose to) adopt, to (choose to) use	49
菜系	菜系	càixì	n.	culinary system, culinary tradition	41
差距	差距	chājù	n.	disparity, contrast	48
插	插	chā	v.	to stick (something) in, to insert	41
插足	插足	chāzú	v. obj.	to put one's foot in (someone else's affairs), to interfere with (other's affairs)	46

Simplified	Traditional	Pinyin	Part of Speech	Definition	Lesson
馋	饞	chán	adj.	gluttonous, drooling over (food), making (somebody) drool over (food)	42
产	產	chǎn	b.f.	product	41
产品	產品	chǎnpǐn	n.	product	48
产生	產生	chǎnshēng	v.	to give rise to, to produce, to emerge	49
厂子	廠子	chǎngzi	s.e.	factory	48
车辆	車輛	chēliàng	n.	vehicles (collectively)	50
尘	塵	chén	b.f.	dust, dirt	50
陈皮牛	陳皮牛	chénpí niú	n.	orange beef	41
成功	成功	chénggōng	v. obj.	to achieve success; (lit.) to complete a meritorious deed	47
成立	成立	chénglì	v.	to set up, to establish	49
成品	成品	chéngpǐn	n.	ready-made product, finished product	41
成药	成藥	chéngyào	n.	ready-made medicine	44
成长	成長	chéngzhǎng	n.	(bodily) development, growth	50
逞能	逞能	chěng néng	s.e.	to brag, to show off one's abilities	45
冲突	衝突	chōngtū	n.	conflict, clash, confrontation	49
筹	籌	chóu	b.f.	to plan, prepare, raise (money)	50
筹备	籌備	chóubèi	v.	to prepare, to arrange, to plan	50
臭氧层	臭氧層	chòuyǎngcéng	n.	ozone layer	50
出路	出路	chūlù	n.	outlet, exit; (lit.) a way out	45
出于	出於	chūyú	v. comp.	to come from	50

Simplified	Traditional	Pinyin	Part of Speech	Definition	Lesson
初	初	chū	b.f.	elementary, beginning, first part of, the first ten day period of a lunar month	42
初中	初中	chūzhōng	n.	middle school	45
除	除	chú	v.	to take away, to divide	42
除此之外	除此之外	chú cǐ zhīwài	conj.	other than this/these, apart from this/these	42
除非	除非	chúfēi	conj.	unless	45
除非…否则	除非…否則	chúfēi…fǒuzé	conj.	unless… otherwise…	45
处	處	chǔ	b.f.	to be placed in/at, to be in/at, to stay in/at, to get along (with somebody)	50
处理	處理	chǔlǐ	v.	to process, to handle, to deal with	49
处于	處於	chǔyú	v. comp.	(formal) to find oneself in (a situation), to be placed in a situation	50
传	傳	chuán	v.	to pass on, to hand down, to circulate	42
传统	傳統	chuántǒng	n.	tradition	42
此	此	cǐ	prop.	the Classical Chinese equivalent of 这/这些	42
凑合	湊合	còuhe	adj., v.	so-so, bearable; to make do, to put up (with a situation, a person).	46
存在	存在	cúnzài	v.	(formal) to have (in existence), to exist, to remain	46
错过	錯過	cuòguò	v.	to miss (an opportunity)	45
措施	措施	cuòshī	n.	(formal) measure, step (to accomplish something)	50
搭	搭	dā	v.	to bring together, to build (by putting pieces together)	44

Simplified	Traditional	Pinyin	Part of Speech	Definition	Lesson
搭配	搭配	dāpèi	v.	to combine, to match up, to intermingle	44
打麻将	打麻將	dǎ májiàng	v. obj.	to play mahjong	43
打牌	打牌	dǎ pái	v. obj.	to play cards	43
打招呼	打招呼	dǎ zhāohu	v.	to say hello	43
大幅度	大幅度	dà fúdù	adv.	on a large scale	50
大量	大量	dàliàng	n.	(lit.) a large amount (of), large quantity (of)	47
大陆	大陸	dàlù	n.	mainland	49
大米	大米	dàmǐ	n.	rice	41
(大)型	(大)型	(dà)xíng	n.	(large-) scale	48
大学	大學	dàxué	n.	college/university	45
大约	大約	dàyuē	adv.	approximately	49
大夫	大夫	dàifu	n.	medical doctor	44
代	代	dài	n.	generation, dynasty, era	42
待	待	dài	b.f.	treatment	49
贷	貸	dài	b.f.	to lend, to borrow	50
贷款	貸款	dàikuǎn	n., v. obj.	loan, credit; (formal) to borrow/lend money	50
担忧	擔憂	dānyōu	v. obj.	to worry; (lit.) to carry anxiety	50
当今	當今	dāngjīn	adv.	nowadays	47
当选	當選	dāngxuǎn	v.	to be elected, to succeed in an election	49
倒	倒	dǎo	v.	to fall, to topple	50
倒闭	倒閉	dǎobì	v.	to go bankrupt; (lit.) to fall and close	50
导致	導致	dǎozhì	v.	(usually negative) to lead to, to result in, to cause	47
到时候你…	到時候你…	dào shíhou nǐ…	s.e.	when the time comes, you would (do something)	44
地区	地區	dìqū	n.	region, area, district, zone	50

Simplified	Traditional	Pinyin	Part of Speech	Definition	Lesson
地位	地位	dìwèi	n.	status, standing, position	46
第三者插足	第三者插足	dìsānzhě chāzú	phr.	a third person stepping in (the marriage)	46
丢人	丢人	diūrén	v. obj.	to lose face; (lit.) to lose one's personal dignity	46
电视台	電視臺	diànshì tái	n.	TV station, TV channel	43
调	調	diào	n.	melody, tune, accent	47
调查	調查	diàochá	v.	to investigate	50
动脑子	動腦子	dòng nǎozi	s.e.	to think; (lit.) to move one's brain	43
动物	動物	dòngwu	n.	animal, the animal kingdom	44
断	斷	duàn	v.	to cut off, to break	44
独(生)	獨(生)	dúshēng	n.	only (child); (lit.) only birth	47
对方	對方	duìfāng	n.	the other; (lit.) the opposite side	46
恶	惡	è	adj.	evil, bad	50
恶化	惡化	èhuà	v.	to become worse, worsen, to deteriorate	50
二氧化硫	二氧化硫	èryǎnghuàliú	n.	sulphur dioxide	50
发生	發生	fāshēng	v.	to occur, to happen, to arise, to emerge	46
发展	發展	fāzhǎn	n., v.	development, growth; to develop, to expand	41
罚	罰	fá	v.	to punish, to penalize	47
罚款	罰款	fá kuǎn	n.	penalty, fine	47
法	法	fǎ	b.f.	way, method, mode	44
法定	法定	fǎdìng	adj.	determined by law, prescribed by law	42
发	髮	fà	b.f.	(formal) hair (on the head of a human being)	48

Simplified	Traditional	Pinyin	Part of Speech	Definition	Lesson
发廊	髮廊	fàláng	n.	hair salon	48
烦	煩	fán	v.	to irritate, to bother	43
烦恼	煩惱	fánnǎo	adj., n.	troublesome, vexing; trouble, vexation	43
反对	反對	fǎnduì	v.	to be opposed to, to object	46
范围	範圍	fànwéi	n.	range, scope	48
方面	方面	fāngmiàn	n.	aspect, side	43
方式	方式	fāngshì	n.	method, pattern, mode; (lit.) direction and pattern	41
放宽	放寬	fàngkuān	v. comp.	to relax (rules, regulations, etc.), to loosen; (lit.) to let go and broaden	47
放弃	放棄	fàngqì	v.	to give up; (lit.) to let go and abandon	42
非但不(没)… 反而…	非但不(没)… 反而…	fēidàn bù/méi… fǎn'ér…	conj.	not only … but on the contrary…	47
非婚	非婚	fēihūn	adj.	out of wedlock	46
废气	廢氣	fèiqì	n.	waste gas/steam, fume	50
废渣	廢渣	fèizhā	n.	waste residue, dross	50
(分数)线	(分數)線	(fēnshù) xiàn	n.	the cut-off point for admission to schools	45
逢	逢	féng	v.	to come upon, to encounter	42
否	否	fǒu	b.f.	not true, negative	47
肤	膚	fū	n.	facial skin, skin	44
幅度	幅度	fúdù	n.	amplitude, range	50
负担	負擔	fùdān	n.	responsibility, burden	47
父母	父母	fùmǔ	n.	parents	45
附近	附近	fùjìn	n.	nearby area, surrounding area	44
复杂	複雜	fùzá	adj.	complicated, complex	49

Simplified	Traditional	Pinyin	Part of Speech	Definition	Lesson
富	富	fù	b.f.	rich, the rich	48
副食	副食	fùshí	n.	non-staple food (soup, vegetables, meat, pastry, etc.)	41
副	副	fù	pref.	side (effect), minor, marginal, vice-	41
改变	改變	gǎibiàn	n., v.	change; to alter, to change	41
改革	改革	gǎigé	n., v.	reform; to reform	48
改善	改善	gǎishàn	n., v.	improvement; to improve, to better, to ameliorate	50
干扁四季豆	幹扁四季豆	gānbiǎn sìjìdòu	n.	crispy beans	41
赶鸭子上架	趕鴨子上架	gǎn yāzi shàng jià	s.e.	(lit.) to force the duck onto the shelf; (met.) to force someone to do something beyond his/her ability	45
感觉	感覺	gǎnjué	n., v.	feeling, sense; to have the feeling	42
岗	崗	gǎng	b.f.	(guard or sentry) post	48
高尔夫(球)	高爾夫(球)	gāo'erfū (qiú)	n.	golf	43
高中	高中	gāozhōng	n.	high school	45
高专	高專	gāozhuān	n.	vocational high school	45
歌曲	歌曲	gēqǔ	n.	(formal) song	43
个体户	個體戶	gètǐhù	n.	individual entrepreneur, (private) merchant	48
各行各业	各行各業	gè háng gè yè	n.	each and every trade and profession, all walks of life	48
根据	根據	gēnjù	prep.	according to	44
更加	更加	gèngjiā	adv.	(formal) even more	42
工厂	工廠	gōngchǎng	n.	factory	48
工程	工程	gōngchéng	n.	engineering project	50
工业	工業	gōngyè	n.	industry	50
工资	工資	gōngzī	n.	salary; (lit.) work money	48

Simplified	Traditional	Pinyin	Part of Speech	Definition	Lesson
公历	公曆	gōnglì	n.	Western calendar; (lit.) public calendar	42
公立	公立	gōnglì	adj.	public; (lit.) publicly owned/established	45
供	供	gōng	v.	to provide, to supply	48
供求	供求	gōngqiú	n.	supply and demand	48
宫保鸡丁	宮保雞丁	gōngbǎo jīdīng	n.	gongbao chicken	41
古代	古代	gǔdài	n.	ancient times	42
古老	古老	gǔlǎo	adj.	ancient	44
鼓励	鼓勵	gǔlì	n., v.	encouragement; to encourage, to promote	47
固	固	gù	adj.	tenacious, solid, hard	44
固然	固然	gùrán	adv.	admittedly, although it is true …	44
关闭	關閉	guānbì	v.	to shut down (a store, a factory, etc.), to block (a road, a street,etc.)	50
关于	關於	guānyú	conj.	concerning, regarding, about	49
关注	關注	guānzhù	n., v.	attention; (formal) to pay close attention to, to focus in on (a topic, a change, etc.), to be concerned with	47
观念	觀念	guānniàn	n.	outlook, viewpoint, standpoint	46
官	官	guān	n.	government official	49
官员	官員	guānyuán	n.	government official	49
管	管	guǎn	v.	to control, to take responsibility for	48
管理	管理	guǎnlǐ	v.	management; to manage (a business, an institution, a group, etc.), to control	50
广	廣	guǎng	adj.	broad, wide, vast	44

Simplified	Traditional	Pinyin	Part of Speech	Definition	Lesson
规定	規定	guīdìng	n., v.	rule, regulation; to set as a rule	45
鬼	鬼	guǐ	n.	ghost	47
国家	國家	guójiā	n.	country, nation, state	42
国民经济	國民經濟	guómín jīngjì	n.	national economy	48
国营企业	國營企業	guóyíng qǐyè	n.	state-owned enterprise	48
国有制	國有制	guóyǒu zhì	n.	state ownership system	48
果然	果然	guǒrán	conj.	as expected, just as one would expect	43
过程	過程	guòchéng	n.	process, course (of an action or event)	49
过分	過分	guòfèn	adj., v. obj.	excessive; to exceed the normal limit, to transgress the limit	47
过去	過去	guòqù	n.	the past	43
海峡两岸	海峽兩岸	hǎixiá liǎngàn	phr.	two shores of the Taiwan strait, referring to mainland China and the island of Taiwan	49
海洋	海洋	hǎiyáng	n.	ocean	50
函	函	hán	n.	(formal) correspondence, letter	45
函授	函授	hánshòu	n.	to teach by correspondence	45
函授大学	函授大學	hánshòu dàxué	n.	correspondence school	45
行业	行業	hángyè	n.	business, trade, profession	48
好处	好處	hǎochu	n.	advantage, benefit; (lit.) good points	47
合	合	hé	b.f., v.	to match each other, to be in harmony; to join, to unite, to combine	44
河川	河川	héchuān	n.	rivers big and small	50
盒	盒	hé	m.w.	box	42

Simplified	Traditional	Pinyin	Part of Speech	Definition	Lesson
衡量	衡量	héngliáng	v.	to measure, to gauge	45
红油抄手	紅油抄手	hóngyóu chāoshǒu	n.	dumplings in hot and spicy oil	41
后果	後果	hòuguǒ	n.	(usually in the negative) aftermath, consequence	50
后悔	後悔	hòuhuǐ	v.	to regret, to repent	44
呼	呼	hu	v.	to call out	43
滑冰	滑冰	huá bīng	v. obj.	to skate (on ice); (lit.) to slide on ice	43
滑雪	滑雪	huá xuě	v. obj.	to ski (in snow); (lit.) to slide on snow	43
化	化	huà	b.f.	-ise, -ize	41
怀	懷	huái	v.	to conceive, to be pregnant with; (lit.) to have in one's bosom	47
环	環	huán	b.f.	to surround, to encircle	50
环境	環境	huánjìng	n.	environment, surroundings, ambience	50
回头	回頭	huítóu	v. obj.	to turn back one's head, to turn backwards	48
回头客	回頭客	huítóukè	s.e.	returning clients/ customers	48
婚外情	婚外情	hūn wài qíng	n. phr.	extramarital affair, illicit love affair	46
婚姻	婚姻	hūnyīn	n.	marriage, wedlock	46
婚姻介绍所	婚姻介紹所	hūnyīnjièshàosuǒ	n.	dating service; (lit.) place for introducing (singles to each other)	46
火鸡	火雞	huǒjī	n.	turkey	42
湖水	湖水	húshuǐ	n.	lake water	50
户外	戶外	hùwài	n.	outdoor	43
机关	機關	jīguān	n.	mechanism, (government) institution	49

Simplified	Traditional	Pinyin	Part of Speech	Definition	Lesson
基本上	基本上	jīběn shàng	adv.	basically, generally speaking	45
基金	基金	jījīn	n.	fund, endowment	50
激烈	激烈	jīliè	adj.	intense, fierce	45
及	及	jí	b.f.	to reach, to extend	42
即	即	jí	adv.	namely, that is, thence; (lit.) the classical Chinese word for 就 or 就是	45
即便/即使	即便/即使	jíbiàn/jíshǐ	conj.	(formal) even if, even though	47
急性	急性	jíxìng	n.	fast-acting, short-tempered nature, impatient personality; (lit.) quick nature	44
急性病	急性病	jíxìngbìng	n.	acute disease; (lit.) quick-natured disease	44
集体	集體	jítǐ	n.	collective; (lit.) collective body	48
集中	集中	jízhōng	v.	to focus, to concentrate	49
计划经济	計劃經濟	jìhuà jīngjì	n.	planned economy	48
计算	計算	jìsuàn	n., v.	calculation; (formal) to calculate, to count	42
纪	紀	jì	b.f.	to write down, to record	42
纪念	紀念	jìniàn	n., v.	commemoration, remembrance; to commemorate, to honor by remembering	42
际	際	jì	n.	boundary, border	43
技	技	jì	n.	skill, ability	47
技术	技術	jìshù	n.	technique, skill, technology	47
既然	既然	jìrán	conj.	since (something has already happened)..., now that...	46

Simplified	Traditional	Pinyin	Part of Speech	Definition	Lesson
济	濟	jì	b.f.	to tide over, to aid; (lit.) to cross (a river)	48
继续	繼續	jìxù	v.	to continue, to keep on	46
继…之后	繼…之後	jì…zhīhòu	phr.	(formal) following…	48
加入	加入	jiārù	v.	to join, to enter, to add, to put in	48
加以	加以	jiāyǐ	conj., v.	in addition; to add (followed by a verb)	49
家常豆腐	家常豆腐	jiācháng dòufu	n.	home-style tofu	41
家庭	家庭	jiātíng	n.	(formal) family, household	43
家务	家務	jiāwù	n.	housework	46
尖子	尖子	jiānzi	s.e.	top, top student	45
减少	減少	jiǎnshǎo	v.	to decrease, to reduce, to cut down	46
剪	剪	jiǎn	v.	to cut or trim with scissors	48
剪发	剪髮	jiǎn fà	v. obj.	to have a haircut; (lit.) to cut hair	48
间接	間接	jiànjiē	adv.	indirectly	49
建	建	jiàn	v.	to build (buildings), to construct, to establish	48
建立	建立	jiànlì	v.	to establish, to build; (lit.) to construct and set up	48
健身	健身	jiànshēn	v. obj.	to strengthen the body, to improve health	43
健身房	健身房	jiànshēnfáng	n.	gymnasium	43
渐	漸	jiàn	b.f.	gradually	43
践	踐	jiàn	v.	to step on, to tread on	47
讲究	講究	jiǎngjiu	adj., v.	fastidious, artistic, sophisticated; (of taste) to be particular about, to be fastidious about	41

Simplified	Traditional	Pinyin	Part of Speech	Definition	Lesson
交	交	jiāo	v.	(of two things) to cross, to interact, to meet (new friends), to hand over, to deliver	43
交际	交際	jiāojì	v. obj.	to socialize with others	43
叫停	叫停	jiàotíng	s.e.	to call for a stop, to shut down	50
教育	教育	jiàoyù	n., v.	education; to educate, to teach	45
接受	接受	jiēshòu	v.	to accept, to bear	46
节目	節目	jiémù	n.	program	43
节庆	節慶	jiéqìng	n.	holiday festivities, holiday celebrations	42
结	結	jié	v.	to knot, to tie up	44
结果	結果	jiéguǒ	conj., n.	as a result; result, consequence	43
结合	結合	jiéhé	v.	to unite, to unify, to join in wedlock	44
解	解	jiě	v.	to dissolve	47
解决	解決	jiějué	v.	to find a solution (to a problem), to remove (obstacles)	47
今后	今後	jīnhòu	n.	future, hereafter	46
仅	僅	jǐn	b.f.	(lit.) the classical Chinese word for 只	45
尽管	儘管	jǐnguǎn	conj.	even though	47
进步	進步	jìnbù	n., v.	progress; to make progress	45
进货	進貨	jìnhuò	v. obj.	to stock goods	48
进行	進行	jìnxíng	v.	to carry on	45
进一步	進一步	jìn yī bù	phr.	(lit.) take one step further	46
京剧	京劇	jīngjù	n.	Beijing Opera	43
经过	經過	jīngguò	n., v.	process; to pass through (an area), to go through (an experience)	43

Simplified	Traditional	Pinyin	Part of Speech	Definition	Lesson
经济	經濟	jīngjì	n.	economy, financial state	47
经济特区	經濟特區	jīngjì tèqū	n.	special economic zone (SEZ)	48
经营	經營	jīngyíng	n., v.	management; to run (a business)	48
景	景	jǐng	b.f.	scenery, view	49
净化	淨化	jìnghuà	v.	to purify	50
竞争	競爭	jìngzhēng	n., v.	competition; to compete	45
竟然	竟然	jìngrán	adv.	unbelievably, beyond imagination	46
境	境	jìng	b.f.	area, place, condition, circumstances	50
就	就	jiù	b.f.	(classical Chinese) to have access to, to get close to	48
就业	就業	jiù yè	v. obj.	to have a job, to get a job, to be employed	48
就…而言	就…而言	jiù…éryán	phr.	in the case of…, as for…; (lit.) talking about…	48
救	救	jiù	v.	to save, to rescue	48
救济	救濟	jiùjì	v.	to provide relief; (lit.) to save and tide over	48
居	居	jū	b.f.	to dwell, to reside	50
居民	居民	jūmín	n.	residents, people living in a certain area	50
居然	居然	jūrán	adv.	unbelievably, unimaginably	46
举重	舉重	jǔzhòng	v. obj.	to lift weights	43
据	據	jù	b.f.	according to, in accordance with	42
据说	據說	jùshuō	phr.	It is said…	42
距	距	jù	b.f.	distance (between two points)	48

Simplified	Traditional	Pinyin	Part of Speech	Definition	Lesson
聚	聚	jù	v.	to gather together	43
聚会	聚會	jùhuì	n.	get-together, party	43
决	决	jué	b.f.	to decide, to determine	47
绝	絕	jué	b.f.	extreme, end	42
绝对	絕對	juéduì	adv.	absolutely, definitely	42
均	均	jūn	b.f.	even, equal, balanced	48
卡拉OK	卡拉OK	kǎlā OK	n.	karaoke	43
开放	開放	kāifàng	v.	to open to the public	41
看法	看法	kànfǎ	n.	way of looking at things	44
科举	科舉	kējǔ	n.	imperial civil service examination system	45
可不	可不	kěbù	s.e.	for sure, ain't that the truth	48
控制	控制	kòngzhì	n., v.	control, supervision; to control, to supervise	43
快速	快速	kuàisù	adj.	fast-paced, high-speed	47
宽容	寬容	kuānróng	adj., v.	tolerant, lenient; (lit.) broad(-minded) and accommodating; to forgive, to allow, to make room for	46
款	款	kuǎn	n.	fund	50
矿物	礦物	kuàngwù	n.	minerals	44
拉倒	拉倒	lādǎo	s.e.	to knock it off, to bring it down, to end and forget about (something)	46
来源	來源	láiyuán	n.	origin, source	45
来自	來自	láizì	v. comp.	to originate from	45
来自于	來自於	láizì yú	phr.	to originate from	45
廊	廊	láng	b.f.	corridor, porch, salon	48
劳动	勞動	láodòng	n., v.	manual labor; to do physical labor, to work physically	47

Simplified	Traditional	Pinyin	Part of Speech	Definition	Lesson
老百姓	老百姓	lǎobǎixìng	n.	ordinary folks, common folks	48
类	類	lèi	n.	category	49
类似	類似	lèisì	v.	to resemble, to be similar to	49
离婚	離婚	líhūn	n., v. obj.	divorce; to get a divorce; (lit.) to leave the marriage	46
礼节	禮節	lǐjié	n.	manners, courtesy, social formalities	41
理	理	lǐ	v.	to put in order, to straighten up	44
理论	理論	lǐlùn	n.	theory	44
历	曆	lì	b.f.	experience	41
历史	歷史	lìshǐ	n.	history	41
立	立	lì	b.f.	to stand (up), to set up, to establish	49
立法	立法	lìfǎ	v. obj.	legislation; (lit.) to establish laws	49
利	利	lì	n.	advantage, benefit, profit	46
利用	利用	lìyòng	v.	to make use of, to utilize (negative connotation), to take advantage of (somebody, opportunity, etc.)	43
励	勵	lì	v.	to urge, to spur on	47
例如	例如	lìrú	conj.	for instance, for example	41
恋爱	戀愛	liàn'ài	n.	romantic love	46
练气功	練氣功	liàn qìgōng	v. obj.	to practice qigong	43
良好	良好	liánghǎo	adj.	(formal) good, fine	49
粮	糧	liáng	n.	grain, cereals	41
粮食	糧食	liángshi	n.	grain, provisions	41
两口子	兩口子	liǎng kǒuzi	s.e.	married couple	46
邻居	鄰居	línjū	n.	neighbor	46

Simplified	Traditional	Pinyin	Part of Speech	Definition	Lesson
领导	領導	lǐngdǎo	n., v.	leader, leadership; to lead	49
令	令	lìng	v.	to cause (someone to do something)	50
另外	另外	lìngwài	conj., adj.	in addition, moreover, on the other hand; other	41
留级	留級	liú jí	v. obj.	to be kept back a grade, to fail to proceed to a higher level	45
流产	流產	liúchǎn	n., v. obj.	miscarriage; to have a miscarriage	47
流行	流行	liúxíng	v., adj.	to be popular, to be in vogue; (lit.) to circulate in a flow; popular, fashionable, in vogue	42
率	率	lǜ	b.f.	ratio, rate, proportion	46
麻	麻	má	adj.	numb	44
麻婆豆腐	麻婆豆腐	mápó dòufu	n.	mapo tofu	41
麻醉	麻醉	mázuì	n.	anaesthesia	44
麦子	麥子	màizi	n.	wheat (the crop)	41
脉象	脈象	màixiàng	n.	pattern of one's pulse	44
馒头	饅頭	mántou	n.	steamed bun (without filling)	41
慢性	慢性	mànxìn	n.	slow-acting nature, slow or phlegmatic temperament	44
慢性病	慢性病	mànxìngbìng	n.	chronic illness, chronic health condition; (lit.) slow-natured disease	44
盲	盲	máng	b.f.	blind	46
盲目	盲目	mángmù	adj.	undiscerning, indiscriminate, injudicious; (fig.) blind	46
贸易	貿易	màoyì	n.	trade, commerce	48
煤	煤	méi	n.	coal	50

Simplified	Traditional	Pinyin	Part of Speech	Definition	Lesson
每逢	每逢	měi féng	adv.	each/every time one encounters somebody or something	42
米	米	mǐ	n.	rice (uncooked) (=米; 大米 is used to distinguish it from other grains)	41
米饭	米飯	mǐfàn	n.	cooked rice	41
密切	密切	mìqiè	adv., adj.	(of relationship) closely, intimately; close, intimate	49
免	免	miǎn	v.	to avoid	47
面	麵	miàn	n.	wheat flour, flour, noodles	41
面对	面對	miànduì	v.	to face, to confront	50
面食	麵食	miànshí	n.	food made out of wheat (noodles, bread, buns, dumplings, etc.)	41
面条	麵條	miàntiáo	n.	noodles	41
民间	民間	mínjiān	adj.	folk, non-governmental	42
民主	民主	mínzhǔ	n.	democracy	49
民族	民族	mínzú	n.	ethnic group	49
明快	明快	míngkuài	adj.	bright and joyful	42
模仿	模仿	mófǎng	v.	to copy, to imitate	48
末	末	mò	n.	tip (of a tree), final period, end	47
磨	磨	mò	n.	grindstone	47
目	目	mù	b.f.	(formal) eye, item	48
目的	目的	mùdì	n.	purpose, goal	48
目前	目前	mùqián	n.	present moment, now; (lit.) in front of one's eyes	48
墓	墓	mù	n.	grave, tomb	42
南方	南方	nánfāng	n.	south, southern direction	41
南瓜饼	南瓜餅	nánguā bǐng	n.	pumpkin pie	42

Simplified	Traditional	Pinyin	Part of Speech	Definition	Lesson
难道	難道	nándào	adv.	(used in a rhetorical question) could it be possible that…	45
难怪	難怪	nánguài	conj.	no wonder; (lit.) difficult to blame	42
恼	惱	nǎo	v.	to anger, to annoy	43
能	能	néng	b.f.	energy	50
能源	能源	néngyuán	n.	energy source	50
你瞧	你瞧	nǐ qiáo	s.e.	take a look (around), often used to direct someone's attention to something	48
年代	年代	niándài	n.	decade, generation	47
年级	年級	niánjí	n.	grade, year (in school)	45
年轻	年輕	niánqīng	adj.	(of adults) young; (lit.) light in years	46
念	念	niàn	b.f.	to constantly think of, to miss, to feel anxious about, to worry	42
尿	尿	niào	n., v.	urine; to urinate	44
宁可	寧可	nìngkě	conj.	(despite the disadvantage) would rather	50
农村	農村	nóngcūn	n.	countryside, village	47
农历	農曆	nónglì	n.	traditional Chinese lunar calendar; (lit.) the agricultural calendar	42
农民	農民	nóngmín	n.	peasantry, peasant, country folks	48
农业	農業	nóngyè	n.	agriculture	47
努力	努力	nǔlì	adj., n, adv.	to exert one's strength, to exert oneself; effort; hard	45
爬山	爬山	pá shān	v.obj.	to climb a mountain	43
牌	牌	pái	n.	cards	43

Simplified	Traditional	Pinyin	Part of Speech	Definition	Lesson
排放	排放	páifàng	v.	to discharge, to dump (pollutants, waste); (lit.) to expel and release	50
攀岩	攀岩	pān yán	v. obj	to climb rocks	43
培	培	péi	b.f.	to add soil to (plants to encourage growth), to cultivate	47
培养	培養	péiyǎng	v.	to cultivate, to raise	47
批评	批評	pīpíng	n., v.	criticism; to criticize	46
皮肤	皮膚	pífū	n.	skin	44
贫	貧	pín	b.f.	poor, the poor	48
贫富不均	貧富不均	pínfù bù jūn	phr.	inequality between the rich and the poor	48
品	品	pǐn	n.	article, product, commodity	41
乒乓球	乒乓球	pīngpāng qiú	n.	ping-pong; (lit.) ping-pong ball	43
平等	平等	píngděng	adj.	of equal status	46
评估	評估	pínggū	v., n.	to assess, to appraise; assessment, appraisal	50
平衡	平衡	pínghéng	n., v., adj.	balance, equilibrium; to balance; balanced	47
破	破	pò	v.	to break, to damage	50
破坏	破壞	pòhuài	n., v.	destruction, damage; to destroy, to damage	50
普	普	pǔ	b.f.	common, ubiquitous, pervasive	42
普及	普及	pǔjí	adj.	widespread, far-reaching	42
普通	普通	pǔtōng	adj.	ordinary, common, average	45
普通话	普通話	pǔtōnghuà	n.	standard spoken languaage, Mandarin	49
妻子	妻子	qīzi	n.	wife	46

Simplified	Traditional	Pinyin	Part of Speech	Definition	Lesson
其中	其中	qízhōng	phr.	(in) the midst (of something); (lit.) its midst	43
企业	企業	qǐyè	n.	enterprise, business	48
(起)作用	(起)作用	qǐ zuòyòng	v. obj.	to have an effect, to be effective	48
气功	氣功	qìgōng	n.	(lit.) qi cultivation	43
气候	氣候	qìhòu	n.	climate	41
弃	棄	qì	v.	abandon	42
气味	氣味	qìwèi	n.	(formal) smell, odor	44
强	強	qiáng	adj.	strong, powerful	47
强调	強調	qiángdiào	v.	to put emphasis on	47
瞧	瞧	qiáo	v.	(colloq.) to look	48
切脉/号脉/把脉	切脈/號脈/把脈	qiē mài / hào mài /bǎ mài	v. obj.	to feel/take a pulse	44
亲戚	親戚	qīnqi	n.	relatives	46
轻	輕	qīng	adj.	light (weight)	47
清亮	清亮	qīngliàng	adj.	clear and bright	42
情	情	qíng	b.f., n.	feeling, emotion, passion, romantic love, love affair; situation, circumstance, condition; (lit.) feeling	44
情况	情況	qíngkuàng	n.	situation, condition, circumstance	50
求	求	qiú	v.	to seek, to request, to need	46, 48
区	區	qū	b.f.	region, area	50
权	權	quán	n.	power, authority, right	46
权力	權力	quánlì	n.	power, authority	49
权利	權利	quánlì	n.	right, power, authority	46
全球	全球	quánqiú	n.	the entire world	50
劝	勸	quàn	v.	to persuade, to advise, to urge	44

Simplified	Traditional	Pinyin	Part of Speech	Definition	Lesson
却	卻	què	adv.	on the contrary, in contrast to what one would expect	43
燃	燃	rán	v.	(formal) to burn	50
然而	然而	rán'ér	conj.	(formal) (in spite of the fact that…) yet, nevertheless (indicating a contrast to what one would expect)	43
热题	熱題	rètí	n.	controversial topic; (lit.) heated subject	49
热心	熱心	rèxīn	adj.	warm-hearted, eager to help	46
人工	人工	réngōng	adj.	artificial, human-induced, (lit.) human work	47
人工流产	人工流產	réngōng liúchǎn	n.	abortion	47
人口	人口	rénkǒu	n.	population	47
人力	人力	rénlì	n.	manpower, manual labor	47
人权	人權	rénquán	n.	human rights	49
人数	人數	rénshù	n.	number of people	45
任命	任命	rènmìng	v.	to appoint (someone to a certain position)	49
仍然	仍然	réngrán	adv.	(formal) still, as before	48
日益	日益	rìyì	adv.	day by day, more and more, increasingly	50
如此	如此	rúcǐ	adv.	like this	48
如此一来	如此一來	rúcǐ yīlái	phr.	given the above situation; (lit.) once it happened like this	48
如何	如何	rúhé	interrog.	(written) how	41
散步	散步	sàn bù	v. obj.	to take a walk, to take a casual stroll	43
扫墓	掃墓	sǎo mù	v. obj.	to sweep graves, to go to one's ancestors' graves and pay respects	42

Simplified	Traditional	Pinyin	Part of Speech	Definition	Lesson
善	善	shàn	adj.	(morally) good, kind-hearted, charitable	50
商品	商品	shāngpǐn	n.	merchandise, goods, commodity	42
商业	商業	shāngyè	n.	commerce, business, trade	49
赏月	賞月	shǎngyuè	v.	to appreciate or admire the moon	42
上	上	shàng	v.	to reach the level of	48
上百个	上百個	shàng bǎi ge	s.e.	nearing a hundred	48
上马	上馬	shàngmǎ	s.e.	to launch (a new project); (lit.) to mount the horse	50
上瘾	上癮	shàng yǐn	s.e.	to get addicted to, to get hooked on	43
少数	少數	shǎoshù	n.	minority; (lit.) small number	49
奢侈	奢侈	shēchǐ	adj.	extravagant, luxurious, wasteful	50
奢侈品	奢侈品	shēchǐ pǐn	n.	luxury item	50
社会	社會	shèhuì	n.	society	43
设想	設想	shèxiǎng	n., v.	(lit.) planning and thinking; to imagine (the future)	50
什么没有	什麼沒有	shénme méiyǒu	s.e.	what don't they have? (rhetorical), (they) have everything	48
什么的	什麼的	shénmede	s.e.	etc., and so forth	43
审	審	shěn	b.f.	to examine	43
审查	審查	shěnchá	n., v.	investigation, careful examination; to investigate, to carefully examine	43
肾虚	腎虛	shèn xū	phr.	deficiency in kidneys	44
甚至	甚至	shènzhì	adv.	going so far as, even going to the extent that	46
升级	升級	shēng jí	v. obj.	to rise to a higher level, to rise to another grade	45

Simplified	Traditional	Pinyin	Part of Speech	Definition	Lesson
生产	生產	shēngchǎn	v.	to produce, to manufacture	41
生存	生存	shēngcún	n., v.	(continued) existence, survival; to survive	48
生活	生活	shēnghuó	n., v.	life; to live	43
生态	生態	shēngtài	n.	ecology	50
生育	生育	shēngyù	n., v.	giving birth; (lit.) giving birth to and raising (children); to give birth to and raise children	47
省（自治区）	省（自治區）	shěng (zìzhìqū)	n.	province	49
省长	省長	shěngzhǎng	n.	governor of a province	49
失	失	shī	b.f.	to lose, to miss, to fail	43
失去	失去	shīqù	v.	to lose	50
失望	失望	shīwàng	v. obj.	to feel disappointed; (lit.) to lose hope	45
失业	失業	shī yè	v. obj.	to lose a job, to be unemployed	48
师资	師資	shīzī	n.	faculty of an educational institution	45
诗	詩	shī	n.	poetry, poem	42
石油	石油	shíyóu	n.	petroleum	48
时兴	時興	shíxīng	adj.	to be in vogue, to be in fashion, to consider (something fashionable)	43
实	實	shí	adj., n.	solid; reality, actuality, fact	47
实际	實際	shíjì	adj., n.	practical; actuality, reality, the hard facts	50
实际上	實際上	shíjì shàng	phr.	in fact, in reality	50
实践	實踐	shíjiàn	n., v.	putting into practice (of a theory, a policy, etc.); practice	47
实行	實行	shíxíng	v.	(of a theory, a policy) to put into practice	47

Simplified	Traditional	Pinyin	Part of Speech	Definition	Lesson
食	食	shí	b.f.	food	41
史	史	shǐ	b.f.	history	41
使	使	shǐ	v.	to cause, to make/let (somebody do something), to send, to dispatch	43
市场	市場	shìchǎng	n.	market, marketplace	48
市场经济	市場經濟	shìchǎng jīngjì	n.	market economy	48
市长	市長	shìzhǎng	n.	mayor	49
世纪	世紀	shìjì	n.	century	46
世界	世界	shìjiè	n.	the world, (Buddhist) the cosmos	42
是	是	shì	adj.	true, correct	47
是否	是否	shìfǒu	adv.	(formal) (is it) true or not true (that...), (whether it is) true/correct	47
试点	試點	shìdiǎn	n.	test site, pilot project	48
收入	收入	shōurù	n.	income	48
手术	手術	shǒushù	n.	surgical operation	44
首	首	shǒu	m.w.	measure word for songs or poems	42
首先	首先	shǒuxiān	adv.	first of all	49
受	受	shòu	v.	to be the recipient of (an action), to receive	41
受益	受益	shòuyì	v. obj.	to receive profit/benefit	49
授	授	shòu	v.	(formal) to give, to teach	45
属于	屬於	shǔyú	v.	(formal) to belong to	48
术	術	shù	n.	art, skill	44, 47
水源	水源	shuǐyuán	n.	source of water, water supply	50
水质	水質	shuǐzhì	n.	water quality	50
水煮牛	水煮牛	shuǐzhǔ niú	n.	Sichuan-style beef	41
税	稅	shuì	n.	taxes	48

Simplified	Traditional	Pinyin	Part of Speech	Definition	Lesson
硕士	碩士	shuòshì	n.	master's degree	45
私立	私立	sīlì	adj.	privately owned; (lit.) privately established	43
私有制	私有制	sīyǒu zhì	n.	private ownership system	48
死亡	死亡	sǐwáng	n.	(formal) death	47
似乎	似乎	sìhu	adv.	it seems, it looks as if..., seemingly	46
速	速	sù	b.f.	rapid, speedy	41
速度	速度	sùdù	n.	speed	48
速食	速食	sùshí	n.	fast food	41
算不上	算不上	suàn bú shàng	v. comp.	not to be able to count as anything	48
算不上什么	算不上什麼	suàn bú shàng shénme	s.e.	to not amount to anything	48
酸雨	酸雨	suānyǔ	n.	acid rain	50
随着	隨著	suízhe	conj., v.	following, along with...; to follow	41
讨论	討論	tǎolùn	n., v.	discussion; to discuss	45
特	特	tè	b.f.	special, particular	41
特产	特產	tèchǎn	n	product of a specific area	41
特点	特點	tèdiǎn	n.	characteristic, trait	41
特殊	特殊	tèshū	adj.	special	49
提高	提高	tígāo	n., v.	enhancement, improvement; to enhance, to raise, to uplift	48
提名	提名	tímíng	n., v. obj.	nomination; to nominate	49
体系	體係	tǐxì	n.	system, structure	45
天书	天書	tiānshū	s.e.	writing that is too difficult to read and comprehend; (lit.) heavenly scripture	41
挑选	挑選	tiāoxuǎn	v.	to pick and select	45
调	調	tiáo	v.	to mix, to blend	44

Simplified	Traditional	Pinyin	Part of Speech	Definition	Lesson
条件	條件	tiáojiàn	n.	condition, requirement	43
调理	調理	tiáolǐ	v.	to regulate and harmonize (the bodily functions)	44
停工	停工	tínggōng	v. obj.	(lit.) to suspend or stop the work	50
停止	停止	tíngzhǐ	v.	(formal) to stop, to discontinue, to suspend	47
通过	通過	tōngguò	v.	to pass through, to pass (a set standard)	44
同	同	tóng	adj.	the same as	41
同居	同居	tóngjū	v.	to live together (used for lovers or boyfriends and girlfriends), (lit.) to stay (in the) same (place)	46
同时	同時	tóngshí	n.	(at) the same time	45
同事	同事	tóngshì	n.	colleague, fellow worker	46
同意	同意	tóngyì	v.	to agree, to approve	44
统	統	tǒng	b.f.	system	42
统一	統一	tǒngyī	adv.	in a unified way, all together	45
头台	頭檯	tóutái	s.e.	appetizer, starter	41
土豆泥	土豆泥	tǔdòu ní	n.	mashed potatoes	42
团	團	tuán	b.f.	collective, group	42
团聚	團聚	tuánjù	v.	to have a reunion; (lit.) (of a group) to come together and gather in one place	42
团圆	團圓	tuányuán	n., v.	reunion; to have a family reunion; (lit.) to come together and form a circle	42
推	推	tuī	v.	to push	48
推动	推動	tuīdòng	v.	to push forward; (lit.) to push and move	49

Simplified	Traditional	Pinyin	Part of Speech	Definition	Lesson
推广	推廣	tuīguǎng	v.	to spread, to promote, to popularize	44
推磨	推磨	tuīmò	v.obj.	to turn a millstone (for grinding grains)	47
推行	推行	tuīxíng	v.	(for a government) to implement (a policy); (lit.) to push into action	48
退休	退休	tuìxiū	n., v.	retirement; to retire	43
托…福	托…福	tuō…fú	s.e.	to receive blessings, to rely on (someone's) blessing, thanks to the good fortune (of something)	48
外商独资	外商獨資	wàishāng dúzī	n.	businesses owned and run solely by foreign firms	48
完美	完美	wánměi	adj.	(completely) perfect	49
完美无缺	完美無缺	wánměi wúquē	adj.	(lit.) perfect and flawless	49
网页	網頁	wǎngyè	n.	webpage	43
危及	危及	wēijí	v.	endanger; (lit.) to become dangerous to	50
危险	危險	wēixiǎn	adj., n.	dangerous, risky; danger, risk	45
威胁	威脅	wēixié	n., v.	threat; to menace, to threaten	50
为	為	wéi	v.	to be	45
违	違	wéi	b.f.	to disobey, to violate, to defy	50
违法	違法	wéifǎ	v. obj.	to violate the law, to break the law	50
唯一	唯一	wéiyī	adj.	the one and only	45
委员	委員	wěiyuán	n.	committee member, commissioner; (lit.) the appointed person	49
委员会	委員會	wěiyuánhuì	n.	committee, commission	49

Simplified	Traditional	Pinyin	Part of Speech	Definition	Lesson
委员会主任	委員會主任	wěiyuánhuì zhǔrèn	n.	head of a commission	49
未婚	未婚	wèihūn	adj.	not yet married	46
位于	位於	wèiyú	v. comp.	(formal) to be located in/at	49
稳定	穩定	wěndìng	adj.	steady, stable	47
乌	烏	wū	b.f.	black, dark	50
乌烟瘴气	烏煙瘴氣	wūyān zhàngqì	phr.	(lit.) dark smoke and heated (sickness-inducing) air	50
污染	污染	wūrǎn	n., v.	pollution, contamination; to pollute, to contaminate	50
无法	無法	wúfǎ	phr.	no way, no idea	44
无论	無論	wúlùn	conj.	regardless of	41
无论如何	無論如何	wúlùn rúhé	conj.	in any case, no matter what	41
无缺	無缺	wúquē	adj.	without any flaw	49
物价	物價	wùjià	n.	commodity prices	48
西餐	西餐	xīcān	n.	Western food	41
西方	西方	xīfāng	n.	the West, Western countries	41
西药	西藥	xīyào	n.	Western medicine	44
西医	西醫	xīyī	n.	Western medicine	44
戏剧	戲劇	xìjù	n.	musical drama	43
下岗	下崗	xiàgǎng	v. obj.	to be laid off; (lit.) to get off duty	48
下棋	下棋	xià qí	v. obj.	to play chess	43
先进	先進	xiānjìn	adj.	advanced, progressive	48
闲	閑	xián	b.f.	idle, leisurely	43
闲话	閑話	xiánhuà	n.	gossip; (lit.) casual conversation	46

Simplified	Traditional	Pinyin	Part of Speech	Definition	Lesson
险	險	xiǎn	n., adj.	narrow strategic pass, danger, risk; dangerous	47
县	縣	xiàn	n.	county	49
县长	縣長	xiànzhǎng	n.	county magistrate	49
现代	現代	xiàndài	n.	modern times, modern age	43
现象	現象	xiànxiàng	n.	phenomenon, situation	46
限	限	xiàn	v.	to limit, to set boundaries	49
限制	限制	xiànzhì	v.	to limit, to restrict	49
相比	相比	xiāngbǐ	v.	to compare with each other	43
相当	相當	xiāngdāng	adv.	considerably, quite, fairly	50
相反	相反	xiāngfǎn	adj.	opposite	43
相似	相似	xiāngsì	adj.	similar	43
相同	相同	xiāngtóng	adj.	same, identical	41
相同之处	相同之處	xiāngtóng zhī chù	phr.	similar traits, resemblance	41
相信	相信	xiāngxìn	v.	to believe (in), to trust	44
响	響	xiǎng	v.	to echo, to ring, to produce a sound	43
想念	想念	xiǎngniàn	n., v.	(formal) to feel a longing for; longing	42
相声	相聲	xiàngsheng	n.	cross talk, comic dialogue show	43
享受	享受	xiǎngshòu	n., v.	enjoyment; to enjoy, to benefit from	46
象征	象徵	xiàngzhēng	n., v.	symbol, sign; to symbolize	42
消	消	xiāo	b.f.	to reduce, to diminish	43
消费	消費	xiāofèi	n.	expenditure, (of money) spending, consumption	43
消失	消失	xiāoshī	v.	(formal) to disappear, to vanish	43
销售	銷售	xiāoshòu	n., v.	sale; to sell, to market	48

Simplified	Traditional	Pinyin	Part of Speech	Definition	Lesson
小本	小本	xiǎo běn	n.	small capital	48
小本经营	小本經營	xiǎo běn jīngyíng	s.e.	small business; (lit.) to run a business with small capital	48
小看	小看	xiǎokàn	s.e.	belittle	45
小品	小品	xiǎopǐn	n.	a short theatrical piece	43
小学	小學	xiǎoxué	n.	elementary school	45
效果	效果	xiàoguǒ	n.	effect, result	44
心目	心目	xīnmù	n.	(formal) state of mind; (lit.) eyes of the heart/mind	49
信	信	xìn	v.	to believe, to trust	42
信仰	信仰	xìnyǎng	n., v.	belief, faith; to believe in (a religion)	42
兴隆	興隆	xīnglóng	adj.	prosperous	48
行	行	xíng	v.	to walk, to move, to act	47
行政	行政	xíngzhèng	n.	administration; (lit.) to carry out policies	49
形状	形狀	xíngzhuàng	n.	form and shape	41
形成	形成	xíngchéng	v. comp.	to take the form of, to develop into	41
形式	形式	xíngshì	n.	form (as opposed to content)	48
性	性	xìng	b.f.	-ness, nature	45
幸福	幸福	xìngfú	adj., n.	blessed, happy; happiness	46
休	休	xiū	v.	to stop, to rest	43
休闲	休閒	xiūxián	n.	leisure, relaxing in one's spare time	43
选举	選舉	xuǎnjǔ	n., v.	election; to elect	49
选择	選擇	xuǎnzé	n., v.	choice; (formal) to select, to choose	46

Simplified	Traditional	Pinyin	Part of Speech	Definition	Lesson
学费	學費	xuéfèi	n.	school fees, tuition	45
学士	學士	xuéshì	n.	bachelor's degree	45
学位	學位	xuéwèi	n.	academic degree	45
雪豆虾	雪豆蝦	xuědòu xiā	n.	shrimp with snow peas	41
血统	血統	xuètǒng	n.	lineage, nationality; (lit.) blood system	49
压力	壓力	yālì	n.	pressure	45
烟尘	煙塵	yānchén	n.	smoke and dust	50
言	言	yán	b.f.	classical Chinese word for 说	48
严	嚴	yán	adj.	(of a person) strict, severe	46
严重	嚴重	yánzhòng	adj.	(of a situation) severe, grave	46
研究院	研究院	yánjiū yuàn	n.	graduate school	45
仰	仰	yǎng	v.	to look up to, to admire, to adore	42
养	養	yǎng	v.	to nourish, to care for	47
养家	養家	yǎng jiā	v. obj	to support a family	50
腰	腰	yāo	n.	waist, the middle section (of something)	44
要求	要求	yāoqiú	n., v.	formal request, demand; to formally request, to demand	46
药效	藥效	yàoxiào	n.	efficacy of a medicine; (lit.) the effect of a medicine	44
业	業	yè	b.f.	career, profession, study	43
页	頁	yè	n.	page	43
一来	一來	yīlái	phr.	(lit.) once that comes	48
一流	一流	yīliú	adj.	first-rate, first-class	45
一向	一向	yīxiàng	adv.	unwaveringly, steadfastly; (lit.) (constant) in one direction	43

Simplified	Traditional	Pinyin	Part of Speech	Definition	Lesson
医学	醫學	yīxué	n.	medical science; (lit.) the study of medicine	44
以	以	yǐ	prep.	relying, taking, using, by means of	44
以及	以及	yǐjí	conj.	including, going as far as	45
以免	以免	yǐmiǎn	conj.	(so as) to avoid, lest	44
以上	以上	yǐshàng	phr.	above mentioned	47
以…为	以…為	yǐ…wéi	phr.	to take…as, to regard…as, to treat…as	45
亿	億	yì	n.	hundred million	47
议	議	yì	b.f.	to discuss, to express one's idea	47
益	益	yì	b.f.	(classical Chinese) more, increasing; profit, benefit	49
因此	因此	yīncǐ	conj.	therefore	42
引起	引起	yǐnqǐ	v.	to trigger, to give rise to	44
饮	飲	yǐn	n., v.	drinks; to drink	41
饮食	飲食	yǐnshí	n.	food and drink	41
应有尽有	應有盡有	yīng yǒu jìn yǒu	phr.	to have everything needed; (lit.) Whatever one should have one has it all.	42
婴儿	嬰兒	yīng'ér	n.	infant, baby	47
营养	營養	yíngyǎng	n.	nutrition, nourishment	41
影响	影響	yǐngxiǎng	n., v.	influence, effect, impact; to influence	41
拥有	擁有	yōngyǒu	v.	to possess	48
优	優	yōu	adj., b.f.	excellent, outstanding; sorrow, anxiety, worry, concern	49

Simplified	Traditional	Pinyin	Part of Speech	Definition	Lesson
优待	優待	yōudài	n.	privilege, special treatment; (lit.) excellent treatment	49
由于	由於	yóuyú	conj.	because, thanks to, as a result of	41
游戏	遊戲	yóuxì	n.	game, play, recreation	43
游行	遊行	yóuxíng	n.	parade, demonstration	42
有关	有關	yǒuguān	v.	to be related, to be connected; (lit.) to have a connection	46
有害	有害	yǒuhài	v. obj.	to have harmful effects	50
有害于	有害於	yǒuhài yú	v.	to be harmful to, to have harmful effects on	50
有利于	有利於	yǒulì yú	v.	to be beneficial to	50
于	於	yú	prep.	from	45
于是	於是	yúshì	conj.	thereupon, as a result, accordingly, consequently; (lit.) at this	46
鱼香肉丝	魚香肉絲	yúxiāng ròusī	n.	fish-flavored pork	41
娱乐	娛樂	yúlè	n.	entertainment, recreation	43
舆论	輿論	yúlùn	n.	public opinion	46
与	與	yǔ	prep.	(formal) with	43
与此同时	與此同時	yǔ cǐ tóngshí	phr.	at the same time as this	48
与其...不如...	與其...不如...	yǔqí...bùrú...	conj.	rather than... might as well...; (lit.) rather than... not as good as...	50
与...相比	與...相比	yǔ...xiāngbǐ	phr.	in comparison to, comparing with	43
与...相似	與...相似	yǔ...xiāngsì	phr.	to be similar to, to bear resemblance to	43
遇到	遇到	yù dào	v. comp.	to encounter, to come across	44

Simplified	Traditional	Pinyin	Part of Speech	Definition	Lesson
预告	預告	yùgào	n.	advance notification, forecast	43
圆	圓	yuán	adj.	(of shape) circular, round	42
原理	原理	yuánlǐ	n.	fundamental principle; (lit.) the original principle	44
原先	原先	yuánxiān	adv.	originally, at first	44
源	源	yuán	b.f.	source	50
月饼	月餅	yuèbǐng	n.	mooncake	42
月亮	月亮	yuèliang	n.	the moon	42
造成	造成	zàochéng	v. comp.	(usually negative) to create, to bring into being, to give rise to	47
增	增	zēng	b.f.	to increase, to add	47
增高	增高	zēnggāo	v.	to raise, to enhance	46
增长	增長	zēngzhǎng	n., v.	increase, growth; to increase, to rise	47
展	展	zhǎn	b.f.	to unfold, to put on display	41
丈夫	丈夫	zhàngfu	n.	husband	46
障	障	zhàng	b.f.	barrier, screen	47
障碍	障礙	zhàng'ài	n.	obstacle, barrier	49
招	招	zhāo	v.	to wave (hands)	43
招生	招生	zhāo shēng	v. obj.	to recruit students	45
针	針	zhēn	n.	needle	44
针灸	針灸	zhēnjiǔ	n.	acupuncture and moxibustion	44
镇	鎮	zhèn	n.	town	49
镇长	鎮長	zhènzhǎng	n.	mayor, head of a town	49
争	爭	zhēng	v.	to argue, to dispute, to contend, to compete	47
争论	爭論	zhēnglùn	n., v.	controversy, argument; to argue	49

Simplified	Traditional	Pinyin	Part of Speech	Definition	Lesson
争议	爭議	zhēngyì	n., v.	controversy, debate; to dispute, to debate	47
正月	正月	zhēngyuè	n.	the first month of the traditional Chinese lunar calendar	42
政	政	zhèng	b.f.	politics, various aspects of government administration	49
政策	政策	zhèngcè	n.	policy	47
政治	政治	zhèngzhì	n.	politics	49
整体	整體	zhěngtǐ	n.	entirety; (lit.) whole body	44
之外	之外	zhīwài	b.f.	outside of	42
执	執	zhí	v.	to hold in hand, to grasp, to carry	47
执行	執行	zhíxíng	v.	to carry out, to put into practice	47
(直辖)市	(直轄)市	(zhíxiá) shì	n.	city (directly under the central authorities)	49
职	職	zhí	b.f.	job, post, position	50
职工	職工	zhígōng	n.	employee	50
植物	植物	zhíwù	n.	vegetation, plant	44
止	止	zhǐ	v.	to stop	44
止痛	止痛	zhǐ tòng	v. obj.	to stop pain	44
止痛药	止痛藥	zhǐ tòng yào	n.	painkiller	44
至少	至少	zhìshǎo	phr.	at least	50
至于	至於	zhìyú	conj.	as for	49
志愿	志願	zhìyuàn	n.	preference (when choosing a vocation, an academic discipline, a profession, a career); (lit.) aspiration	45
制	制	zhì	b.f.	system	49

Simplified	Traditional	Pinyin	Part of Speech	Definition	Lesson
制定	制定	zhìdìng	v.	to draw up (a new regulation), to make...into a rule/law/plan, etc.	47
制度	制度	zhìdù	n.	rules, regulations, institution, system	45
制造	製造	zhìzào	v.	to make, to manufacture	49
治本	治本	zhì běn	v. obj.	to treat the root of the problem	44
治标	治標	zhì biǎo	v. obj.	(标 = surface) to treat symptoms only (not the underlying	44
中成药	中成藥	zhōng chéngyào	phr.	ready-made traditional Chinese medicine	44
中(草)药	中(草)藥	zhōng(cǎo)yào	n.	traditional Chinese (herbal) medicine	44
中外合资	中外合資	zhōngwài hézī	phr.	Chinese-foreign joint venture	48
中西医	中西醫	zhōngxī yī	phr.	traditional Chinese and Western medicine	44
中央	中央	zhōngyāng	n.	center, central authorities	43, 49
中医	中醫	zhōngyī	n.	traditional Chinese medicine	44
中专	中專	zhōngzhuān	n.	vocational middle school	45
终于	終於	zhōngyú	adv.	finally, at last	45
重	重	zhòng	adj.	weighty, significant	47
重点	重點	zhòngdiǎn	n.	the most important (point, center, etc.)	45
重视	重視	zhòngshì	v.	to take seriously, to highly value, to pay special attention to	50
逐	逐	zhú	b.f.	one by one, in succession	43
逐渐	逐漸	zhújiàn	adv.	gradually	43
主菜	主菜	zhǔcài	s.e.	entrée	41

Simplified	Traditional	Pinyin	Part of Speech	Definition	Lesson
主任	主任	zhǔrèn	n.	director; (lit.) the main (official) post	49
主食	主食	zhǔshí	n.	staple food (rice, noodles, bread, etc.)	41
主席	主席	zhǔxí	n.	chairman (of a government, political party, etc.)	49
专心	專心	zhuānxīn	v. obj.	to focus one's mind/heart, to concentrate	45
专业	專業	zhuānyè	n.	profession, area of specialization	45
转变	轉變	zhuǎnbiàn	v.	to turn and change; (lit.) to make turns and changes	48
转换	轉換	zhuǎnhuàn	v.	to undergo changes, to shift; (lit.) to turn and change	48
转型	轉型	zhuǎn xíng	v. obj.	to change into a different form/shape; (lit.) to change the form	48
状况	狀況	zhuàngkuàng	n.	state of affairs, condition	49
追	追	zhuī	v.	to run after, to chase	46
追求	追求	zhuīqiú	v., n.	to pursue, to go after; pursuit, aspiration	46
子	子	zi	n.	child, children, sons	47
资金	資金	zījīn	n.	capital, fund	48
自由	自由	zìyóu	adj., n.	free; freedom	46
自主权	自主權	zìzhǔquán	n.	autonomy; (lit.) the power to make one's own decisions	49
宗	宗	zōng	n.	ancestor	42
宗教	宗教	zōngjiào	n.	religion	42
总	總	zǒng	adj., adv.	total; always	47
总理	總理	zǒnglǐ	n.	premier	49

Simplified	Traditional	Pinyin	Part of Speech	Definition	Lesson
总统	總統	zǒngtǒng	n.	president, chief of state	49
总之	總之	zǒngzhī	conj.	in short; (lit.) to sum it up	50
粽子	粽子	zòngzi	n.	glutinous rice cake wrapped with large bamboo leaves	42
走后门	走後門	zǒuhòumén	s.e.	(lit. and met.) to go through the back door	45
足	足	zú	b.f.	sufficient, enough	47
族	族	zú	n.	clan, tribe, ethnic group	49
组织	組織	zǔzhī	n., v.	organization; to organize; (lit.) to weave	48
嘴	嘴	zuǐ	n.	mouth	41
醉	醉	zuì	adj.	intoxicated	44
左右	左右	zuǒyòu	suff.	approximately	47
作用	作用	zuòyòng	n.	function, role, effect	44
做操	做操	zuò cāo	v. obj.	to do calisthenics	43

Glossary of Proper Nouns

This vocabulary glossary includes all regular vocabulary, spoken expressions, and supplementary vocabulary from *Chinese Odyssey*, Volumes 5 & 6.

Simplified	Traditional	Pinyin	Definition	Lesson
重庆	重慶	Chóngqìng	Chongqing, formerly a city in Sichuan Province, now a district under national jurisdiction	41
楚国	楚國	Chǔ guó	Chu, an ancient state in China	42
灯节	燈節	Dēngjié	Lantern Festival; the same as 元宵节	42
端午节	端午節	Duānwǔjié	Dragon Boat Festival (fifth day of the fifth lunar month)	42
福建	福建	Fújiàn	Fujian (Province)	49
感恩节	感恩節	Gǎn'ēnjié	Thanksgiving Day; (lit.) feeling gratitude holiday	42
广东	廣東	Guǎngdōng	Guangdong Province	41
国际劳动节	國際勞動節	Guójì Láodòngjié	International Labor Day (May 1)	42
国庆节	國慶日	Guóqìngjié	National Day; (lit.) national celebration holiday	42
国务院	國務院	Guówùyuàn	the State Council (of China)	49
好莱坞	好萊塢	Hǎoláiwū	Hollywood	43
汉族	漢族	Hànzú	the Han nationality	49
湖南	湖南	Húnán	Hunan Province	41
肯得鸡	肯得雞	Kěndéjī	Kentucky Fried Chicken	41
龙井茶	龍井茶	Lóngjǐngchá	Dragon Well Tea, a famous green tea	41
麦当劳	麥當勞	Màidāngláo	McDonald's	41
闽南	閩南	Mǐnnán	south of Fujian	49
茉莉花茶	茉莉花茶	Mòlihuāchá	Jasmine tea	41
清明节	清明節	Qīngmíngjié	Pure-and-Bright Festival (approximately April 5, for paying respect to one's ancestors who have passed away)	42
情人节	情人節	Qíngrénjié	Valentine's Day; (lit.) lover's holiday	42
屈原	屈原	Qū Yuán	Qu Yuan (ca 340 - 278 BC, considered one of China's first great poets)	42

Simplified	Traditional	Pinyin	Definition	Lesson
全国人民代表大会	全國人民代表大會	Quánguó Rénmín Dàibiǎo Dàhuì	The National People's Congress of China	49
山西	山西	Shānxī	Shanxi Province	41
神农本草经	神農本草經	Shénnóng Běncǎojīng	The Divine Farmer's Classic of Pharmacology	44
圣诞节	耶誕節	Shèngdànjié	Christmas; (lit.) the saint's birth holiday	42
四川	四川	Sìchuān	Sichuan Province	41
台湾	臺灣	Táiwān	Taiwan	49
万圣节	萬聖節	Wànshèngjié	Halloween; (lit.) ten thousand saints holiday	42
新浪网	新浪網	Xīnlàng wǎng	www.sina.com	43
亚洲	亞洲	Yàzhōu	Asia	49
元旦	元旦	Yuándàn	New Year's Day; (lit.) the first dawn	42
元宵节	元宵節	Yuánxiāojié	Lantern Festival (fifteenth of the first lunar month); (lit.) sweet dumplings holiday	42
原住民	原住民	yuán zhù mín	native people	49
中华人民共和国	中華人民共和國	Zhōnghuá Rénmín Gònghéguó	the People's Republic of China (P.R.C.)	49
中秋节	中秋節	Zhōngqiūjié	Mid-Autumn Festival	42
中央电视台	中央電視臺	Zhōngyāng Diànshìtái	China Central Television (CCTV)	43